Executive Education after the Pandemic

Santiago Iñiguez · Peter Lorange
Editors

Executive Education after the Pandemic

A Vision for the Future

Editors
Santiago Iñiguez
IE Business School
Madrid, Madrid, Spain

Peter Lorange
Lorange Institute of Business Zurich
Horgen, Switzerland

ISBN 978-3-030-82342-9   ISBN 978-3-030-82343-6 (eBook)
https://doi.org/10.1007/978-3-030-82343-6

© The Editor(s) (if applicable) and The Author(s), under exclusive license to Springer Nature Switzerland AG 2022

This work is subject to copyright. All rights are solely and exclusively licensed by the Publisher, whether the whole or part of the material is concerned, specifically the rights of translation, reprinting, reuse of illustrations, recitation, broadcasting, reproduction on microfilms or in any other physical way, and transmission or information storage and retrieval, electronic adaptation, computer software, or by similar or dissimilar methodology now known or hereafter developed.

The use of general descriptive names, registered names, trademarks, service marks, etc. in this publication does not imply, even in the absence of a specific statement, that such names are exempt from the relevant protective laws and regulations and therefore free for general use.

The publisher, the authors and the editors are safe to assume that the advice and information in this book are believed to be true and accurate at the date of publication. Neither the publisher nor the authors or the editors give a warranty, expressed or implied, with respect to the material contained herein or for any errors or omissions that may have been made. The publisher remains neutral with regard to jurisdictional claims in published maps and institutional affiliations.

This Palgrave Macmillan imprint is published by the registered company Springer Nature Switzerland AG
The registered company address is: Gewerbestrasse 11, 6330 Cham, Switzerland

Foreword

The pandemic has proved to be the ultimate test of our community's resilience and agility, as well as our capacity to strategize and implement tactical adaptations in a highly uncertain environment. As painful as it has been was for humanity, the crisis has forced us to change how work is performed and accelerated the digitalization of all aspects of life, learning included. The episode can be regarded as an enormous unwarranted experiment, which hopefully we can channel as a force for renewal in legacy and legitimacy in management practices.

Never before have we had to embrace fluid leadership to such an extent, nor pursue vertiginous decision-making cycles, or resort to intuition and humanism over deliberate data-backed strategies. This unprecedented context has helped us reframe the way we think about executive education through the lens of life-long learning, technology, collaboration and the well-being of communities.

The global crisis has also created an opportunity for us to reflect on our missions, purpose, values, role, and impact on the society and world we inhabit.

Even before the pandemic, we were witnessing the unbundling of education, with different shapes and forms coexisting rather than competing. This includes classroom-based vs workplace education, mass vs personalized programs, campus-based vs online, structured vs unstructured, taught vs facilitated, and increasingly, degree-based vs skill-based education.

In this increasingly complex learning ecosystem, established education providers like business schools and corporate universities compete and collaborate with EdTech start-ups and other emerging players in the world of executive education. With digitalization featuring more prominently in executive education, the future of learning is blended. This creates a plethora of opportunities for experimentation and innovation.

Set against global challenges such as the COVID-19 pandemic and the climate emergency, these developments magnify the need for all stakeholders to be part of the transformation ecosystem, including the educational sector, the corporate sector, the public sector and individuals.

This very timely book, edited by my two dear friends and esteemed thought-leaders, Santiago Iñiguez and Peter Lorange, sheds new light on these vital issues and initiates an important debate about a whole range of aspects of executive education development in this very dynamic context.

Eric Cornuel
President and CEO of EFMD
Brussels, Belgium

Eric Cornuel is President and CEO of EFMD (European Foundation for Management Development), as well as an affiliated professor of HEC (France), member of different corporate boards and regular contributors at Emerald journals.

Introduction: Business Education in Times of Disruption and Resilience

Our World Has Changed Abruptly

We are living through special times, possibly the most challenging in recent years. The crisis resulting from the COVID-19 pandemic has tested our resilience, leadership and ability to manage organizations amid radical, ever-changing uncertainty.

In this environment, all the skills associated with business leadership become particularly relevant. Entrepreneurial initiative; formulating a vision of the future, even if the scenarios to be evaluated are unpredictable; leading and motivating people; and the determination to implement actions in an agile and effective manner, changing direction if necessary. Darwin's conclusion that it is not the strongest or the biggest that survives, but the species with the best capacity to adapt has never been more apposite.

However, it is precisely under these circumstances that business schools, executive education centres and corporate universities are called upon to play a decisive role in the development of companies. Our mission as trainers of tomorrow's leaders must be linked to several objectives: rebuilding a global governance system that enables effective integration and can quickly deal with challenges such as pandemics; adopting norms and practices that promote sustainable economic activity; and achieving standards of freedom, equality and justice on all continents that allow for full human development that respects the environment.

In recent decades, the education sector has undergone profound changes as a result of irreversible globalization, the impact of technologies and social transformations. These changes have become more acute as a consequence of the current crisis, where lockdowns have stretched the possibilities of virtual interaction and online training. Indeed, the pandemic has accelerated many changes in education that would have occurred much more slowly if they had come about organically.

As the contributions in this book illustrate, the future of education, and also of work, will be increasingly hybrid. Face-to-face classroom learning will be complemented by multiple educational resources, synchronous and asynchronous, to facilitate greater flexibility and adaptation to the learner's personality and circumstances. In this transformed educational environment, education will have a greater impact on both developing global citizens and enhancing their employability. In short, the best is yet to come.

There is another major lesson to be learned from the pandemic. Contrary to the predictions that robots will take over humans, lockdowns across the world have enhanced the role of technologies in bringing us closer by providing powerful platforms for group working, virtual meetings and delivering effective education programs.

Indeed, the post COVID-19 world enhances adaptation and change. Professionals will live blended lives and the work environment will become increasing hybrid and liquid. Professionals will work in teams face-to-face and on social platforms, from home or at their company offices, in a continuum that blurs distance, time and that increases productivity. They will increasingly deal virtually with colleagues from different hemispheres and time zones, making friends who belong to diverse cultures and possess different visions of the world.

Hybrid formats and various online forms of delivery are here to stay, as many contributors to this book explain. Not just because social distancing and cross-border mobility may still pose problems for attending face-to-face classes on a regular basis, but rather because they provide better results than just traditional presential learning. This flexibility will also be reflected through the creation and distribution of knowledge, teaching methodologies, and other university activities, including extracurricular experiences, which may become partly virtual.

The main engine for the transition to a more flexible and adaptable learning world has to be, naturally, the faculty and staff at business schools and executive education centres. The key to success in any educational format is not the technology, nor the contents. These are necessary components of online learning, but they quickly become commodities. It is the experience orchestrated by the faculty, instructors and coaches, be it presential or remote that makes the difference.

There's a general consensus among analysts that the pandemic will have an enduring negative impact on globalization. However, we believe that progress in controlling the virus—which will come about through breakthroughs in finding a vaccine and better treatments, along with the spread of prudent social habits—will foster consumer confidence and reignite international mobility, favouring cross-border trade and the next expansion phase of global business.

Three further drivers will help rekindle this optimism: the international appetite of young entrepreneurs from all latitudes; the spread of new technologies, platforms and apps that facilitate cross-border business; and the reactivation of the economy, also fuelled by opportunities brought from the endorsement of sustainable policies.

A New Learning Environment

Even though the focus of our book is on executive education, especially on how this might be taking shape after the pandemic, it is worthwhile putting this issue in a broader societal context. The post-COVID world will not necessarily mean a return to a non-pandemic world. Severe, new epidemic waves will regrettably become the norm (1) and there will probably be long-term impacts from future pandemic threats on society and thus on executive education.

The post-pandemic reality may be that executive development will increasingly take major global changes into account. We might see a gradual return to a focus on macro-political issues as part of executive education: most business schools have in general given a relatively low emphasis to such macro-political shifts. This is likely to change with the new circumstances.

This new reality will change the face-to-face dimension of executive education and learning. So-Young Kang, the founder and CEO of Gnowbe, which specializes in macroenvironmental advice, argues that there will be a post-COVID shift in mind-sets from digital as nice-to-have to digital as must-have. (2) Face-to-face will be just one way of teaching in the future, to be used in parallel with digital, social, participatory approaches based on participants' perspectives. Students participate through their screen and are seen/heard by the other participants, in addition to interacting with the instructor/professor, who now acts more as a catalyst to bring out the participants' experiences, rather than giving a lecture.

New know-how will be required to make this happen:

- Mobile instructional design (MID).
- Retraining teachers to become better catalysts, more focused on listening and/or synthesizing, rather than on traditional lecturing.

The key decision-making criteria driving executive education will also change:

- A gradual shift towards more focus on global/national macro-societal trends.
- A relatively higher input from line managers regarding the needs they might be facing, so as to facilitate more exchange and debate regarding such issues among participants.
- Less focus on strategic, managerial, and leadership principles.

Some of the trends mentioned in this volume and that we identify from interviews with key stakeholders include:

1. *Hybrid and online courses.* The present already belongs to the programs best able to adapt to the availability and location of managers, given reduced international mobility, which will take time to resume, if it ever reaches the previous levels. Experience shows that the integration of technology and learning, thus prolonging the momentum beyond the traditional in presential sessions that characterize classroom learning may also enrich the experience and contribute to consolidate the corporate culture among participants.
2. *Learning orchestrators.* Academics, along with practitioners and consultants with relevant experience in the business world, interaction with companies, and contact with senior management, are the best deliverers of in-company training. They combine a thorough technical knowledge of their disciplines with the necessary neutrality to be able to efficiently and independently advise companies on their training needs but are also capable of transcending traditional disciplines through understanding from within of the decisive issues facing a company.
3. *Courses and knowledge applied to the development of corporate needs*, linked to the company's mission. The time of cut and paste from open programs available at schools or executive education centres is over, with companies demanding courses designed to suit their needs and context.

4. *Integrated learning platforms*, shared by business schools or consultancies and their corporate clients. These would offer participants access to content adapted to their needs and environment, while allowing them to interact with other directors in the company. Such platforms would also allow clients to use assessment schemes to measure personal or group learning progress.
5. *Mechanisms to measure the efficacy or impact of learning*, along with the use of learning analytics. We have seen that many companies believe this need is not being met. It is increasingly possible to develop methods to measure the impact of a program on the personal development of participants, thanks to new apps and technology developments, and subsequently to assess how they carry out their tasks within the company. We are entering a fascinating period in the construction of tools based on technology that will allow us to better measure the effects of educational products on the development of directive skills and the behaviour of participants.
6. *Multiple partnerships*. We may see alliances between schools and consultancies, coaching networks, software, and technology and content platforms, which provide integrated solutions to corporate customers. An example is the IE Business School/Financial Times Headspring, a global supplier of custom programs for corporations, represented in this volume by two of the contributors.
7. *Increasing and varied competition*. The preponderance of business schools in the in-company training sector has been challenged during the pandemic by the arrival of many new players, particularly online platforms, which have in many cases doubled their revenues, as shown by some case studies included in this book. In addition, we may expect engineering schools and departments of psychology and international relations entering the tailor-made segment, as are universities' continuous education and extension units. At the same time, consultancy firms see in-company training as part of their professional services portfolio and are able to offer myriad synergies for their business units, as well as the possibility of implementing their programs in multinationals on every continent via their subsidiaries. Competition is further increasing thanks to the growing number of freelancers and coaches, whose services are available on an individual basis or as consociates.
8. *Timing and pricing*. Finally, to further complicate matters, we are witnessing an increasing demand of just-in-time education, as well as corporate customers demanding increasingly competitive prices and shorter design and execution times, given the relevant budget reductions over the pandemic, while at the same time requiring programs to fit in

with participants' schedules and locations and expecting deliverers to scale up their offer for larger groups when needed. Again, online and hybrid courses has proven to be a good solution to meet most of these demands.

Structure of the Book

This volume consists of 30 chapters that can be read independently, grouped into three main parts.

The first part focuses on the values and purpose of business schools and centres of executive education, whose role has been reinforced after the pandemic by the need to train managers and entrepreneurs who will be the architects of a sustainable and just global society.

Julian Birkinshaw draws on the experiences at London Business School to propose reinforcing the three different modes of leadership development through executive education in a hybrid and challenging environment.

Paolo Boccardelli outlines the major macro trends that will mark the development of the post-pandemic society and how they will affect educational institutions, and in particular the training of managers.

Santiago Iñiguez proposes associating management teaching and research with the humanities, as opposed to the traditional ties to the social sciences.

Daniel R. LeClair draws on his cross-cultural experience to explain how business schools have developed their purpose, in different ways, according to their cultural context and mission, which affects the nature of their activities, their mission and their activities from research to teaching.

Johan Roos proposes reconfiguring campuses as educational hubs, diversifying programs and taking advantage of all online educational resources.

Richard Straub summarizes some of the perennial teachings of Peter Drucker, who lived through the great crisis of the 1930s, and whose ideas are even more topical than before the pandemic.

Nick Van Dam focuses on how the future of work will change, the need for digital skills, leading teams in virtual environments and enhancing well-being.

The first part of the book is completed with case studies that illustrate the professional experiences of senior managers like Michael Arena of Amazon Web Services and General Motors; Caryn L. Beck Dudley piloting AACSB; Birgitte Holter at Yara, the leading global fertilizer company; Jose Maria Palomo at Santander bank, one of the world's leading financial institutions; and Claire Pérez-Redondo at the United States Postal Service. The selection has attempted to capture diverse examples in terms of sectors, geographies and organizational cultures.

The second part of this book focuses on specific areas of business school activity, and how they are expected to transform in the coming years. Diego del Alcázar and Santiago Iñiguez address the impact of new technologies on the learning process, proposing a concept of liquid learning that transcends traditional learning references.

Gabriela Alvarado and Iñiguez analyse whether it makes sense to speak of MBA maturity, explaining that the diversification of formats, specializations and markets will continue to grow in the future.

Salvador Carmona explains how the new development needs of companies in the wake of the pandemic justify the adoption of new content in management programs.

Jerry Wind proposes reimagining executive education and reformulating all its basic aspects, using six models.

The part concludes with case studies of Haier, with an interview with CEO Zhang Ruimin, who has been dubbed the Asian Steve Jobs. Two large professional services and auditing companies are also reviewed: PWC, through the veteran experience of Blair Sheppard, founder of Duke Corporate Education, and Mazars, with the outside-the-box vision of Laurent Choain. It is completed by complementary views on management education and executive development on the Asian continent from the perspectives of two increasingly influential countries: Rebecca Taylor, head of Southampton University Malaysia, and Jikyeong Kang, president of the Asian Institute of Management in the Philippines.

The third and final part of the book addresses issues within the field of executive education related to technological applications.

Bala Chakravarthy raises the importance of differentiating online courses and offering quality programs in these formats as a clear opportunity for business schools.

Ignacio Dahl Rocha and Nicole Michel explain how the learning space has two dimensions, the real and the virtual, and that the challenge is how to manage both so that their boundaries are blurred.

Kurt Haanaes and Katherine Brown emphasize the importance of system leadership in the current era, analysing all the drivers of significant change at a meta level.

Jean François Manzoni shares experiences at IMD on how technology-mediated interactions complement face-to-face experiences.

Karin Mugnaini presents arguments to justify how family businesses, traditionally closed to in-company training, have development needs similar to other corporations.

Martin Rodriguez Jugo illustrates the advantages of implementing learning analytics in programs to improve the learning experience and increase its effectiveness.

Finally, this part is completed with three case studies: edx, one of the most successful online program platforms, founded by Harvard University and MIT, and the vision of its founding CEO, Anant Agarwal; an alternative case in Europe, OpenClassrooms, whose youthful founder, Pierre Dubuc, comments on the social focus of its programs, as well as the boom during the pandemic; and finally Cheung Kong, the Beijing private school focused on CEO training, from the perspective of its dean since its founding, Bing Xiang.

We trust that these chapters will be a learning opportunity for readers, and that they will enjoy and learn from them as much or more than the editors have.

Madrid, Spain	Santiago Iñiguez
Horgen, Switzerland	Peter Lorange

Contents

Part I Values and Purpose

1. Rethinking Executive Education for the Virtual World 3
   Julian Birkinshaw

2. Megatrends Impacting Higher Education After the Pandemic 13
   Paolo Boccardelli

3. The Enlightened Executive: Management and the Humanities 29
   Santiago Iñiguez

4. Business Schools as Catalysts for Sustainable Development 37
   Daniel R. LeClair

5. Executive Education 2.0 Coming Right Up 47
   Johan Roos

6. Perennial Insights from Peter Drucker 57
   Richard Straub

7. The Role of Business Education in Supporting the Future of Work 67
   Nick van Dam

8	**The Innovative Ecosystem** *Michael Arena*	79
9	**AACSB: Paving New Ways in Business Education** *Caryn L. Beck Dudley*	89
10	**Traditional Corporations Going Green: Yara** *Birgitte Holter*	99
11	**Diversity and Inclusion: Banco Santander** *Chema Palomo*	103
12	**Reinventing Public Service: US Postal Service** *Claire Pérez-Redondo*	111

Part II The Renaissance of Business Schools

13	**Abracadabra: How Technology-Enhanced Education Personalizes Learning** *Diego del Alcázar Benjumea and Santiago Iñiguez*	121
14	**The MBA Is Dead: Long Live the MBA** *Gabriela Alvarado Cabrera and Santiago Iñiguez*	135
15	**Covid-19: Organizational Responses to Societal and Business Challenges** *Salvador Carmona*	147
16	**Reimagine Executive Education** *Jerry Wind*	157
17	**Bridging Academia and Business: Mazars** *Laurent Choain*	171
18	**Executive Education in Southeast Asia: Asian Institute of Management** *Jikyeong Kang*	181
19	**Learning to Learn: PWC** *Blair Sheppard*	191
20	**International Campuses Abroad: The University of Southampton Malaysia** *Rebecca Taylor*	201
21	**Transforming Organizations: Haier** *Ruimin Zhang*	211

Part III Innovation: Formats, Methods, Platforms

22 Using the Pandemic to Reset Executive Programs 223
Bala Chakravarthy

23 Post-Pandemic Architecture and Education 231
Ignacio Dahl Rocha and Nicole Michel

24 How the Pandemic Has Demonstrated the Importance of System Leadership in Executive Education 237
Knut Haanaes and Katherine Brown

25 Executive Education Post-Pandemic: Some Reflections on the Role of Technology-Mediated Interactions Going Forward 245
Jean François Manzoni

26 Executive Education for Family Owned Portfolio Corporations: Needs and Challenges 257
Karin Mugnaini

27 Learning Analytics: A Science in Rapid Expansion That Is Shaping the Future of Education 265
Martin Rodriguez Jugo

28 Learning Platforms: edX 277
Anant Agarwal

29 Enhancing Social Reach: OpenClassrooms 287
Pierre Dubuc

30 Chinese Executive Education in Perspective: CKGSB's Innovations in Business Education 297
Bing Xiang

Editors and Contributors

About the Editors

Santiago Iñiguez is the president of IE University and founding member of the board of IE Business School/Financial Times Headspring.

Peter Lorange is the founder and Chairman of Lorange Network. He is a former President of IMD and of BI (Oslo) and the President Emeritus of the Zurich/CEIBS Institute of Business Education. He was formerly a professor at MIT and at Wharton. He has also been in charge of the successful investment company S. Uglestad Invest for more than 35 years. He has published more than 20 books and 120 articles related to multinational management and strategy.

Contributors

Anant Agarwal is the founding CEO of edX, a professor of electrical engineering and computer science at MIT and a member of the international commission in global education financing at Education Commission, as well as founder of several start-ups.

Michael Arena is VP Talent and Development at Amazon Web Services (AWS) and member of Organizational Dynamics Faculty, University of

Pennsylvania (US). He has been Chief Talent Officer at General Motors and Visiting Scientist at the MIT Media Lab.

Julian Birkinshaw is Professor of Strategy and Entrepreneurship at London Business School (UK). He is a member of the British Academy, has been listed among the Top 50 Management Thinkers and has published 15 books.

Paolo Boccardelli is Dean and CEO at Luiss Business School, and Full Professor of Corporate Strategy and Management. Member of the EQUIS Committee and Advisor of Quality Services and Processes to schools, he is expert of International Standing at the Australian Research Council, and Chairman of the Scientific Committee of the Ericsson Foundation.

Katherine Brown is a specialist in ESG investing, former Head of Sustainable and Impact Investing and Global Leadership Fellow at the World Economic Forum, and a Senior Advisor to IMD Business School.

Gabriela Alvarado Cabrera is Professor of Marketing at IPADE Business School where she also serves as Associate Director of Research and Academic Processes. She is member of the EFMD Research Committee and her research focuses on management education, business schools' reputation, international accreditations, and rankings.

Salvador Carmona is the Rector at IE University (Spain) and Professor of Accounting and Management Control. He has served as President of the European Accounting Association and Editor of the European Accounting Review.

Bala Chakravarthy is Professor Emeritus of Strategy & Leadership at IMD; and a former professor at INSEAD and Wharton. He has worked with leading multinational companies as a management consultant and educator. He is a Fellow of the Strategic Management Society; and has served on the editorial boards of top journals in the field.

Laurent Choain is the Chief Leadership, Education & Culture at Mazars, CEO of Mazars University, executive coach, affiliate professor at Université Paris Pantheon-Assas and a senior fellow at ESCP. A long-standing member of the EFMD and EQUIS boards, he also serves on the Peter Drucker Society of Europe.

Diego del Alcázar Benjumea is CEO of IE University, member of the board of Spain StartUp, member of the board Headspring (FT-IE).

Pierre Dubuc is the co-founder and CEO of OpenClassrooms, B-Corp and mission-driven leading online education platform in Europe with more than 2 million unique visitors every month. He created it with Mathieu Nebra in 2013 in order to make education accessible. Pierre Dubuc was featured among the "30 under 30" by Forbes magazine in 2016.

Caryn L. Beck Dudley is President and CEO of AACSB International and a scholar in law and ethical organizations. She has been dean at the business schools of Santa Clara University, Florida State University and Utah State University.

Knut Haanaes is a Professor and the Lundin Sustainability Chair at IMD. He was previously Dean of the Global Leadership Institute at the World Economic Forum as well as senior partner at the Boston Consulting Group.

Birgitte Holter is Business Development Director of Climate Neutrality at Yara International, the world's leading fertilizer company and a provider of environmental solutions. As a former VP at Hydro Aluminium she has also contributed to taking new and sustainable solutions both to the automotive- and building markets.

Jikyeong Kang is the president and dean of the Asian Institute of Management, Philippines. Previously, she was a professor of marketing at Manchester Business School and IE Business School, and visiting professor at CEIBS and ESSEC. She serves on the boards of AACSB, EFMD, AAPBS, and PRME.

Daniel R. LeClair is CEO of the Global Business School Network (GBSN), advisory board member for several start-ups and business schools, and former EVP & chief strategy and innovation officer of AACSB International.

Jean François Manzoni is the Nestlé Professor of Leadership and Organizational Development at IMD, where he also serves as the President. He has been working in Executive Development for more than 30 years and over the years has initiated a number of ground-breaking technology-enabled tools and programs.

Nicole Michel is an Architect from Buenos Aires, Argentina. She holds a Master of Architecture degree from the Massachusetts Institute of Technology (MIT), where she won the William Everett Chamberlain Award for Excellence in Architecture, the Imre Halasz Award for the Best Thesis, and the AIA Award and Certificate.

Karin Mugnaini is the President and COO of The Lorange Network, former Global Head of Communications at Intertrade Group and in charge of business development at CEO Positions AG.

Chema Palomo is Human Resources Group VP at Banco Santander. Previously he was HR business partner head for EMEA at Johnson and Johnson, HR manager at CEMEX and financial controller at LVMH.

Claire Pérez-Redondo is Director International Civilian and Military Transportation and Networks Logistics, US Postal Service, and was previously international affairs specialist at Correos (Spain).

Ignacio Dahl Rocha is Senior Partner in RDR Architectes, a leading architectural firm based in Lausanne. He holds a master's degree from Yale School of Architecture and in an undergraduate in Architecture from Buenos Aires.

Martin Rodriguez Jugo is the Director of IE Publishing and Executive Education Online at IE University, and Adjunct Faculty of Operations Management, focusing his area of teaching in how to manage creative projects.

Johan Roos is Chief Academic Officer and professor at Hult Business School, co-inventor of LEGO Serious Play, board member of Imagination Lab Foundation. A Swedish national he is a member of the Danish Academy of Technical Sciences.

Blair Sheppard is the Global Leader Strategy and Leadership for the PWC network, Dean Emeritus and Professor Emeritus at Fuqua School of Business and former CEO of Duke Corporate Education.

Richard Straub is the Founder and President of the Peter Drucker Society Europe and the Global Peter Drucker Forum.

Rebecca Taylor is the CEO of the University of Southampton Malaysia and a Pro Vice-Chancellor & Professor of Economics at the University of Southampton UK. Rebecca is also the former Executive Dean of the Open University Business School, UK.

Dr. Nick van Dam is Chief Learning Officer of IE University and the Chair of the IE Center for Liquid Learning. He is a visiting Professor at Nyenrode Business University (The Netherlands) and the University of Pennsylvania. He is a former Partner and Global Chief Learning Officer at McKinsey & Company.

Jerry Wind is Lauder Professor Emeritus and Professor of Marketing at The Wharton School at the University of Pennsylvania, co-founder of the Reimagine Education global competition, author of over 300 articles and 30 books and received all the major marketing awards.

Bing Xiang is the founding Dean and professor of China business and globalization at Cheung Kong School of Business, was professor at Guanghua School of Management, Beijing University, and serves on the boards of several companies.

Ruimin Zhang is the current Secretary of the Haier Group Party Committee, Chairman of the Board of Directors and CEO of Haier Group. He has been recognized as one of the World's 50 most respected business leaders by the Financial Times and as a leading business influencer by Thinkers50.

List of Figures

Fig. 7.1	The top ten competencies by 2025 (Elaborated by the author based on sources of the World Economic Forum, 2020)	73
Fig. 7.2	The foundations of learning sciences (Elaborated by the Author)	77
Fig. 24.1	A timeline of industry-wide initiatives (Elaborated by the Authors)	239
Fig. 25.1	*Summarized responses from 350 senior executives, collected online during IMD's Leading High Impact Learning Day, March 3, 2021 On a 1 (low) to 5 (high) scale (Source* Elaborated by the author)	255
Fig. 27.1	Engagement evolution tracked in a five week-long executive education online program	271
Fig. 27.2	Mastery of concepts and competency evolution tracked in a five-week long executive education online program	272

List of Tables

Table 1.1	Three different modes to leadership development	7
Table 14.1	Top 10 full-time MBA	141
Table 14.2	Top 10 executive MBA	142

Part I

Values and Purpose

1

Rethinking Executive Education for the Virtual World

Julian Birkinshaw

It is no secret that the executive education industry was hit hard by the Covid pandemic, with face-to-face programmes put on hold and corporate spending on learning and development being cut. A study by UNICON (the consortium for university-based executive education) noted that "many of the world's leading business schools suffered a fall in executive education turnover" (Hammergren 2021). The Financial Times reported that "the global university based executive education market, worth close to $2bn in 2019, fell by a third in 2020" (Moules 2021).

Like others, we at London Business School had already built competencies in digital learning, for example, through MOOCs (massive open online courses) and SPOCs (small private online courses). It was surprisingly easy to shift all our teaching to online delivery as soon as the pandemic hit, and indeed to develop interactive and engaging learning formats that replicated much of what we had always done in the classroom. We developed a variety of formats—live online, asynchronous online, hybrid—and we worked tirelessly with custom clients to create virtual alternatives to the face-to-face programmes they had already signed up for. We managed to keep the business ticking over, though at lower levels of demand. Satisfaction ratings were

---

J. Birkinshaw (✉)
London Business School, London, UK
e-mail: jbirkinshaw@london.edu

as good if not better than for face-to-face teaching. The experience of faculty and professional staff was mostly positive.

So that's the good news. The less-good news is that virtual working has enabled and accelerated big changes in the executive education market. Moving classes and workshops online was the easy bit—now comes the harder challenge of rethinking our overall value proposition to prepare for the "new normal" which will likely involve a blend of face-to-face and virtual working.

In this article, we share some of our ideas about what comes next, based on our own experiences as well as insights we have picked up from others. We tackle two linked issues—the specific challenge of rethinking leadership development for a hybrid world and the broader challenge of rethinking the *raison d'etre* of business schools.

Rethinking Leadership Development for a Hybrid World

A major part of the LBS offering is leadership development, defined as the growth process individuals go through to become more effective in leadership roles. Thinking about leadership development has evolved over the years, but there is a growing view that it involves three elements: (a) knowledge-development, i.e., the accumulation of cognitive insights about the world of business and management; (b) action-taking, i.e., individuals having the confidence to do things differently and to learn from their actions, and (c) identity-development, i.e., individuals becoming better at influencing others and developing a clear sense of who they are (Day 2000; Day et al. 2014; Ibarra 2015; Snook et al. 2012). Stated more simply, successful executives are knowledgeable, good at making things happen, and good at relating to and getting the best from others. And our value proposition is to help them with all three.

Which is why the changes unleashed by Covid are only just beginning. Every aspect of leadership development is made harder when we work remotely, though some are harder than others. Let's look at each in turn.

Knowledge-development. As already noted, moving classes online was straightforward and basically works well. There are still challenges in getting participation and engagement in Zoom-based classes, and it's much harder for speakers to get feedback on *their* performance, but these are relatively small problems. If the demand is for cognitive development—helping leaders to accumulate a new body of knowledge and understand the world better—virtual teaching works fine. It's not as good—or as much fun—as classroom teaching, but as long as participants are motivated, they will get what they need.

Action-taking. A landmark book in the field of leadership development was Lessons from Experience by McCall et al. (1988) which famously claimed (without much evidence) that 70% of learning occurs on-the-job through challenging work assignments. It is only when we are thrown into new or difficult situations, the book argued, that we really grow and develop as individuals. Another useful concept from the literature is situated learning (Lave and Wenger 1991), which says people develop new skills in an apprentice-like way, first of all as a peripheral observer on a team, and then gradually becoming an active participant and contributor.

Our sense is that executives are not getting enough of these challenging new assignments when working virtually. Many are building new skills (e.g., around crisis management) within roles, but the opportunities for changing roles, and developing entirely new skills, are much harder to come by. In our conversations with clients, it seems many organisations decided to put these lateral development opportunities on hold until face-to-face working returned.

Another well-known concept from the literature is David Kolb's (1984) learning cycle which argues for a deep symbiosis between active experimentation (doing things differently) and reflective learning (making sense of what you have done). Our programmes at LBS were always designed to stimulate that iterative process of development, and in the pre-Covid world there were usually ample opportunities for leaders to try things out when they got back to the office on Monday morning. But such opportunities are now few and far between. And even when leaders are able to try out something new, they don't get the same richness of feedback from colleagues because there are no informal opportunities to talk to them. The learning cycle has to a large degree broken down.

Identity-Development. The third pillar of leadership development is about making sense of ourselves and our relationships with others—our identity (Ibarra 2015). This might sound a bit flaky to a hard-nosed plant manager or finance director, but the reality is that the more senior an executive becomes, the more important it is that they understand their own strengths and weaknesses, and the effect they have on others. Many of the components of our successful programmes, including 360 feedback, personal biography exercises, and group discussions, are all about helping participants become more self-aware. As Petriglieri and Petriglieri (2010) argued, business schools can be viewed as "identity workspaces" because they provide a setting for leaders to take time out to reflect, get help from peers and coaches, and try out low-risk experiments in how they interact with others.

It seems clear that this type of identity-development work is less effective in a virtual environment. Our experience suggests that Zoom calls are fine for maintaining existing relationships, but they are not good for difficult conversations, and they don't work so well when you are trying to forge new relationships. Indeed, a lot of organisations put their leadership development activities on hold during the first lockdown because they could see this type of development was compromised.

So how do we overcome these obstacles to leadership development? What should business schools be doing to help organisations create more fully rounded leaders in a world with less face-to-face contact than before? A few practical thoughts.

First, ensure a good balance across the three dimensions of leadership development. Covid has reminded us that a lot of knowledge-based learning can be done asynchronously and alone, which is why we increasingly provide video recordings of faculty introducing topics for people to view before a programme starts. This leaves more time in live sessions for discussion and sense-making. We also use live sessions to design and commit to new actions that participants pursue after the programme or between modules.

As we plan for a post-pandemic hybrid workplace, it is clear that we need to match the medium to the message more carefully. Consider Table 1.1, which illustrates how each dimension of leadership development (knowledge-development, action-taking, and identity-development) can be addressed through some combination of three formats (live face to face, live virtual, asynchronous). The best leadership development experiences, we believe, will involve a combination of these approaches, and often with frequent iterations between them. For example, we created a new format with 90-minute 'live online' sessions twice a week, interspersed with asynchronous learning and application exercises.

Second, use technology creatively. When a new piece of technology comes along we first of all use it as a substitute for what came before, then we gradually figure out all the exciting new opportunities it opens up. We have already moved from using zoom to replicate a traditional class to a more interactive form of teaching with video, chat, and PowerPoint operating simultaneously. But there is scope for taking these emerging technologies much further. As my colleague Tim Sylvester notes "technology opens up learning experiences that were previously inconceivable, such as exploring self-awareness and personal presence using virtual reality." We need to become a lot more creative in

Table 1.1 Three different modes to leadership development

	Live face to face structured sessions	Live virtual structured sessions	Asynchronous—in your own time
Knowledge-development	In class lecture or seminar, emphasising dialogue, interaction, spontaneity, multiple voices	Zoom-style lecture or seminar, more structure required than face to face especially when in a large group	Reading a book, watching a webinar or lecture when convenient. Works well for one-way communication, but hard to concentrate for long periods. Exercises and quizzes can be used to reinforce learning
Identity development	Physical co-location is good for personal coaching, one-to-one or one-to-few, and also for larger group sessions for sharing personal insights and getting feedback (used to be called "t-groups")	One-to-one or one-to-few sessions can be effective in virtual setting, and they are very efficient. But generally not as good as when people are in the same physical space. Larger group sessions do not work well in virtual setting	Many ways to work on identity development on a day-to-day basis, for example, ongoing observation of colleagues in meetings, whether face to face or virtual, also use of 360 surveys and other codified forms of feedback, that the individual reads and reviews in their own time
Action-taking	Role plays in classes and small meetings are helpful in trying out new ways of acting, but they can be a bit sterile and simplistic. useful	It's possible to do role playing in virtual sessions, but this is even more challenging given the limited opportunity for feedback and interaction	This is simply "doing your job" but if you want to learn from your day-to-day activities you need to deliberately stretch yourself and take on challenging assignments, and also to link these activities up to some of the more reflective activities mentioned above

(Developed by the Author)

trying out these new applications. And we need to ensure our students and faculty keep developing their digital literacy skills.

Third, work with organisations to increase the experiential components of learning. There are limits to how much leaders can develop if they are confined to a narrowly defined job and, as discussed above, people have been more "stuck" than usual during the pandemic. This is starting to change, and we have had conversations with several progressive organisations about putting in place schemes explicitly designed to counteract this problem. For example, some have provided senior mentors to high-potential employees to provide help during lockdown, and others have put in place shadowing or apprenticeship schemes.

Rethinking the Purpose of Executive Education

While it is important to think creatively about our clients' changing needs, its equally important to reflect on our own purpose—our *raison d'etre* as business schools. And here, as above, the pandemic has unleashed a set of forces for change that have potentially far-reaching consequences.

Consider a brief analogy—the newspaper industry. In the traditional print-based world, everyone bought the same paper and it bundled together news, classified ads, gossip, TV listings, and so forth. The Internet made it possible for these things to be unbundled, leading quickly to the emergence of specialist offerings in all these areas, and a collapse of the traditional business model that was based on selling advertising space alongside what people wanted to read.

Business schools face the prospect of a similar unbundling of their executive education programmes. It is well understood that executives don't sign up for a week at LBS just to hear the latest research insights from faculty. They want to meet interesting people. They want time out to reflect on a challenging business problem. They are looking for advice. They want to put the LBS logo on their LinkedIn profile. Some are looking for a new job. Some want to go shopping and to the theatre.

Because of this multitude of reasons for coming to LBS, we created "bundled" offerings where all these needs could be addressed during a one-week programme. But moving online has enabled the process of unbundling. Of course, this was happening to some degree before the pandemic already. But the shift to 100% virtual learning (even if only temporarily) has accelerated this trend and has exposed the fragility of the business model in a couple of ways.

First, it is clear that some things are lost altogether when you take a virtual programme—we cannot, in all honesty, provide the social experience or the London connection some people are looking for.

Second, participants vote with their feet (or rather, with their mouse) in terms of deciding what activities to take part in during a programme.

Whereas in pre-Covid times, people would immerse themselves in the whole week of activities as a cohort—and would typically join in whether they thought they were useful or not—there is no such obligation when working virtually. You can quit with a click of the mouse. It is not unusual to see a drop-off in participation in evening events or group sessions.

The core of the offering—the faculty-led sessions—remains solid, and many executives will still pay a premium for this type of high-quality content (just as the Financial Times and the New York Times continue to attract subscribers to their online formats). But there are likely to be potential participants who don't want the whole bundle. Some might be attracted to the faculty sessions and nothing else. Others might be particularly keen on the coaching and reflection piece, in which case they could sign up for a free online course to cover the academic content and then pay for half a dozen sessions with an executive coach—a much cheaper option.

In sum, and whether we like it or not, the greater transparency and the "modularisation" of a virtual programme design allows it to be unbundled. This creates both threats and opportunities for incumbent business schools. Fortunately, there are lessons to be learned from other industries, such as newspapers, financial services, and retailing, about how to respond. Here are a few that might be useful.

Double down on your core offering. From newspapers to movies to music, the axiom that "content is king" still prevails. The world of business is awash with blogs, commentaries, surveys, and opinions, and most is pretty poor quality. Executives will pay a premium for high-quality content, and business schools are uniquely positioned to provide one form of quality, i.e., rigorous, research-led insight into practical business challenges.

High-quality insight isn't the only thing at the core of the business school offering. We are good at creating stimulating and fun learning experiences, we offer "identity workspaces" as noted earlier, we operate in exciting locations. As we leave lockdown and we offer more hybrid or blended programmes, these characteristics will come increasingly to the fore.

There is also increasing interest in *micro-credentialing*—providing learners with certificates and badges of achievement for completing short training courses. Business schools have traditionally resisted these types of schemes, preferring to keep their degree-granting and non-degree activities completely separate. But Covid has spurred on real growth in this area, on both the supply and demand sides, so it's not an opportunity we can afford to ignore.

Be creative about offering ancillary services. Another lesson from the unbundling of the newspaper industry is that specialist competitors emerged quickly, especially in the profitable parts of the business such as classified advertising (Craigslist, finn.no in Scandinavia, Autotrader in the UK). In the world of executive education, there is a similar dynamic in evidence, with specialist providers in such areas as coaching, consulting, networking and corporate event management. Rather than simply cede ground to these specialists, there is scope for business schools to fight back, and to create dedicated offerings in some of these specific market areas.

Look for rebundling opportunities in hybrid and blended formats. The legendary venture capital investor Jim Barksdale reputedly said "There are two ways to make money in business: You can unbundle, or you can bundle." So even while traditional executive programmes are being pulled apart thanks to the Internet and the Covid pandemic, we can start thinking about creative ways to develop new offerings that bundle together the best of virtual and face-to-face learning. There is an emerging consensus that the "new normal" for business won't involve as much international travel as before, so the learning interventions that companies invest in are likely to require a more careful mix of asynchronous, face-to-face and virtual components. And who better to design those interventions than business schools?

**

The executive education market has always been cyclical, with demand rising and falling broadly in line with the economic conditions of the time. But there has never been a "shock" anywhere near as severe as the Covid pandemic. The short-term hit to the industry has been significant, and business schools have successfully adapted to a temporary world of 100% virtual learning. But the longer term impact of Covid is not yet clear. In this paper we have sketched out some initial thoughts on how the world of learning and development might change, and how business schools will need to change with it, to prepare ourselves for the new normal.

References

Day, D. V. 2000. Leadership development: A review in context. *The Leadership Quarterly*, 11(4): 581–613.

Day, David V., et al. 2014. Advances in leader and leadership development: A review of 25 years of research and theory. *The Leadership Quarterly*, 25(1): 63–82.

Hammergren, L. 2021. Executive education is changing for good. AACSB report. https://www.aacsb.edu/insights/2021/february/executive-education-is-changing-for-good.

Ibarra, H. 2015. *Act like a leader, think like a leader*. Boston, MA: Harvard Business Review Press.

Kolb, D. A. 1984. *Experiential learning: Experience as the source of learning and development*. Upper Saddle River, NJ: Prentice Hall.
Lave, J., & Wenger, E. 1991. *Situated learning: Legitimate peripheral participation*. New York, NY: Cambridge University Press.
McCall, M. W., Lombardo, M. W., & Morrison, A. M. 1988. *Lessons of experience: How successful executives develop on the job*. Lexington, MA: Lexington Books.
Moules, J. 2021. Financial Times, Business School briefing. February 15.
Petriglieri, G., & Petriglieri, J. L. 2010. Identity workspaces: The case of Business Schools. *Academy of Management Learning & Education*, 9(1): 44–60.
Snook, S., Nohria, N., & Khurana, R. 2012. *The handbook for teaching leadership: Knowing, doing, and being*. Thousand Oaks, CA: Sage.

2

Megatrends Impacting Higher Education After the Pandemic

Paolo Boccardelli

The current challenging environment demands that business leaders adopt a holistic vision, with a wide view of the world where technical and human perspectives converge. Our global society is undergoing a profound transformation, in which megatrends will impact business models and organizational structures, threatening to transform the world in the coming years.

Demographic and climate change, globalization, middle-class growth, workforce evolution, and digitalization are the main drivers of demographic and socio-economic change. These mega-trends are transforming and will transform the world over the next decade. In a work environment characterized by complexity, volatility, and ambiguity, leaders must achieve their goals by navigating between different challenges and by learning the art of balancing sciences and Humanities, the ability to develop soft skills such as creativity.

P. Boccardelli (✉)
Luiss Business School, Rome, Italy
e-mail: pboccard@luiss.it

© The Author(s), under exclusive license to Springer Nature Switzerland AG 2022
S. Iñiguez and P. Lorange (eds.), *Executive Education after the Pandemic*, https://doi.org/10.1007/978-3-030-82343-6_2

Demographic Changes

One of the main megatrends that will transform the world in a disruptive way over the next few years is represented by demographic evolution. According to the United Nations, "the world's population is expected to increase by 2 billion persons in the next 30 years, from 7.7 billion currently to 9.7 billion in 2050".[1] According to the same report, nine Countries will contribute to more than 50% of the projected growth of the global population in the period 2019–2050: India, Nigeria, Pakistan, the Democratic Republic of the Congo, Ethiopia, the United Republic of Tanzania, Indonesia, Egypt, and the United States of America.

A further phenomenon that generates a significant impact on society is related to the aging of the population, associated with the lengthening average life span, higher costs of services, and the complexity of financing welfare systems that often do not meet expectations. Globally, the median age has increased from 21.5 years in 1970 to over 30 years in 2019, and by the end of the century, the United Nations estimates a global population of 11.2 billion.[2] With an increase in women's longevity, the elderly population is predominantly female: in 2020, women accounted for 55% of the global population aged 65 and over and 62% of those aged 80 and over.[3] In the decades to come, no substantial change in the gender balance of the elderly population is expected at a global scale.[4]

Nowadays, the immigration phenomenon is also relevant. In 2019, one out of thirty individuals was an international migrant; to date, there are nearly 272 million international migrants, which counts for about 3.5% of the world population and more than half of them are male.[5]

Also, urbanization plays a central role in the development of urban centers and in the implementation of investments that can favor companies and jobs. By 2050, it is estimated that at least 68% of the world's population will reside in urban areas.[6] One of the continents that records the highest rates of urbanization growth is Africa, which is still one of the least prepared for this "urban

---

[1] Report: World population prospects 2019: Highlights. United Nations.
[2] https://ourworldindata.org/age-structure#:~:text=The%20global%20median%20age%20has,bracket%20between%2025%20and%2065.
[3] World population ageing 2020 Highlights.
[4] Ibid.
[5] International Organization for Migration (IOM), World Migration Report 2020.
[6] United Nations, Department of Economic and Social Affairs (2018), *World urbanization prospects 2018. Highlights*, https://population.un.org/wup/Publications/Files/WUP2018-Highlights.pdf.

explosion". For instance, Lagos is the largest Nigerian city where an expansion of 77 people is expected every hour by 2030.[7] A crucial issue in this phase of uncontrolled expansion is represented by the current ability of these countries to absorb the increasing population with the use of a small number of resources.

Finally, the growth of the middle class, which is the engine of global economic growth, comes essentially from Asia and is expanding day by day with about 140 million people.[8] A recent report published by the World Economic Forum revealed that over half of the world's population, corresponding to approximately 3.8 billion people, is represented by individuals living in families with an expense that can be considered "average" or "rich".[9] By the end of 2020, the middle class can be represented by around 4 billion people, which could be more than 5 billion by 2030.

Climate Change and Sustainability

Even the effects produced by human action on climate change deserve specific discussion. About half of young people aged 18–35 consider climate change to be the first serious global issue, even more significant than large-scale wars, conflicts, income inequality, and discrimination. Furthermore, 69.6% of them strongly agree that human activity is responsible for the substantial climate change that is taking place.[10]

Since the industrial revolution began, the concentration of carbon dioxide (CO_2) in the atmosphere has increased due to the burning of fossil fuels and emissions. During this time, the pH of the surface ocean waters decreased by 0.1 pH units, resulting in a 30% increase in acidity.[11] Additionally, air pollution causes an estimated 4.2 million deaths every day (World Health Organization, 2021),[12] and the rate of deforestation was estimated at 10 million hectares per year in the period 2015–2020 (FAO 2021).[13]

---

[7] Myers, J. (2016), *These are Africa's fastest-growing cities*, World Economic Forum.
[8] Kharas, H. (2017), *The unprecedented expansion of the global middle-class, An update*, in Global Economy and Development Working Paper 100.
[9] Kharas, H., Hamel, K. (2018), *A global tipping point: Half the world is now middle class or wealthier*, World Economic Forum.
[10] Global Shapers Community, *Global shapers survey 2017*, World Economic Forum.
[11] National Oceanic and Atmospheric Administration (2013), *Ocean acidification*.
[12] https://www.who.int/health-topics/air-pollution#tab=tab_1.
[13] http://www.fao.org/state-of-forests/en/#:~:text=Between%202015%20and%202020%2C%20the,80%20million%20hectares%20since%201990.

Globalization

A considerable and evolving phenomenon is that of globalization, which affects the sharing of resources and skills, the connection between individuals and organizations that are physically distant from each other, and the creation of new distribution channels. The development of a world without borders reveals the importance of opening markets in terms of competitiveness: companies can operate according to a "win–win" logic, favoring the rapid transfer of ideas and innovation. Therefore, the economies participating to a greater extent in the new global system prove to be the most competitive. In countries where the economic growth is mainly driven by exports, globalization has several positive effects, including higher living standards of a considerable part of the population. The use of technologies and the opening of borders are even more encouraged by the fourth industrial revolution, which is redefining the way we work, live, and interact. In fact, over the years, technological evolution has grown rapidly and has transformed the very concept of globalization. In the new world, organizations are increasingly focused on decentralizing value chain activities and internal regulations in each country. Also, thanks to greater connectivity and increased mobility, companies are becoming increasingly customer oriented and dynamic.

Even though markets have opened, supply chains have gone global, middle classes have emerged, and new connections have been established, more recently the free flow of information, ideas, money, jobs, and people has been thwarted. We are witnessing a tightening of immigration rules, and new barriers to trade and investments. In addition, supply chains shorten, and technologies separate. To sum, this phenomenon of "de-globalization" risks reducing international cooperation and increasing conflicts. At the same time, the current Covid-19 pandemic has contributed to boosting this situation by reducing movements and contacts, which represent the lifeblood of cities, thus generating a sort of de-urbanization. It is a fact that the pandemic has increase inequalities worldwide and has bare the already existing disparities in a variety of segments such as gender, wealth, etc. According to the WEF, "low- and middle-income countries that were growing at about 3–4% per capita annually before the global financial crisis have been averaging 1–2% growth thereafter".[14] Many of these countries that before had accelerated their growth thanks to active participation in international trade, now will have to start looking actively within.

---

[14] World Economic Forum. *How deglobalization is hurting the world's emerging economies*. Sept 2020.

Similarly, the job market has been impacted by the pandemic and emphasis on new needs is been made, for instance, according to the latest assessment of the impact of COVID-19 on job and skills demand using online job vacancy data it is "key for governments to support the development of skills that foster individuals' resilience by meeting the demand from labor markets".[15]

Digitalization

The phenomenon of digitization is undoubtedly one of the most influential characterizing of the twenty-first century. As MIT Sloan Management Review reported, although more than half of companies adopt digital technologies to run their business, almost 40% of the same organizations believe that it is necessary to foresee an advancement in terms of digital strategy.[16] All of us are aware that automation represents the real engine of future development, capable of giving a strong boost to productivity and global GDP growth. Digital transformation has the potential to create a significant number of jobs: by 2025, its overall impact in sectors is expected to produce a net gain of 2.1 million jobs.[17]

The advent of Artificial Intelligence and robotics, the use of 3D printing, and the collection of data through cloud technology force organizations to assess their degree of digital maturity, transform their structure, and improve and customize the offering. One of the potential issues related to the use of the Internet of Things (IoT) concerns the threat of job replacement. McKinsey Global Institute showed that 60% of all occupations have at least 30% of technically automatable activities, although few worldwide activities (less than 5%) can be considered fully automatable.[18] In any case, it is evident that non-routine activities—analytical and interpersonal—are rising, while the routine ones—manual and cognitive—and non-routine manual ones are reducing. Furthermore, the real challenge is consolidating the interaction between machines and humans who can leverage on their intuitive thinking that technology lacks.

---

[15] OECD. *An assessment of the impact of COVID-19 on job and skills demand using online job vacancy data.* 2021.
[16] Kane, G.C., Palmer, D., Phillips, A.N., Kiron, D., Buckley, N. (2017), *Achieving Digital maturity adapting your company to a changing world*, MIT Sloan Management Review.
[17] World Economic Forum, *Creating a workforce for the machine age.*
[18] McKinsey Global Institute (2017), *A future that works: Automation, employment, and productivity.*

The digital transformation generates impact in every sector. For instance, with regards to education, Universities are more focused on delivering innovative and continuous students' experience. Moreover, the development of digital and collaborative skills is at the core of the training offer. Concerning pharma, the use of devices facilitates the exchange of patient data between different hospitals and departments, thus reducing the time that staff must take to record, manage, and monitor information.

Facing a context like the one described above, the analysis of strategic leadership theories allows us to identify the essential traits of the leader of the future: the ability to question traditional paradigms, sustainable orientation, innovation, collaboration, and value creation.[19]

Toward a Creative Leader

We often underestimate the scale and speed of change. Nowadays, leaders have the responsibility to navigate these transformations with integrity and to provide positive, impactful leadership while the global scenario evolves. Since predicting the future is impossible, leaders in the new business landscape should learn from the past and be ready to adapt. In order to manage the current complexity and to deal with the rapid technological advancements, there are few but key processes that new leaders need to plan and implement:

- **Analysis**. It involves the management, the collection, as well as the interpretation of the big amount of big data, which represent an important source of competitive advantage. Today, the big data market amounts to more than 55 billion dollars of revenues and it is expected to grow up to 103 billion dollars by 2027, according to Statista.
- **Decision**. This strategic step is related to the opportunity to study and to focus on every decision-making process with the aim to plan not only by considering current events but also by forecasting future trends. Therefore, the adoption of an *ambidexterity* approach allows organizations to be long-term oriented. At the same time, new leaders should possess the ability to innovate by starting from the observation of real and emerging problems.
- **On-boarding**. The involvement and the cooperation between multiple stakeholders is really crucial to align different interests and objectives.

---

[19] De Smet, A., Lurie M., St. George, A. (2018), *Leading agile transformation: The new capabilities leaders need to build 21*st-century organizations, McKinsey & Company.

Moreover, it mainly focused on the real strategy execution to deal with the organizational complexity and evolution.
- **Outcomes.** The monitoring as well as the analysis of the effects of determined actions is really helpful to understand the consequences of specific decisions. In some cases, it is needed to revise and adjust the current strategy in order to respond to the new external conditions.

Essential Traits of the New Leaders

In 2001, Mitchell and James emphasized the link between a leader's skills and performance; in the same year, Boal and Hooijberg (2000) suggested that absorption capacity, the ability to change, and managerial wisdom represent the essence of strategic leadership. Later, Avey et al. (2012) argued that "personality strengths influence performance in creative tasks". Additionally, recent research focusing on the interconnectedness between character and competence of leaders has highlighted the positive effects on performance.[20] In particular, this study provided a distinction between "character" and "competence" as parts of the context in which informal learning opportunities link together, so that character development and skill growth are generated. More in general, new leaders must be creative, no longer authoritarian. Linda Hill, the Harvard University expert, said *"the true innovative leaders are not soloists, but open spaces for others, they are concerned with bringing out talents, turning innovation into a routine also made of confrontation and contrasts in which everyone can contribute. In practice, a continuous process of co-generation"*. Therefore, leaders should act like conductors who guide harmonically their teams in the rapidly evolving scenario. They should be talent oriented: once talent has been intercepted, investment strategies must focus on talent retention and retraining policies, useful for improving the quality of the recruiting service. Near 70% of executives believe that digitization favors these human resources processes.[21] Also, creative leaders should be a symbol of inspiration, open in tone, think like artists or designers, able to take risks, improvise when necessary, learn from their mistakes, and accept criticism.[22] Moreover, leaders should innovate by overturning routines, radically rethinking organizational models and business models, questioning traditional paradigms. Finally,

---

[20] Sturm, R.E., Vera, D., Crossan, M. (2017), *The entanglement of leader character and leader competence and its impact on performance*, The Leadership Quarterly, 28 (2017) 349–366, https://doi.org/10.1016/j.leaqua.2016.11.007.

[21] SAP Center for Business Insight (2017), *SAP digital transformation executive study: 4 ways leaders set themselves apart*.

[22] Maeda, J. (2011), Redesigning leadership, The MIT Press.

leaders should act balancing reason and feelings, trying to be charismatic and effective.[23]

To sum, the new leadership model requires leaders who are:

- Able to manage complexity, trying to collect and analyze the information available in the most effective way, to be as rational as possible;
- Expert decision-makers focused on every step of the decision-making process;
- Optimistic, able to adopt an approach that can stimulate positive thoughts and discourage a hostile mindset;
- Aware of their skills, able to exploit their strengths to influence performance;
- Go beyond their fears, to improve the quality of decisions and face the challenges of society;
- Strategy oriented, and focused on the entire decision-making process, to achieve specific and long-term goals.
- Emotionally intelligent, capable of implementing those actions that adapt and integrate with the strategy of the entire organization;
- Follow their intuition, so that can produce brilliant ideas and push toward solution approaches;
- Long-term thinker, able to plan strategic plans that take into account the current scenario and future business needs with a view to ambidexterity[24];
- Team-builder, cultivating relationships with the entire team and communicating with relevant stakeholders.

As discussed, the secret of the new leadership lies in the ability to carry out the mission concretely and flexibly, by ensuring that every employee is valued and strengthened. Some studies linked financial performance to collective organizational commitment, which is relevant for pursuing the strategic objectives of the company.[25] More practically, the majority of leaders say that an open and diverse workforce encourages the development of ideas

---

[23] Antonakis, J., Bastardoz, N., Jacquart, P., Shamir, B. (2016), *Charisma: An ill-defined and ill-measured gift*, Annual Review of Organizational Psychology and Organizational Behavior, 3(1), 293–319, https://doi.org/10.1146/annurev-orgpsych-041015-062305.

[24] O'Reilly, C.A., Tushman, M.L. (2008), *Ambidexterity as a dynamic capability: Resolving the innovator's dilemma*, Research in Organizational Behavior, 28, 185–206, https://doi.org/10.1016/j.riob.2008.06.002.

[25] Barrick, M.R., Thurgood, G.R., Smith, T.A., Courtright, S.H. (2015), *Collective organizational engagement: Linking motivational antecedents, strategic Implementation, and firm performance*, Academy of Management Journal, 58(1), 111–135.

and stimulates innovation.[26] Therefore, the adoption of a flexible working model, the creation of inter-functional teams, and the high spirit of adaptation are crucial aspects. Defining, implementing, and monitoring strategies are no longer enough. In the new world, leaders must ask themselves whether transformations can impact in a disruptive way, how the leadership approach must change, and what are the needed characteristics to lead modern organizations. The "chameleon" leader is increasingly sought after today, able to combine a multidisciplinary and broad knowledge of the various disciplines.

In response to the transformation, numerous organizations are seeking to develop an increasingly digital market environment, adding professions with a focus on technologies or changing traditional roles toward a more innovative orientation. While therefore increasing the "digital" business functions, there is still a shortage of qualified leaders who know how to lead their organization in the digital context. In fact, according to MIT, only 33% of companies in their development phase declares that they have leaders ready to navigate these transformations. This leadership gap is lower in the case of companies that are in a phase of digital maturity, where the development of determining skills has already begun.

Leaders for the new world need to know the art of balancing the new and the old models, technical knowledge and soft skills, income and well-being goals, productivity, and quality of life. Moreover, they should be prepared to overcome the potential crisis. In this sense, the education of new leaders should be founded on the following skills:

- **Vision for the future**, to understand the potential of a specific action; to identify suitable strategies to achieve the final goal; to involve the entire team and the various stakeholders in the business project;
- **Creative thinking**, stimulates ideas and innovation and therefore provides the whole team with the right motivations and the right incentives. Furthermore, this competence is linked to the ability to adopt a different perspective in dealing with problems; the visual representation of events or situations; identifying solutions for specific problems;
- **Focus on Execution**, to react quickly to changes by adapting capacities, structures, business models, and working methods. This skill is essential for the entire growth process of the organization. A recent report published in MIT Sloan Management Review shows that top-performing companies

---

[26] Kane, G.C., Palmer, D., Phillips, A.N., Kiron, D., Buckley, N. (2016), *Aligning the organization for its digital future*, MIT Sloan Management Review.

have invested more time in executing strategies[27]; focus on execution also implies the ability to mobilize the energies and attention of others in liquid and unstructured contexts, often dominated by unstructured collaborative relationships with external professionals who participate in core functions in the value chain;
- **Shared value orientation**, essential for generating opportunities and benefits for the stakeholders involved and, more generally, for society. Co-creating in a sustainable way: this is one of the main objectives of organizations, and therefore of leaders. To foster transformation and innovation, it is necessary to establish solid strategic partnerships with all the stakeholders around the company; we need to look in a single direction; it is necessary to think in a shared perspective, to undertake initiatives that can create value beyond the individual company reality; a common agenda must be defined and followed to best implement the development process.

A leader for the new world needs to know the art of balancing the new and old, technical knowledge and soft skills, the drive for income and the well-being of the team, maximize productivity as well as quality of life. The unique ability to read what is coming, of sensing soft signs of change raising on the business horizon and a strong empathy with employees and/or colleagues are part of the soft skills that should be intrinsic for every new leader.

The Role of Creativity

In this new scenario a particular role is played by creativity. Creativity can be defined as the tendency to generate or spot ideas, or alternatives that are helpful to solving problems. A creative leader is a fundamental piece in changeling times like the pandemic, not only for the capacity to innovate and find solutions but for being able to boost their team morale up, with purpose and keep it motivated to reach goals. The way to incentivize creativity and cultivate it among your team is a subtle art. In this sense it is widely accepted among business school, that some of the main best practices used to develop creative skills are:

---

[27] Kane, G.C., Palmer, D., Phillips, A.N., Kiron, D., Buckley, N. (2017), *Achieving digital maturity adapting your company to a changing world*, MIT Sloan Management Review.

- Brainstorming, to stimulate debate and to produce one or more innovative solutions that might not occur otherwise. By having an excess of creative potential solutions, it gets easier to reach one with the highest level of quality.
- "What if" or sliding doors approach. Alternative solutions can be obtained through the modification of the main aspects of the problem itself or introducing a new component. Questions as "what if we execute a strategy in a completely different way from how we currently do it?" can be the source of a new idea or vision to deal with complex situations
- Provocation, to help and stimulate creative thought.
- Lateral thinking. Lateral thinking is a process to go where you would not usually choose to go. It consists of the presentation of a problem under different perspectives or reverses it to look and analyze it differently.
- Mind mapping. This process results in a chart where participants (individual or a group) input ideas and connect them. As a result, a full picture of what you are trying to deal with can be traced and new alternative solutions can be identified.

In the new society, the figure of the leader emerges as the guarantor of the inclusive and innovative processes of organizations. Being aware of the importance of fostering the previous mentioned competences such as problem solving and creativity, many business schools, like Luiss Business School, have integrated Design and critical thinking into the offering since are some of the most strategic approaches to innovation and students learn to apply it according to their professional requirements. As well as, specific labs oriented to boost Life Skills such as Empathy and Emotional Intelligence, Transformative Decision-Making, among many others.

Creative leaders represent a fundamental piece in changing times like the ones we are living. The way to develop and cultivate creativity as well as to involve the entire team is a subtle art that stimulates all the senses.

Bibliography

Ahmed, S.A. (2015), *How are global demographics changing?*, World Economic Forum.

Antonakis, J., Bastardoz, N., Jacquart, P., Shamir, B. (2016), *Charisma: An ill-defined and ill-measured gift*, Annual Review of Organizational Psychology and Organizational Behavior, Vol. 3, No. 1, pp. 293–319, https://doi.org/10.1146/annurev-orgpsych-041015-062305.

Avey, J.B., Luthans, F., Hannah, S.T., Sweetman, D., Peterson, C. (2012), Impact of employees' character strengths of wisdom on stress and creative performance, *Human Resource Management Journal*, Vol. 22, pp. 165–18, https://doi.org/10.1108/dlo.2012.08126faa.005.

Barley, S.R., Meyer, G.W., and Gash, D.C. (1988), Cultures of culture: Academics, practitioners, and the pragmatics of normative control, *Administrative Science Quarterly*, Vol. 33, pp. 24–60.

Barrick, M.R., Thurgood, G.R., Smith, T.A., Courtright, S.H. (2015), Collective organizational engagement: Linking motivational antecedents, strategic Implementation, and firm performance, *Academy of Management Journal*, Vol. 58, No. 1, pp. 111–135, https://doi.org/10.5465/amj.2013.0227.

Bennis, W. C., and J. O'Toole. (2005). How business schools lost their way, *Harvard Business Review*, p. 3.

Blanchard, M. (2009), From 'Écoles de commerce' to 'management schools': Transformations and continuity in French business schools, *European Journal of Education*, Vol. 44, No. 4, Part II., pp. 587–603.

Boal, K.B., Hooijberg, R. (2000), Strategic leadership research: Moving on, *The Leadership Quarterly*, Vol. 11, No. 4, pp. 515–549, https://doi.org/10.1016/S1048-9843(00)00057-6.

Bradley, J., Loucks, J., Macaulay, J., Noronha, A., Wade, M. (2015), *Digital Vortex, How digital disruption Is redefining industries*, Global Center for Digital Business Transformation.

Colby, A., Ehrlich, T., Sullivan, W.M., and Dolle, J, foreword by Shulman, L.S. (2011), *Rethinking undergraduate business education: Liberal learning for the profession*, New York, NY: The Carnegie Foundation for the Advancement of Teaching/Jossey Bass.

Cruikshank, J.L. (1987), *A delicate experiment: The Harvard business school 1908–1945*, Boston, MA: Harvard Business School Press, p. 8.

De Smet, A., Lurie M., St. George, A. (2018), *Leading agile transformation: The new capabilities leaders need to build 21st-century organizations*, McKinsey & Company.

Drabble, S., Ratzmann, N., Hoorens, S., Khodyakov, D., Yaqub, O. (2015), *The rise of a global middle class, Global societal trends to 2030: Thematic report 6*, RAND.

Dworkin, R. (1991), Pragmatism, right answers, and true banality, in *Pragmatism in law & society: New perspectives on law, culture, and society*, ed. M. Brint and W. Weaver, Boulder: Westiview Press, p. 359.

Felin, T., and Foss, N. (2005), Strategic organization: A field in search of microfoundations, *Strategic Organization*, Vol. 3, pp. 441–455, https://doi.org/10.1177/1476127005055796.

Frey C.B., and Osborne, M.A. (2017), The future of employment: How susceptible are jobs to computerization?, *Technological Forecasting and Social Change*, https://doi.org/10.1016/j.techfore.2016.08.019.

Gavetti, G. (2012), PERSPECTIVE, Toward a behavioral theory of strategy, *Organization Science*, Vol. 23, No. 1, pp. 267–285, https://doi.org/10.1287/orsc.1110.0644.

Global Shapers Community, *Global Shapers Survey 2017,* World Economic Forum.

Hambrick, D.C., and Mason, P.A. (1984), Upper Echelons: The organization as a reflection of Its top managers, *The Academy of Management Review*, Vol. 9, No. 2, pp. 193–206, http://www.jstor.org/stable/258434.

Hartley, S. (2017), *The Fuzzy and the Techie: Why the Liberal Arts will rule the digital world*, Boston and New York, NY: Houghton Mifflin Harcourt, pp. 5–6.

How the ideas of 10 female philosophers bring value into the workplace. (2020). Palgrave Macmillan.

Hodgkinson, G.P., and Healey, M.P. (2011), Psychological foundations of dynamic capabilities: Reflection and reflection, *Strategic Management Journal*, Vol. 32, pp. 1500–1516, https://doi.org/10.1002/smj.964.

Iñiguez de Onzoño, S. (2011), *The learning curve: How business schools are re-inventing education*, London: Palgrave Macmillan, p. 126.

Iñiguez de Onzoño, S., and Carmona, S. (2016), The academic triathlon: Bridging the agora and the academia, *Journal of Management Development*, Vol. 38, No. 7, 8 August.

Kane, G.C. (2018), *Common traits of the best digital leaders*, MIT Sloan Management Review.

Kelland, K. (2018), *Bill Gates has a warning about population growth*, World Economic Forum.

Keenan, R.J., Reams, G.A., and Achard, F. et al. (3 more authors). (2015), Dynamics of global forest area: Results from the FAO Global Forest Resources Assessment 2015. *Forest Ecology and Management*, Vol. 352, pp. 9–20. ISSN 0378–1127.

Kane, G.C., Palmer, D., Phillips, A.N., Kiron, D., and Buckley, N. (2016), *Aligning the organization for its digital future*, MIT Sloan Management Review.

Kane, G.C., Palmer, D., Phillips, A.N., Kiron, D., and Buckley, N. (2017), *Achieving digital maturity adapting your company to a changing world*, MIT Sloan Management Review.

Kharas, H. (2017), *The unprecedented expansion of the global middle-class, An update*, in Global Economy and Development Working Paper 100.

Kharas, H., and Hamel, K. (2018), *A global tipping point: Half the world is now middle class or wealthier*, World Economic Forum.

Landrigan, P.J., Fuller, R., Acosta, N., Adeyi, O., Arnold, R., and Basu, N., et al. (2018), The Lancet Commission on pollution and health, *The Lancet*, https://doi.org/10.1016/S0140-6736(17)32345-0.

Lorange, P. (2008). *Thought leadership meets business: How business schools can become more successful*, Cambridge: Cambridge University Press, p. 1.

Markides, C. (2007), In search of ambidextrous professors, *Academy of Management Journal*, Vol. 50, No. 4, pp. 762–8.

Maeda, J. (2011), *Redesigning leadership*, The MIT Press.

Mayne, T. (2011), *Architecture and Education*, presentation at the International Architectural Education Summit, IE University, June 30.

McKinsey Global Institute. (2017), *A future that works: Automation, employment, and productivity*.

Mitchell, T.R., and James, L.E. (2001). Building better theory: Time and the specification of when things happen, *The Academy of Management Review*, Vol .26, pp. 530–547, https://doi.org/10.5465/amr.2001.5393889.

MIT SMR Strategy Forum. (2018), *Will restricted U.S. immigration drive business operations abroad?*.

Modis. (2018), White Paper, Il Digital Mismatch.

Monahan, K., Chmiola, A., and Roos L. (2017), *How effective leaders drive digital change*, MIT Sloan Management Review.

Myers, J. (2016), *These are Africa's fastest-growing cities*, World Economic Forum.

National Oceanic and Atmospheric Administration. (2013), *Ocean acidification*.

O'Reilly, C.A., and Tushman, M.L. (2008), Ambidexterity as a dynamic capability: Resolving the innovator's dilemma, *Research in Organizational Behavior*, Vol 28, pp. 185–206, https://doi.org/10.1016/j.riob.2008.06.002.

Pfeffer, J., and Fong, C. T. (2002), The end of business schools? Less success than meets the eye, *Academy of Management Learning and Education*, Vol. 1, No. 1, pp. 8–85.

Price Waterhouse Coopers. (2016), *Industry 4.0: Building the digital enterprise, 2016 Global Industry 4.0 Survey*.

Rigby, D. (2001), Management theory and techniques: A survey, *California Management Review*, Vol. 43 , pp. 139–60.

Rometty, G. (2018), *We need a new era of data responsibility*, World Economic Forum

Roser, M. (2017), *Future population growth*, Published online at OurWorldInData.org, [Online Resource], Retrieved from https://ourworldindata.org/future-population-growth/.

Roser, M., and Ortiz- Lajcák, M. (2018), *Why we need a global understanding of migration*, World Economic Forum.

SAP Center for Business Insight. (2017), *SAP digital transformation executive study: 4 ways leaders set themselves apart*.

Shoemaker, P.J.H. (2008). The future challenges of business: rethinking management education and research, *California Management Review*, Vol. 50, No. 3 (Spring 2008), pp. 119–39, at 120.

Sorrell, M., Komisar, R., and Mulcahy, A. (2010), How we do it: three executives reflect on strategic decision making, *McKinsey Quarterly*, Vol. 2, pp. 46–57.

Sturm, R.E., Vera, D., and Crossan, M. (2017), The entanglement of leader character and leader competence and its impact on performance, *The Leadership Quarterly*, Vol. 28, pp. 349–366, https://doi.org/10.1016/j.leaqua.2016.11.007.

The state of the World Forest. (2020). Food and Agriculture Organization of the UNIted Natios. http://www.fao.org/state-offorests/en/#:~:text=Between%

202015%20and%202020%2C%20the,80%20million%20hectares%20since%201990.

United Nations, Department of Economic and Social Affairs. (2014), *World urbanization prospects: The 2014 revision highlights*, http://esa.un.org/unpd/wup/Highlights/WUP2014-Highlights.pdf.

World Economic Forum, *Creating a workforce for the machine age*.

World Trade Organization. (2018), *Statistics on trade in commercial services*.

https://www.un.org/development/desa/pd/sites/www.un.org.development.desa.pd/files/files/documents/2020/Sep/un_pop_2020_pf_ageing_10_key_messages.pdf.

https://www.un.org/development/desa/publications/world-population-prospects-2019-highlights.html.

International Organization for Migration (IOM), World Migration Report 2020. https://publications.iom.int/system/files/pdf/wmr_2020.pdf.

3

The Enlightened Executive: Management and the Humanities

Santiago Iñiguez

Executive Summary

The Humanities have been part of the higher education curriculum since the first universities were created. Their fundamental purpose was to nurture the virtues or habits required for social coexistence and civic behavior within a tradition of human values dating back to antiquity.

It could be argued that business education has two objectives: on the one hand, to train competent and employable entrepreneurs and managers who are knowledgeable in the most up-to-date management techniques; on the other hand, personal development as committed and responsible citizens. To achieve these objectives, management programs should include not only technical courses in traditional disciplines such as finance or marketing, but also subjects or sessions imported from the humanities, which develop facets related to personal development and a worldview. Business schools aim to create well-rounded managers, enlightened directors who are cultured with a solid grounding in the arts and history of their own and other cultures, thus better enabling them to lead multicultural teams. Studying history provides key references that enable directors and executives to take better business decisions on the basis of an understanding of the experiences of the past.

S. Iñiguez (✉)
IE University, Madrid, Spain
e-mail: santiago.iniguez@ie.edu

Moreover, professional practice would benefit from ascribing management, as an academic discipline, not only to the social sciences but also to the humanities, broadening the topics and methodologies of research, as well as breaking down the silos between the different areas. The humanities act as the mortar of knowledge, holding fundamental management topics together while exploring integrated visions and tempering excessive specialization.

The Academic Evolution of Management. From the Social Sciences to the Humanities

The advent of management as an academic discipline is a relatively recent phenomenon. The écoles de commerce that emerged in France in the late nineteenth century offered vocational education but were not recognized by universities [1]. In the United States, the first business schools appeared at the beginning of the twentieth century, also to provide a technical education and prepare executives in nascent industries such as railroads and steel, [2] as well as professionals tasked with setting up the international trade structures of the U.S. federal administration.

The technical nature of the knowledge developed and taught in business schools experienced a turning point at the end of the 1950s, when a report by the Ford and Carnegie Foundations in the United States recommended that these centers develop more academic research, following the methodology characteristic of other social sciences, such as economics or sociology [3]. Since then, there has been a boom in research output in the field of management, along with the creation of new academic journals in various disciplines, driven by the strength and resources generated by business schools. [4] The result is a self-sustaining academic marketplace.

This impressive deployment of academic research in management, relevant insiders and academics has sparked a debate about whether its nature has been distorted and has lost impact. As Wharton's Paul Schoemaker has observed: "the field has strengthened its academic position by promoting professors with deep scientific roles (…) over time, however, these academics often took business research in directions that are no longer understandable or relevant to business students and managers" [5]. Criticism of irrelevant research produced by business schools is a constant theme in articles written by many]top academics [6].

In their 2005 landmark article for the Harvard Business Review, *How Business Schools Lost Their Way*, Warren Bennis and James O'Toole lay the blame for what they see as business schools' failings on a system in which academics fear being seen as interested in disseminating their ideas to the general public, which could be seen as demeaning their research. To avoid this risk, they seek to satisfy the interests of their colleagues, looking only at methodology-related topics and avoiding issues of real use in the professional world. In their view, the system creates pressure on academics to publish articles on specific topics of interest mainly to other academics, but not to the world of business [7].

Similarly, Jeffrey Pfeffer and Christina T. Fong of Stanford University [8] have questioned the direction academic research has taken in recent years and its impact on the professional world. They point to three barometers to assess the impact of research conducted by business schools in the real world. The first is an analysis of the origin of BusinessWeek's top ten business books over two decades, during which only four of the 10 most popular books were written by academics.

The second is based on the list of the concepts and analytical frameworks used to illustrate management practices and to enable decision-making prepared by Darrell Rigby, author and head of Boston-based consultancy Bain & Company's Global Innovation and Agile Practices [9]. Rigby selected the 25 most popular management tools, based on a list of books published by Dow Jones Group, together with interviews with academics and company managers. His conclusion was that only eight of these analysis tools originated in business schools, while 17 came from consultants or corporations.

Pfeffer and Fong's final source for demonstrating the gulf between academic research and the real world is based on a study by Barley, Meyer, and Gash [10] of the language and tone used by academics and managers, respectively, when discussing organizational practice. They conclude that while academics are increasingly influenced by the literary constructs of managers, the reverse is not true for managers. These three barometers led Pfeffer and Fong to the conclusion that business research and the actual problems faced by business managers in their daily lives are increasingly diverging.

Business schools are not alone in being criticized for the irrelevance of their research. There is also debate about the disconnect between academic output and professional interests in the fields of, for example, the philosophy of law, [11] or architectural theory [12], both areas of eminently applied character, where the subjects of analysis should be the problems of actual practice. I suspect that lack of relevance is a potential problem for all areas of research, particularly in clinical disciplines.

In his Theory and Practice, the Enlightenment philosopher Immanuel Kant argued that there is no substantial difference between what might be called theoretical research and applied research. There is simply good and bad research: good research is consistent with the real world and compatible with applied problems; bad research is sterile intellectual speculation [13]. His assessment is equally relevant today.

If business schools are to produce more relevant research, they will need to find ways to strengthen the links between academia and business. The London Business School's Costas Markides, talked about "ambidextrous professors" [14], arguing that it may be a mistake to underestimate both the value of academic research and that we need to see things in global terms. This in turn will lead to the demise of a fundamental and highly valuable approach that has endowed the management knowledge base with rigor. According to Markides, it may also be a mistake to encourage organic separation in the structure of schools between academics who are interested in academic research and what he calls professors of practice. Markides' proposals to encourage younger academics to publish not only in academic journals, but also in professional publications, are one way forward. This can stimulate the transfer of academic research to the teaching and outreach environment, as well as encouraging cooperation between companies to identify new ideas and research models.

Drawing on his experience in executive education at IMD, Peter Lorange [15] has also highlighted the need for business schools to adopt a "two-way interactive approach, where propositional knowledge meets prescriptive knowledge." This virtuous cycle can be seen in executive education programs, or MBAs, where participants have considerable experience, giving teachers the opportunity to benefit from feedback from the professionals who attend their classes.

In the same vein, myself and my colleague at IE University Salvador Carmona have argued that the increasing irrelevance of some business school research may be down to reward folly, that is, the system of recognition and compensation that exists in general in the academic world [16]. In this sense, relevance to external stakeholders is expected, but relevance to academic stakeholders is rewarded by evaluating the performance of their researchers, primarily by publication in academic journals. It would be desirable for business school research to combine internal and external validity, which would involve business school faculty members conducting rigorous and relevant research and interacting with practitioners. Persuading faculty members to combine research and teaching activities, as well as interacting with industry to disseminate their research results, would require a comprehensive transformation of recognition and compensation systems, as well as an emphasis on the external impact of research, a Herculean task. In addition, these changes would have implications for leadership, the structure of business schools, and the resources available to faculty members.

Perhaps part of this change could be brought about by broadening the ascription of management research from the social sciences to the humanities. An interesting proposal sponsored by the Carnegie Foundation, which sponsored the aforementioned scientific turn in management sixty years ago, could offer a way forward. The Carnegie Foundation's 2011 report, *Rethinking Undergraduate Management Education: Liberal Learning for the Profession*, [17] recommends that the BBA (Bachelor in Business Administration), which has become one of the most in-demand programs in both America and Europe, adopt an open approach, similar to that of undergraduate programs in the liberal arts. This could also give the humanities a greater presence both in the curriculum of management courses and in the research carried out in business schools. It would also help break down the silos that so much academic research takes place in at university departments, promoting cross-disciplinary research between Humanities and STEM areas and breaking down the fallacious separation between "soft" and "hard" areas in the process.

The professional reality also belies this separation between the sciences and the Humanities: many of today's most successful technology entrepreneurs have bachelor's degrees in the liberal arts, even if they later specialized in technical studies at the master's level. As *The Fuzzie and the Techie* author Scott Hartley explains, the professional profiles of "techies" have traditionally been contrasted with "fuzzies," the terms used at Stanford University to designate STEM students versus humanities students, respectively [18]. However, in my opinion, the ideal graduate profile integrates both facets; that of a professional with a broad worldview, cultivated and enlightened, yet with a solid understanding of technology, programming and data management. Hartley provides a long list of current business leaders who combine these two indissoluble parts of the true entrepreneur. He also provides powerful arguments about how to solve the problems posed by the development of technology and the new inventions of artificial intelligence, insisting that they require a philosophical and humanistic perspective.

This evolution toward the humanities is also reflected in the growing number of business schools that have introduced liberal arts subjects into their curricula. Making the Humanities a core part of all degrees will cement the learning experience and develop open-minded and well-rounded graduates. This spirit inspired the Executive MBA program launched a decade ago by IE Business School and Brown University. We believe that by teaching modern art, for example, we nurture in participants skills such as perception and observation, typical of artists and architects, which may help managers, traditionally oriented toward action, to be more reflective while assessing risk. Courses on foreign cultures may help them better lead cross-cultural teams in their global companies. Modules on critical thinking may be of use to question unethical decisions imposed by their bosses in the future. Indeed, it is time to bring all the benefits of classical education to business schools [19].

References

1. Blanchard, M. "From 'Écoles de commerce' to 'Management Schools': Transformations and Continuity in French Business Schools," *European Journal of Education* vol. 44, no. 4, (2009); Part II.; pp. 587–603.
2. Cruikshank, J. L. *A Delicate Experiment: The Harvard Business School 1908–1945*, (Boston, MA: Harvard Business School Press, 1987), p. 8. It is commonly accepted that the first business school was Wharton (1881), though the first MBA program was launched by Tuck Business School at the University of Dartmouth (1900), with the antecedents of the mentioned écoles de commerce. https://www.businessbecause.com/news/mba-degree/352/who-invented-the-business-school.
3. Iñiguez de Onzoño, S. *The Learning Curve: How Business Schools Are Re-Inventing Education* (London: Palgrave Macmillan, 2011), p. 126.
4. According to *Scopus* data as of April, there are more than 468 journals in management and business studies worldwide, counting just those published in English. https://www.scimagojr.com/journalrank.php?category=1408.
5. Shoemaker, P. J. H. "The Future Challenges of Business: Rethinking Management Education and Research," *California Management Review*, vol. 50, no. 3 (Spring 2008), pp. 119–39, at 120.
6. Iñiguez, S. (2011). op. cit., Ch. 2.
7. Bennis, W. C., and O'Toole, J. "How Business Schools Lost Their Way," *Harvard Business Review* (May 2005), p. 3.
8. Pfeffer, J., and Fong, C. T. "The End of Business Schools? Less Success Than Meets the Eye," *Academy of Management Learning and Education*, vol. 1, no. 1 (2002), pp. 8–85.
9. Rigby, D. "Management Theory and Techniques: A Survey," *California Management Review*, vol. 43 (2001), 139–60.
10. Barley, S. R., Meyer, G. W., and D. C. Gash, "Cultures of Culture: Academics, Practitioners, and the Pragmatics of Normative Control," *Administrative Science Quarterly*, vol. 33 (1988), pp. 24–60.
11. Dworkin, R. "Pragmatism, Right Answers, and True Banality," in Pragmatism in Law & Society: New Perspectives on Law, Culture, and Society, ed. M. Brint and W. Weaver (Boulder: Westiview Press, 1991), p. 359, affirmed: "For more than a decade American legal theory has been too occupied in metatheoretical debates about its own character and possibility. "
12. Mayne, T. "Architecture and Education," presentation at the *International Architectural Education Summit*, IE University, June 30, 2011.

13. Kant, I. *Teoría y Práctica* (Madrid: Tecnos, 1986).
14. Markides, C. "In Search of Ambidextrous Professors," *Academy of Management Journal* vol. 50, no. 4 (2007), pp. 762–8.
15. Lorange, P. *Thought Leadership Meets Business: How Business Schools Can Become More Successful* (Cambridge: Cambridge University Press, 2008), p. 1.
16. Iñiguez de Onzoño, S., and Carmona, S. "The academic triathlon: Bridging the agora and the academia", *Journal of Management Development*, vol. 38 no. 7 (8 August 2016).
17. Colby, A., Ehrlich, T., Sullivan, W. M., and Dolle, J, foreword by Shulman, L.S., *Rethinking Undergraduate Business Education: Liberal Learning for The Profession* (New York, NY: The Carnegie Foundation for the Advancement of Teaching/Jossey Bass, 2011).
18. Hartley, S. *The Fuzzy and the Techie: Why the Liberal Arts Will Rule the Digital World* (Boston and New York, NY: Houghton Mifflin Harcourt, 2017), pp. 5–6.
19. See also an argument in support of the Humanities in management education in S. Iñiguez, In An Ideal Business: How The Ideas of 10 Female Philosophers Bring value into The Workplace" (London: Palgrave Macmillan, 2020), Ch. 7, p. 91.

4

Business Schools as Catalysts for Sustainable Development

Daniel R. LeClair

Many readers will be surprised by what has been happening at Monash Business School in Melbourne, Australia. Scholars at the school have been studying strategies for managing urban water supplies, policies for supporting Pakistan's horticulture markets, and guidelines for handling national blood supplies. These projects have been led by research centers that are intentionally interdisciplinary and supported by an associate dean responsible for research impact. Not to be left out, students at the school have pitched social enterprises for the Australian African community and participated in sustainable tourism study tours. And these are just a few examples from Monash—similar ones can be found at hundreds of other business schools around the world.

Myriad forces are transforming schools of business and management into catalysts for sustainable development. In business, the dominant paradigm is shifting from narrow, short-term profit maximization toward broader, more responsible, and sustainable strategies. Executives can no longer afford to ignore issues like inequality, climate change, and poor health. Meanwhile, local and international development initiatives are increasingly reliant on

---

D. R. LeClair (✉)
Global Business School Network, Washington, DC, USA
e-mail: dleclair@gbsn.org

private-sector and people-first solutions, which play to the strengths of business schools. After all, the Sustainable Development Goals (SDGs) are a call to action to business and higher education, as well as government and civil society. Finally, the changing landscape of higher education has itself been an important factor in the transformation. Funders are holding business schools more accountable for generating knowledge that benefits society, students are demanding curricula that do more to address sustainability, and technological advances are expanding the diversity of education programs and extending their reach into underserved communities.

For more than two decades I have had a privileged view of business schools, including 19 years in various leadership responsibilities at AACSB International, an accrediting body, and two years and counting as CEO of the Global Business School Network (GBSN), which improves access to management education in the developing world. During this time, I have seen the forces of change at work, motivating and enabling business schools to become catalysts for sustainable development. More and more business schools, like Monash, have been going beyond the historical boundaries of business education to make the world a better place.

But it is still early in the transformation and far from clear what it means for business schools. This chapter attempts to fill this gap by offering five strategies to unlock the full potential of business schools as catalysts for sustainable development.

Explore and Articulate Purpose

The venerable dean, Dipak Jain, often said that "business schools have put performance over purpose." His observation was not entirely critical. At AACSB I witnessed a remarkable rise in the overall quality of business education and research. Aspiring schools recruited increasingly talented students, connected graduates to better jobs with higher salaries, and produced more, and more rigorous, articles in peer-reviewed journals. The number of ranked and accredited business schools increased, as did the overall popularity of business education. I was especially impressed by the rapid rise of business schools in Asia and in the Global South.

As professor Jain pointed out, these improvements were motivated by performance. And performance in business education has historically been reflected in the criteria for rankings and accreditations. It was not unusual for a business school to state that its formal vision was to become a top 50 business school, or to join the top echelon of all schools by earning AACSB or EQUIS accreditation, or both.

Now, however, being good is no longer good enough. The time has arrived for every business school to put purpose first; to explore and articulate why its efforts matter to society. That means asking important questions. What positive difference or impact does my school intend to have on the communities it serves? At what scale and scope? Does the school prepare students to work in business as it currently is, or to shape the development of business in positive ways? What are the grand challenges or wicked problems we want to inform the school's research agenda?

The breadth of societal issues and ways to address them, as well as the variety of contexts in which schools operate, allows for considerable diversity when it comes to purpose. Every business school can and should be more distinctive when it acts as a catalyst for sustainable development. There are no formal rules about expressing purpose. Schools describe it in different forms and at various levels of granularity. GBSN member, Fundação Dom Cabral (2021) in Brazil, is quite clear in its mission statement "to contribute to the sustainable development of society by educating, developing and building the skills of executives, entrepreneurs and public managers." The Suliman S. Olayan School of Business (2021) at American University of Beirut, also a GBSN member, articulates purpose in its vision statement, which is to "transform business thinking in the MENA region."

Clarity about social purpose acts as a powerful motivator. It helps scholars to discover or rediscover why their work matters beyond simply publishing papers. It guides students as learners in longer, increasingly dynamic careers. It describes why alumni, donors, government officials, and community leaders should support the school, with time as well as money. In my experience engaging these stakeholders and others in exploring the questions matters as much as the ultimate answers, because that is when innovation and buy-in happens.

Diversify Research Approaches

Since joining GBSN, I have been surprised by the enormous thirst for evidence to inform efforts related to sustainable development. I hear regularly from leaders in government, NGOs, and business about the need for credible research to navigate a world that is more complex, interconnected, and uncertain than ever. They can't afford to continue pouring resources into policies and projects that work in theory, but are ineffective or financially unsustainable in practice. They want better insights about relevant markets and behaviors, and need it now. They want useful knowledge about managing strategy, finances, operations, and marketing for their own organizations and in the organizations they support.

At the same time, serious doubts have emerged inside and outside of academia about the dominant model of research and whether it can effectively support the changing roles and responsibilities of business schools. Critics argue that the system motivates scholars to address gaps in the academic literature rather than important problems in business and society. Others worry that the commercialization of higher education has already compromised the independence of scientific research. Some people say that scholars don't care to communicate effectively with the public about what they learn through research—and that increasing political partisanship, expanding social media, and weaknesses in education have exacerbated the challenge by blurring the boundaries between facts and opinions in the minds of policy-makers, as well as the public. Whether you believe these criticisms or not, the reality is that the current model is well established, as are the incentive structures and cultures that support it.

I maintain that the best way forward in the near term is to build around the current model by diversifying research approaches in business schools. As Andrew Hoffman (2021) writes in *The Engaged Scholar*, "The goal in this book's pages is not to change the role of academic scholars such that all must engage. Instead, the goal is to widen the range of definitions of what it means to be an academic scholar, allowing more diversity within the scholarly ranks." Individual scholars find their best fit, while departments and schools generate greater impact from a more diverse portfolio of faculty and methods.

There are many approaches to research that can serve business schools well, as catalysts for sustainable development. Randomized controlled trials (RCTs) have limitations but have demonstrated utility in the field of development economics. Yet, the approach is hardly ever used by scholars in business schools. I also believe there is great value in the abductive reasoning approach of the Academy of Management *Discoveries* Journal, field-based approaches, research case studies, and large-scale international collaborations such as the Global Leadership and Organizational Behavior Effectiveness (GLOBE) project, which engages more than 500 scholars across 160 countries.

Create Opportunities for Action

I thought I knew a lot about Hanken School of Economics because it is a GBSN member. Still, less than a month after the World Health Organization (WHO) declared Covid-19 a pandemic, I was surprised to learn that the school is a global leader in humanitarian logistics, a field concerned with responses to disasters, both natural and human-generated. By then, the Helsinki Graduate School of Economics (a joint unit of Hanken, Aalto University and the University of Helsinki) had already established the "situation room" to support ministries and other public authorities in economic policy-making during the coronavirus crisis. And the school was already working on a European Union grant called Health Emergency Response in Interconnected Systems (HERoS) to improve the effectiveness and efficiency of the response to the Covid-19 outbreak.

As business schools prioritize sustainable development, we are starting to see more scholars influencing policy and practice, and working in the field themselves, applying what they learned, testing and refining ideas. In their wonderful book, *Good Economics for Hard Times*, Nobel Laureates Abhijit Banerjee and Esther Duflo (2019) compare their work as economists to medical research, "like in medicine, our work does not stop once the basic science is done and the core idea is established; the process of rolling out the idea in the real world then begins."

Schools are also engaging students more directly in social impact activities. As technological advances make educational content more accessible, business schools have made learning more experiential. And, in response to changing student preferences as well as their own changing roles, schools are including more sustainable development projects in their action-learning portfolios. Students are also making a difference through hackathons and competitions. In 2020, GBSN partnered with Hanken's Humanitarian Logistics (HUMLOG) Institute to plan a global student competition. The HUMLOG Challenge ultimately brought together 120 teams from 36 countries to work on local food and medical supply problems. First prize went to a team representing GBSN member, Universidad de Los Andes School of Management, which developed a water supply chain solution for La Guajira, Colombia.

Of course, the benefits of engaging faculty and students directly in sustainable development go beyond having a positive impact on society. Projects provide opportunities for academics to make new connections and co-create knowledge with practitioners. Students learn to apply content in context and gain feedback from professionals beyond the classroom. They also learn how to engage the creative capacity of teammates and develop valuable social capital. While others have focused more on changing the content of business curricula to support sustainable development, I believe schools can make a bigger difference, sooner, by shifting the kinds of experiences available to students and scholars.

Empower Local Initiative

Reflecting its mission "to develop principled, innovative leaders who improve the world and to generate ideas that advance management practice," the MIT Sloan School of Management (2021) has always done a lot for sustainable development. I have been especially interested in their Regional Entrepreneurship Acceleration Program (MIT REAP), which is designed to strengthen local innovation-driven entrepreneurial (IDE) ecosystems. Participating communities form teams of eight representatives from corporations, higher education, government, risk capital, and entrepreneurial ventures. These teams engage in a series of action-learning activities over a two-year period, while constructing and implementing a regional strategy to enhance their IDE ecosystems (MIT Sloan Global Programs 2021).

The MIT program empowers local leaders to create solutions from within their own context. Participants can and do learn from other communities, but it is not about importing solutions from other parts of the world. Every business school can and should contribute to sustainable development by investing in, and participating in, local and regional entrepreneurial ecosystems. That means providing entrepreneurship education, of course. It also means operating incubators, accelerators, innovation labs, makerspaces, and the like, and doing more to connect founders to funding. Many leading business schools are also prioritizing different kinds of entrepreneurship. At IE University, for example, social innovation has become a key driver for its work at home in Madrid and in other parts of the world, such as West Africa.

When the focus is entrepreneurship, it is easy to equate progress with business development. As catalysts for sustainable development, however, business schools must think more broadly. Real progress means building better communities and working closely with local governments, civic organizations, and other stakeholders, as well as business organizations. Going further, business schools generate value by facilitating collaboration across sectors, a point that is explored further below.

To be sure, achieving the SDGs will require global leadership as well as local initiative. By coordinating across multiple IDE ecosystems, MIT Sloan is also building global knowledge and leadership capacity. Similarly, network organizations like GBSN play an important role by connecting schools and communities across borders. It helps schools from the countries to learn from each other and provides a global platform for resource sharing and collective action. International diversity is an important source of innovation and action for sustainable development.

Connect Across Sectors and Silos

At the World Economic Forum's annual meeting in January 2020, the Thunderbird School of Global Management and the Foundation for Climate Restoration brought together global leaders across sectors to release a report on carbon capture as a multitrillion dollar set of business opportunities. (Thunderbird School of Global Management 2020) Convening people with different perspectives is one of the most powerful ways that business schools catalyze sustainable development. Yet, it is still rare for business schools to take a lead role in convening across sectors like Thunderbird has for climate restoration.

Ron Burt, sociologist, is one of my academic heroes for pioneering work on social networks and capital. He called attention to the importance of bridging structural holes, which are knowledge gaps in the space between tightly-knit clusters of individuals in and across organizations. While there is value in the dense connections within clusters, Burt's research shows that people who bridge structural holes (brokers) have better, more innovative and robust, ideas. Similarly, organizations with collaboration networks that more often bridge structural holes tend to "learn faster and are more creative" (Burt 2005). By connecting people across sectors and silos, business schools can facilitate brokerage and generate more innovative ideas for sustainable development.

A large part of the value created in executive education programs comes from bringing together experienced people from different industries. I have been following a program offered by a large international executive search firm. High-potential managers are recruited from a diverse set of industries to work together for a day on a challenging problem. At the time of this writing, the program was recruiting a cohort to address a software development challenge at the heart of the rapidly changing market for mobility. Everybody wins: the program yields innovative solutions, participants gain experience and contacts, and the search firm gets familiar with the leadership skills of executives in a wide range of industries.

GBSN has been working hard to generate more non-academic connections for business schools. For example, by partnering with the Global Alliance for Improved Nutrition (GAIN) and the World Business Council for Sustainable Development (WBCSD), GBSN will bring academic institutions into cross-sector collaborations to shape the demand for nutritious and sustainable foods. By working with the Center for International Private Enterprise (CIPE) on anti-corruption research, GBSN is connecting scholars to NGOs and SMEs in Indonesia, South Africa, Nigeria, Brazil, and Colombia. In both cases, business schools also serve as connectors to other units, such as the policy school, on campus. GBSN has started similar initiatives at the nexus of business, government, and civil society in other areas, such as health, financial technology, and cybersecurity.

Before closing this chapter, I offer three additional notes about the five strategies. First, the five strategies are not meant to be exhaustive. There are other initiatives that business schools can and should pursue. I left out, for example, a discussion of the curriculum revisions and changes in admissions criteria, extra-curricular activities, and career development activities that can contribute to sustainable development.

Second, the strategies are intended to be complements for each other. Schools are encouraged to take a holistic approach to their work to foster sustainable development. By thinking more comprehensively, schools can generate synergies across various activities, accelerate development, and amplify the impact of their work. For example, the work to build stronger ties between business, government, and civil society can connect the school to companies willing to host sustainability-focused action-learning projects for students. Empowering local initiative can lead to new insights about the overarching purpose of the school, as well as reveal interesting phenomena for scholars to study.

Third, there are risks to pursuing these strategies. For example, if a school moves too far, or too quickly, ahead of others, it could suffer a reputational fall in the rankings. That is a real risk for now. However, in recent years I have been excited to see the Positive Impact Rating (PIR) gain traction as an alternative to rankings, FT consider revisions to its criteria in order to recognize responsibility and sustainability efforts, and AACSB add an accreditation standard for societal impact. All of these developments suggest that the business education ecosystem will adapt as business schools change. Rankings and accreditations will continue to be important, but as means to an end rather than as ends in and of themselves.

While the transformation of schools into catalysts for sustainable development is already quite far along, it is far from complete. And the positive societal dividends are certainly not guaranteed. This chapter outlined five strategies for business school leaders who see sustainable development as a central, or essential, part of their school's future. It also invites readers from other organizations in the broader ecosystem to consider ways to be supportive. What can business leaders, students, and faculty do to accelerate the transformation of business schools? How can university presidents and provosts connect the business school to other parts of the institution to foster sustainable development? How can publishers steward the development of more diverse research models, especially for the developing world? What can global networks, like GBSN, do to create productive cross-sectoral collaborations to achieve the Sustainable Development Goals?

References

A. Barnerjee and E. Duflo, *Good Economics for Hard Times* (New York: Hachette Book Group 2019).

A. Hoffman, *The Engaged Scholar: Expanding the Impact of Academic Research in Today's World* (Stanford: Stanford University Press 2021).

Fundação Dom Cabral, "About FDC". https://www.fdc.org.br/en/aboutfdc. Accessed April 4, 2021.

MIT Sloan Global Programs, "About REAP". https://reap.mit.edu/about/. Accessed March 27, 2021.

MIT Sloan School of Management, "About MIT Sloan". https://mitsloan.mit.edu/about/why-mit-sloan. Accessed March 27, 2021.

R. Burt, *Brokerage & Closure: An Introduction to Social Capital* (Oxford: Oxford University Press 2005).

Suliman S. Olayan School of Business, "About Us". https://www.aub.edu.lb/osb/about/Pages/default.aspx. Accessed April 3, 2021.

Thunderbird School of Global Management, "New Investments and Research Indicate Multi-Trillion Dollar Market for Climate Restoration Through Carbon-Capture". *Newswise*, January 21, 2020. https://www.newswise.com/articles/new-investments-and-research-indicate-multi-trillion-dollar-market-for-climate-restoration-through-carbon-capture.

5

Executive Education 2.0 Coming Right Up

Johan Roos

For many institutions involved in executive education, the future arrived abruptly in early 2020 when the Covid-19 pandemic began profoundly changing the fundamental patterns of how we teach, learn, research, and even enjoy each other's conversation. Most things for us will never be the same and we cannot go back to how it used to be. The sudden shift tested the very fabric of universities and business schools with executive education offerings.

Ironically, many consequences of the pandemic were already evident in emerging trends every leader in executive education already noted; only the urgency to change was new. Traditional multi-year degrees, in-person classroom delivery, and academic year calendars had already made less sense to many. We might say the future for executive education arrived inconveniently early, but the writing was on the wall.

But the pandemic is not the only force pushing on executive education. Before the pandemic hit, an assortment of for-profit providers was already delivering short bursts of education to working professionals, competing de facto with traditional executive education from universities and stand-alone business schools. Commercial providers already offered an abundance of non-degree short courses of one or a few days, or several blocks of sessions over

---

J. Roos (✉)
Hult International Business School, London, UK
e-mail: johan.roos@hult.edu

a few months, capped off with badges, diplomas, and certificates for specific online skill training. Many corporations and working professionals already valued these and relied on them for their executive education needs.

We know that post-pandemic, employers will still need and seek to strengthen the capabilities of their existing workforce. Managers at all levels will need to be prepared to face the rapid changes driven by digitalization, global trade, and demographic shifts. Corporate Learning and Development Officers will continue to demand skills training and broader education for their staff, but in what chunks, from whom, in what delivery format, and at what price remain open questions.

In the years ahead, universities and business schools involved in executive education will face both uncertainty and strong competition from increasingly successful commercial providers. The days of relying on their assumed superiority are gone forever. They must begin making, at a minimum, incremental innovations in their executive education offerings and demonstrate a willingness to try out radical innovations that hopefully create a new growth curve.

These are, in my view, the top three areas that universities and business schools need to strengthen if they intend to survive as leading providers of executive education.

Enlarge the Variety of Offerings (Law of Requisite Variety)

In the infancy of the Internet, Noam (1996) sagely predicted that emerging technologies would enable free information anywhere, anytime and that this would challenge the stable university model from Antiquity. His prescient picture of universities did not arise, burst, and disappear in flames. Rather it gradually emerged over the last decades and has now firmly taken hold and led to an undeniable fact: traditional academic institutions only retain a monopoly on granting degrees, not on who gets to provide education.

The pandemic has fuelled Noam's prediction. If the demand for education among private, public, and third sector organizations is getting more diverse, the offerings from providers need to match that diversity, and vice versa. Used as a metaphor, *Ashby's law of Requisite Variety*, one of the cornerstones of systems theory, helps shed light on what must happen in the executive educational sector. Put simply, Ashby's law holds that a system's ability to deal with change in the environment depends on the variety of actions available to it internally. The meaning of this is clear: *in order to survive, if not thrive, the perspectives, mindsets and ways of working in an organization must be as diverse as the market they are serving.* In short, the law of Requisite Variety suggests that the diversity in the demand of executive education calls for a boost in the diversity of the supply.

This is precisely what we see already happening, yet universities and business schools are not keeping up. The explosion of diversity of commercial providers and offerings of executive education courses is overtaking what traditional institutions have been offering. Education for working professionals is entering a new era of enormous variation in provisions, offered in many forms and sizes over an assortment of time periods and in a variety of learning environments that mix the best of the analogue and digital worlds.

The future thus means that many more non-academic players seeking a share of this multi-billion-dollar action in executive education are vying to take over the market unless universities and business schools respond and catch up. And there is a lot to learn and do to catch up!

The entire higher education system is quickly becoming more complex and dynamic with digital platforms for on-demand and personalized learning. The workforce's Gen Y (and Z coming down the pike) are digital natives who demand and are willing to pay for short bursts of education offered at low cost, at a distance, powered by the latest learning technologies and online pedagogies. This advantages upstart non-academic providers of education that tend to be more digitally native, multi-media savvy, and flexible than traditional business schools and their parent universities.

Looking ahead from now, universities and business schools need to become creative and imagine new possibilities for how they conduct executive education. We're talking about things like combining physical-learning and digital-learning environments, where experience at one real life location is then overlaid with richer, virtual, and even augmented perspectives. Case discussions, guest speakers from all corners of the world, simulations, and role-playing exercises as well as virtual coffee chats and other forms of social engagement outside the classroom might evolve into what resembles advanced computer gaming, especially if they are combined with equipment that engages more of our senses during the experience. Imagine totally immersive live streaming courses based on "holopresence" that will make today's online sessions look old fashion. This kind of education delivery will resemble production of film, carefully crafted by media-savvy experts and delivered by screen-savvy professionals.

Pay Attention to the Infinite Need for Upskilling

In 1995, Jeremy Rifkin published *The End of* Work. His message was rather bleak: technology and synthetics would lead to mass unemployment on a global scale. He was right in that many jobs have disappeared. However, Rifkin did not consider the tremendous growth of new work and jobs that technological advances have also brought. In the same vein as the famous Schumpeterian notion of creative destruction, innovation at its best destroys what does not work but it also builds something new and great.

In view of this prediction, the demand for upskilling existing workforces seems infinite and an obvious growth sector for executive education. There is clear data that universities and business schools need to study to chart their pathways. In fact, in early 2021, a research firm called Burning Glass Technologies analyzed more than 1 billion current and historical job postings in the US to anticipate what jobs will be most important after the pandemic (Siegelman et al. 2021). In line with Rifkin's thesis, employers are prioritizing automation over hiring back low-value workers. Jobs involved with developing and driving automation will thrive. In the spirit of creative destruction, new jobs are being created in brand new fields, e.g., cybersecurity and software engineering, project management, advanced logistics, advanced manufacturing, network systems, and the Internet of Things. Likewise, work and jobs that analyze and visualize data and that apply artificial and virtual reality will play a larger role in the new economies. There will also be many new types of work in the emerging global "green economy."

However, many providers will want a piece of this market. Already the supply of providers offering short, vocational skills courses is growing fast. While corporate academies will likely become masters at skills learning in the practical applications needed within their own organizations and industries, there is still plenty of space for universities and business schools. The market for short bootcamps and quick chunks of classes focused on new skills and resulting in non-credit badges and certificates is sure to grow. This is where new players like LinkedIn Learning, Salesforce Trailblazing, professional service firms, and Big Tech will probably play an ever-increasing role, but for traditional business schools who dare to venture outside the conventional boundaries of executive education, the future can be bright.

Use Your Strengths in Human Skills Development

One ongoing strength of universities and business schools that they can hold tightly onto their executive education in the fields of human skills. Education has always been about more than vocational skills building and upskilling. Just as important is to cultivate the behavioural dimensions of organized life. Self-management, relational skills, leadership, emotional intelligence, self-confidence, politics, working with diversity and inclusion, work-life balance, critical reflection, resolving ethical dilemmas, supporting others, persuasion, learning from mistakes, dealing with failure—all these make up essential "evergreen" human skills necessary to succeed in society and business organizations. This is why individual mentoring and coaching, roleplaying, and staged group activities have been and will continue to be vital in executive education. It is why physical, eye-to-eye contact has always been a core value proposition in learning, and perhaps especially true in executive education.

A correct liberal education should empower individuals and prepare them to deal with complexity, diversity, and change as well as resist dogma and detect fake news. Years ago, I argued hard for the need to build STEM skills into business education, but equally hard for not neglecting the humanities (Roos 2015). Consider the progress in bioengineering, nano-engineering, and personalized medicine as foretold by futurists. Within a few decades, humans will live to age 120, disease will be eradicated, and we will start to colonize Mars. Alternate realities will be visible with the naked eye, and information of any type will be available even faster than today. Let us also assume that we will quickly move from artificial *narrow* intelligence that some cars and refrigerators have today, to artificial *general* intelligence, in which computers are as smart as humans, to the scarier artificial *super* intelligence, in which machines become smarter than us.

The point is, as science and technology advance the machine capacity to do ever-greater actions, we must equally advance our human capacities *to think ever greater thoughts and do even greater deeds*. We must use all our human capacities to ensure that we remain masters of the machines. There is much to be discovered and created in the emerging field of digital humanism. The ability to make decisions and take actions that are not just good for me, but for the organization and community I am part of, is essential for anyone aspiring to lead others. Aristotelian virtue ethics insists that practical wisdom—not just natural science—is required to advance the human race, even as we engage online.

Traditional executive education providers would do well to remember their roots in humanities education that broaden and liberate the mind.

The continuous demand for content about leadership, change management, and more recently, mindfulness and diversity provide evidence that most organizations still take the notion of cultivating core human skills seriously.

Can such teaching be done online or by the commercial executive education upstarts? Perhaps. An example of successfully doing it online is the Virtual Leadership Experience offered by my own school, Hult. We produce an immersive simulation that condenses years of leadership experience and practice responses to extremely challenging situations into a few days. What used to be an in-person exercise is delivered virtually but with intensive and personalized coaching and feedback, including a heart rate report and coping strategies from a sports coach, that aim to improve participants' self-awareness and their ability to think and lead under pressure.

But my bet is that eye-to-eye, hands-on, multi-sensuous, and even playful learning experiences are how we best nurture this kind of practical wisdom (Roos 2006; Statler et al. 2006; Statler and Roos 2007). It is in personal learning environments that we cultivate our intuition, improvisation, and our fleeting state of spontaneity. From what we know today, machines are still at a disadvantage here.

Postscript About Business Schools

I have led or been part of the leadership team of four double- or triple-accredited business schools. All have undergone significant change during my tenure. I know first-hand how difficult it can be to adapt an old organization to quickly changing circumstances and that it is even harder to change the mindsets of its residents. We often call for radical innovation to meet a new world, but to innovate successfully and repeatedly, you must derive your unique innovation approach from your organizational culture (Penker, 2021). Because of the guild-like culture and rigid governance model in academia, most business schools are at a disadvantage in terms of their capacity to innovate to meet new technology, competition, and demand. Many are simply not nimble enough for more than incremental innovations among regulations and self-imposed constraints.

What can business schools do today in the face of the competition, the need for increased variety, the infinite types for upskilling, and the need to teach students to keep man over machines? Here are some nudges for further contemplation or immediate action.

First, campuses need to be converted into attractive hubs for learning experiences of all kinds. Studying and working from home is likely to stick, but *Digital First* does not mean the automatic death of the physical campus.

Many institutions have the convening power to attract busy people to their campus for eye-to-eye interaction and a retreat-like atmosphere. However, most schools should not expect busy professionals to willingly struggle through traffic, wait in check-in lines, sit for 3 hours in a large lecture hall, stay in a modest hotel room for a weekend, and then return home after a day or two. How can we ask students and working professionals to gather in the same physical space and be taught using centuries-old pedagogies, especially after a year ever-more useful innovations supporting studying and working from home? Given their vast sunk costs in bricks and mortar with donor names on brass plates, some schools will strive to slow the movement away from campus-taught courses, but the trend is clear: they can't.

Recognize that mass-digital learning will naturally replace mass face-to-face learning and executive education is likely at the forefront of this shift. In-person engagement will remain a high-perceived value, but too expensive to maintain. Count on massive investments to modernize your technology towards Digital First and beyond, using new hybrid experiences resembling interactive Netflix or gaming productions more than traditional education. Installing the best tracking microphones, cameras, and screens in traditional classrooms is a necessary but insufficient step on a long and expensive journey to create a new generation of learning spaces for more immersive experiences. Future education offerings need to be like blockbuster movies or media events, with professional facilitators, curators, and producers creating augmented digital learning with a corresponding transformed pedagogy.

Second, schools need to develop a dualistic strategy, adapting for today and innovating for tomorrow. While some things remain stable, much will change, in sudden and often surprising ways. This kind of emergent behaviour is a fundamental property of complex systems that describe today's higher education eco-system.

Being accredited by the leading system of quality assessment of business schools—EQUIS and AACSB—necessitate highly documented "strategic plans", list of competitors, and "robust" processes and clearly defined goals, precise timelines, and success metrics. That was a fine idea for a stable yesterday, but not adequate for a more complex tomorrow. The difficult part of the dualistic strategy is preparing for the unexpected. We must begin tackling the void that we do not know much about and, hence, are unprepared for. This means actively scouting the dynamic landscape, picking up early and weak signals, developing an institutional capacity to quickly absorb these, and ensuring fast decision-making and execution among new players in dynamic and competitive eco-systems. As far as I know, this is not yet an accreditation standard.

Third, we need to integrate non-degree awards like certifications and skills badges used by commercial providers into our own learning offerings, starting with executive education. This runs counter to common academic quality standards, but business schools cannot ignore close to a million and growing non-degree badges, certificates, and diplomas offered in the US alone. My school, Hult, has used this tactic in partnering with EY to quality assure and integrate their internal badges curated and taught by their seasoned professionals with our academic content in a personalized MBA for EY employees. In theory, hundreds of thousands of people can enlist on this extended journey of academically sound and practically useful education.

This may feel like cheapening one's reputation for leaders and faculty in the higher echelons of branded schools, who see such initiatives as disrupting the conventional boundary between academia (supplier) and business (buyer), between a degreed education (higher status) and vocational training (lower status). Mohan Sawhney, Associate Dean of Digital Innovation at the renowned Kellogg School of Management, recently did a webinar on the future of executive education and noted that disruptive "barbarians at the gate" innovated much more than branded incumbents. Indeed, my own school was cited as an example, but only the future will tell if we can maintain it:

> *Innovations always come from the periphery. People like us working at Harvard and Kellogg, we are too lazy, fat and rich. We already have a name and we do not innovate enough. While we were sleeping, the ones who used to be small took the lead on disruption and are today the pioneers. We need to look at Hult to understand where executive education is going. They are the future!* (Sawhney 2021)

Universities and business schools should actually be inspired by how Netflix, Spotify, Uber, Klarna, Tesla, and many others are transforming their competitive ecosystems. What is clear from them is that a wait-and-see mindset is not an option. Sawhney called it out to in his webinar: *"Do not sit on your moral highchair and say you will not do it!"* I agree.

References

Noam, E.M. 1996, *Electronics and the Dim Future of the University*, Bulletin of the American Society for Information Science, June/July 1996: 6–9.

Penker, M. 2021, *Play Bold*, Leaders Press, New York, N.Y.

Rifkin J. 1995, *The End of Work*, New York, N.Y., G.P. Putnam's Son.

Roos, J. 2006, *Thinking From Within: A Hands-On Strategy Practice*, Palgrave Macmillan, Basingstoke.

Roos. J. 2015, Build STEM Skills, but Don't Neglect the Humanities, *Harvard Business Review*, online edition, 4 June.

Sawhney. M. 2021, *What Lies Beyond: The Future of Executive Education*, Webinar, Harvard Business School Publishing, March 4. https://tinyurl.com/5c9jv3z6.

Siegelman, M., Brittle, S., Hodge, N., O'Kane, L. and Taska, B. 2021, *After the Storm: The Jobs and Skills that will Drive the Post-Pandemic Recovery*, Burning Glass Technologies, February.

Statler, M. and Roos, J. 2007, *Everyday Strategic Preparedness: The Role of Practical Wisdom in Organizations*, Palgrave Macmillan, Basingstoke.

Statler, M., Roos, J., and B. Victor, 2006, Illustrating the Need for Practical Wisdom, *International Journal of Management Concepts and Philosophy*, 2(1): 1–30.

6

Perennial Insights from Peter Drucker

Richard Straub

As a prolific writer who published some 40 books, Peter Drucker has left us with an abundant and wide-ranging legacy—such that it is sometimes hard to decide the heading his most significant and lasting lessons belong under. Unlike other management writers and gurus, Drucker did not start out as a thinker about organizations and management. Rather, he made his mark as a young man as a political scientist studying the seismic shifts of the twentieth century that gave rise to totalitarianism, in both its fascist and communist forms. This preoccupation remained central to his outlook and output all his life.

Analyzing the roots of these epochal developments in his first major book, *The End of Economic Man*, Drucker concluded that, as became apparent in the Great Depression of the 1930s, capitalism had failed to give people meaning beyond the purely economic. That left them open to the new fascist or communist creeds that promised not only a better world but a perfect one, based on a seemingly rational logic that used scientific language and theories to legitimize their world view. As examples, consider dialectic materialism, race theory and eugenics. Drucker was intrigued, and alarmed, by the way

---

R. Straub (✉)
The Global Peter Drucker Forum, Vienna, Austria
e-mail: richard.straub@druckersociety.eu

the Enlightenment and its unbounded belief in absolute reason and rationality had paved the way for the most murderous ideologies in human history. He saw the havoc that violent upheavals such as the Bolshevik and Mao's Cultural Revolution had wreaked in pursuit of their utopian goals, for which the French revolution with its Reign of Terror and the Vendée massacres had established a terrible precedent. He understood how the desperate yearning of the masses for a place, a status and a function in society made them easy targets for the rhetoric of toxic leaders—the charismatic preachers of death and destruction. By contrast, he perceived the American revolution of 1776 as marking a decisive turn of the absolutist and rationalist tide, the new constitution providing a pragmatic and carefully balanced design for both a functioning and a free society.

Management—A Vital Role in Society

In the course of his enquiries Drucker also uncovered a phenomenon, new to the twentieth century, that—not for the only time—he perceived while others missed. He called it 'the new society of organizations'. And this is where he placed his hopes—on those organizations in which, as they sprang up across all domains of society, he saw the potential to improve people's lives by affording them roles, function, meaning, and community as well as material sustenance. The emergence of large industrial corporations, growing public-sector services institutions and numerous social-sector and non-profit organizations were already generating employment and dignity for many. But to turn their potential into reality—to allow them to endure and help create Drucker's functioning society—it was clear that they needed to develop structures and systems to enable effective performance. In other words, they needed to be consciously managed.

Yet when in the 1950s Drucker searched for methods and tools to guide managers in these tasks, he found—inconceivable as it now sounds—that they barely existed. There were bits and pieces, but no coherent body of knowledge. His conclusion: if management was to become a discipline, something that could be researched, learned, taught, and systematically practised, he would have to create and codify it himself. 'I sat down and made a discipline of it',[1] he would tell an interviewer. This by itself was an enormous intellectual and personal endeavour—the chief of the 'widening circles' in which following the poet Rilke he lived his life, and whose outward ripples

---

[1] Quoted in Jack Beatty, *The World According to Drucker* (1998), 104.

drove, and still drive, subsequent explorers in the field to build on the foundations he had laid.

Coming to 'management' through a concern for the workings of society as a whole, Drucker always viewed the discipline in a broad social context. His argument was simple and fundamental. To function, a free society required strong self-governing institutions across every sector; the only alternative was totalitarianism. In turn, effective organizations required high-performing management: 'Performing, responsible management is the alternative to tyranny and our only protection against it'.[2] Hence his description of management as a 'constitutive organ' of a functioning society: by comparison, making a profit, while important, indeed essential to fulfilling its function, was a means and a validation, not an end. From social purpose derives management's further duty to minimize an organization's social impacts and externalities. Like medicine, it should first do no social harm.

The 'Why' as the Starting Point

Specific to Drucker is the way he treats management as a whole, giving appropriate weight to the three dimensions of what we might call the 'what', the 'how', and the 'why' of management, where the 'what' represents the theories and concepts, the 'how' the tools and methods, and the 'why' the values, principles, and purpose of the work of managers. Most management thinkers address the 'what' and the 'how', eliding the 'why'. For Drucker, the 'why' was the starting point.

The why is the area where what Drucker calls 'the educated person' is needed. For Drucker, management was always a 'liberal art'—as he put it, '"liberal" because it deals with the fundamentals of knowledge, self-knowledge, wisdom, and leadership; "art" because it deals with practice and application'.[3] Management is to the social sciences what medicine is to the natural ones. Following this formulation, those versed in humanities and social sciences will be more at ease with tackling the big questions around purpose and values, because they have learned to think in a broader context. To ignore the 'why' is to turn management into a mere technique and run the risk of nudging us on to the slippery slope to technocracy.

---

[2] Quoted in J.A. Maciarello, *The Daily Drucker* (2004). Accessed at http://meaningring.com/2017/01/10/management-as-the-alternative-tyranny-by-peter-drucker/.
[3] *The New Realities* (1988), 223.

Performance: The Litmus Test for Any Organization

To fulfill its social function, an organization must perform: it must satisfy the needs of customers, innovate to create new offerings, deliver effective public-sector services, and provide the cultural and spiritual experiences that humans need for meaningful lives. For Drucker, the *sine qua non* of management is therefore achieving results, a word that recurs throughout his work. As he put it: 'Performance of his function is his first social responsibility. Unless [the organization] discharges its performance responsibility, it cannot discharge anything else. A bankrupt business is not a desirable employer and is unlikely to be a good neighbour in a community'.[4] Without effective, well-performing institutions, society can't survive, and if an individual cannot play their part in achieving performance that is more than the sum of its parts they are not a manager.

One of the human aspects of enabling performance is the requirement to place people in the organization where their strengths are made the most of and their weaknesses neutralized—a difficult job that imposes high demands on managers and on the individual. This is one reason why self-assessment and self-management were always a touchstone in Drucker's thinking. After all, how can you expect others to perform at the highest level if you don't expect it from yourself? In 'Managing Oneself', one of his most influential articles, Drucker argued that in a knowledge-driven world, it was the responsibility of managers to act as their own CEO: only when you operate from a combination of strength and self-knowledge can you achieve true and lasting excellence. But since management is a social as well as an economic technology, with individual freedom and dignity at its heart, executives have a double goal: as Jim Collins noted on their first encounter, the big question for Drucker is how to make society more productive *and* more humane, at the same time.

Self-Renewal Through Abandonment

Unfortunately, excellence doesn't sustain itself, whether in individuals, organizations, the economy, and society at large. His studies in politics made Drucker profoundly aware of the vital need for rejuvenation and self-renewal in all human affairs. This leads to one of his most important principles,

---

[4] *Management: Tasks, Responsibilities, Practices* (1985 [first published 1974]), 343.

one that many outstanding managers, including Jack Welch and Steve Jobs, publicly took to heart. He called it 'abandonment'. To make it actionable—something a manager could do on Monday morning—Drucker ingeniously turned renewal on its head. He observed that without a 'not-to-do' list a 'to-do' list just proliferated. Deciding what to stop doing was therefore just as important as what to start. 'Every three years, an organization should challenge every product, every service, every policy, every distribution channel with the question, If we were not in it already, would we be going into it now?'[5] Without this challenge to its fundamental assumptions about the 'theory of the business', entropy would set in and the organization would be overtaken by events. It was in the same spirit that Drucker urged managers to pay as much attention to the majority of consumers who didn't buy their products as to the minority who did. Non-customers always outnumbered customers: *ergo*, the first signs of fundamental change were more likely to emerge outside your immediate field of vision, in the parts of the market you weren't currently addressing.

Seeing Reality and the Future That Has Already Arrived

'I never predict. I just look out of the window and see what's visible – but not yet seen', Drucker told a Forbes interviewer in 1997. Given his lived experience, it is hardly surprising that Drucker's radar was perpetually sweeping the horizon for weak signs of what lay ahead. In Jack Beatty's nice phrase, his work constantly 'walks the faint line between the known and the unknown'.[6] Consider the strikingly future-looking titles of many of his books: *America's Next Twenty Years*, *The Ecological Vision* (1993), *Landmarks of Tomorrow: A Report on the 'Post-Modern' World* (1959), *The Age of Discontinuity*, *Managing for the Future*, *The New Realities*, *Post-Capitalist Society* (1993). Drucker claimed to have been the first to use the terms 'post-modern' and 'knowledge work' and 'knowledge worker'. While eschewing prediction, he foresaw the collapse of communism and the fall of the Berlin Wall, the rise of Japan in the 1980s (partly because its manufacturers were quicker to absorb his ideas than their US competitors), and later that of China and India. Alive today, Drucker would be writing about what comes after VUCA, AI and social media, and their consequences for society. Know it or not, the authors

---

[5] 'The Theory of the Business', HBR, September–October 1994.
[6] Beatty, *The World*, 29.

of today's management models that put the focus on experiential learning, experimentation and a high degree of reactiveness and agility are all following Peter Drucker's theory-informed but practically oriented management philosophy. Many of them have been presented and vigorously debated at the annual Global Peter Drucker Forum in Vienna.

The Power of Metaphor

Drucker considered himself as 'a writer'; as such, as Charles Handy observed, he was a master of the creative use of metaphor, low-definition but memorable concepts, to amplify weak signals from the future and as 'the art which draws men's minds to the love of true knowledge',[7] as Drucker himself defined the art of rhetoric. Sharp Drucker quotes, both true and apocryphal, abound, and those metaphors are still in use. Often they seem obvious at first, but deliver added layers of meaning the more time goes by. 'The essence of management is to make knowledge productive'.[8] 'There is only one valid definition of business purpose: to create a customer'.[9] 'Leadership is defined by results, not attributes'.[10] 'So much of management consists of making it hard for people to work'.

Linked together, two of his apparently simple thoughts encapsulate the entire management problematic, today and every day. 'Efficiency is concerned with doing things right; effectiveness is doing the right thing'.[11] 'There is surely nothing quite so useless as doing with great efficiency what should not be done at all'.[12] Efficiency and effectiveness are not the same thing. Sometimes they conflict. Deceptively, while efficiency is essential, if applied to the wrong thing it is useless or worse. Take the obsession with production efficiencies to meet Wall Street's demands of the last few decades. Without a clear purpose and strategy for the business, maximizing efficiencies at any one moment diminishes possibilities for the longer term. In effect, it trades the future for the present. We call the result short-termism. Hence effectiveness comes before efficiency—what is the right thing to do for the business or specific projects and endeavors in the short and longer term?

---

[7] *Adventures of a Bystander* (1994), 89.
[8] *Managing in a Time of Great Change* (2012), 219.
[9] *The Practice of Management* (1954), 37.
[10] 'Managing Oneself'.
[11] *Management: Tasks, Responsibilities, Practices* (1974) 45.
[12] 'Managing for Business Effectiveness', HBR May-June 1963.

Examples of damage done by efficient accomplishment of pointless tasks are legion. Much bureaucracy comes under this heading. If the right thing is done, the need for box-ticking and other red tape falls away, as demonstrated by accelerated international vaccine research and emergency health procedures developed during the pandemic. In the 1980s IBM efficiently built out plant capacity based on flawed linear forecasts of mainframe demand that brought the company almost to its knees. More recently, the social media giants have developed ever more efficient means of capturing user data and using it to manipulate behavior to benefit advertisers. This is an undeniably lucrative formula in the short run. But it runs foul of management's 'no harm' principle, as people are becoming increasingly aware. In the inevitable backlash, as Drucker predicted, ruthlessly 'doing what shouldn't be done at all' eventually risks 'destroy[ing] society's support for the enterprise and with it the enterprise as well'.

Management and Leadership

Drucker's crucial distinction between 'things right' and 'the right thing' also illuminates the endlessly discussed issue of leadership. Drucker wrote remarkably little about leadership as such. He describes leadership tersely as a means (so the end, i.e., the 'why' and the 'right thing', is critical), conferring responsibility rather than a rank or privilege, and whose essence is performance. It has nothing to do with attributes. 'The only definition of a leader is someone who has followers,' he wrote in 'Managing Oneself'.

The terseness is not because leadership is unimportant. On the contrary: Drucker well knew the terrible potency of charismatic but toxic leaders, and as regularly pointed out that some who qualify as great leaders by their results present as unassuming to the point of colorlessness. For Drucker management and leadership are two poles on the same spectrum. Leadership is more concerned with overall effectiveness and managing with efficient use of resources to hand. A senior executive role includes a larger leadership component than a lower position in operational management. At the same time, as Jim Collins noted in his foreword to the second edition of the seminal *Management: Tasks, Responsibilities, Practices*, Drucker made it abundantly clear that 'the very best leaders are first and foremost effective managers. Those who seek to lead but fail to manage will become either irrelevant or dangerous, not only to their organizations, but to society'.

A Vision to Strive For: The Entrepreneurial Society

Characteristically, Drucker concludes his landmark *Innovation and Entrepreneurship* (1985) with a call not just for entrepreneurial firms to animate an entrepreneurial economy, but for an entrepreneurial society. 'What we need,' he wrote, 'is an entrepreneurial society in which innovation and entrepreneurship are normal, steady, and continuous. Just as management has become the specific and integrating organ of all contemporary institutions, so innovation and entrepreneurship have to become an integral life-sustaining activity in our organizations, our economy and our society'.[13]

In the entrepreneurial society, Drucker's ideas of what we might now call the twenty-first century society come together in a culture of independent but strongly connected individuals, entrepreneurs, organizations, and institutions, that generate progress through a constant flow of innovation. In today's conditions, where companies based on knowledge work and peopled by what we might call knowledge entrepreneurs are inherently disruptive, the price of creative destruction as envisioned by Schumpeter must be accepted and adjusted to as the driving force of improved productivity and value creation. Clayton Christensen continued this line of thought with his notion of disruptive and market-creating innovation.

But although Drucker, unlike many other management writers, reserved a vital role for the state as decider in his entrepreneurial vision, it was not the function of government to act as entrepreneur and innovator on its own account. Like the American constitution in politics, its role is to ensure a balance between destruction and creation, continuity, and change: in this case taking a systemic approach to freeing up entrepreneurship, ensuring fair competition, and preventing the rise of over-dominant players that too often thwart innovation and progress. Innovation and entrepreneurship are needed in society as much as in the economy, in public service institutions as much as in businesses. These qualities are pragmatic rather than dogmatic and bottom-up rather than top-down. They provide the capacity for self-renewal to society, to business, to the public, and to the civil sector. For Drucker, key to an entrepreneurial society that can sidestep the bloodshed and destruction of violent revolution is the ability to self-renew.

---

[13] *Innovation and Entrepreneurship* (1985), 236.

Management at the Crossroads

What would Drucker make of the world we find ourselves in in 2021? Although fundamentally an optimist, in the sense that he believed in human agency and rejected determinism, whether historical or technological, he was also a realist—never shy in pointing out societal failures and fallibilities, including those of managers subject to their own powerful forms of temptation. He was clear that perfect organizations and perfect economies were no more achievable than perfect humans. He deplored companies' overemphasis on short-term efficiency at the expense of long-term effectiveness, and was sharply critical of its outward manifestations in the form of soaring executive pay and wholesale outsourcing of jobs, which he saw as directly linked. He would have detested the financialization of the economy, which reverses social priorities by making the real world of value creation dance to the tune of financial value-extractors who make billions from speculating on their success or failure, irrespective of the effects on society. Believing that the corporation was as important to society as to the economy—'free enterprise cannot be justified as being good for business. It can only be justified as good for society'[14]—he never accepted that managers had a duty only to shareholders.

In sum (although he might have found a different metaphor), I believe Drucker would have placed both management and society today at another of their historic crossroads. This time it would not be between democratic capitalism and brute totalitarianism, as in his first books. Equally important for our and our children's future, it would be between a self-renewing entrepreneurial society imbued with a pragmatic innovative mindset based on the ideas of individual freedom and human agency and a strong sense of reality on the one side, and a post-humanistic, technocratic, and financialized society centered on surveillance, intrusion, and manipulation in the private sphere and an over-regulated, algorithmically controlled, centralized power at an economic and societal level, on the other.

More than ever, safely navigating this fork in the road calls for management to live up to Drucker's Renaissance-style vision of it: an embodiment of unique human competencies combined with a deep understanding of what technology, expertise and science can and cannot do to augment and complement them. Only sound judgement, knowledge mined from experience, and competence-based creativity can keep what Drucker called a functioning and bearable society in place. Yet a pluralistic society must have a set of common values to survive—beyond the ideologies and of the day. This makes

---

[14] *The Practice of Management* (1954).

of management something more than a band of hired hands and mercenaries. For Drucker, 'the moralist of our business civilization', in Beatty's words, it makes it a moral, even noble calling. As someone who considered managers—'ordinary people, people running the everyday concerns of business and institutions, [who] took responsibility and kept on building for tomorrow while around them the world came crashing down'[15]—the unsung heroes of the last century, he would certainly have asked: as individuals, as managers, as educators—which do we want for business and society now? What will we stand up and fight for today?

---

[15] *The Frontiers of Management* (1968), Preface.

7

The Role of Business Education in Supporting the Future of Work

Nick van Dam

The pandemic has accelerated existing organizational trends. Many leaders around the world were surprised by the level of their workforce's resilience—the ability of people to change their way of working and build new digital skills, virtually overnight. Indeed, today we are already living in the future of work—a future most of us imagined would take another decade to reach.

But not just business structures have been challenged. Academic institutions have had to completely rethink their approach to education. The walls, both literal and figurative, of educational institutions have fallen away as hybrid models of learning and pure online courses have supplanted traditional in-person classroom experiences.

It is expected that many of these changes to business and education are here to stay—and may even be taken to the next level. Organizations are reflecting on the key learnings of the pandemic, the new realities of the future work, and the opportunities in the post pandemic era. Below, we discuss a number of trends that will define work in this new era, as well as the implications of these trends for the workforce and the critical role of business education through business schools in enabling students to thrive in the new future of work.

N. van Dam (✉)
IE University, Madrid, Spain
e-mail: Nick.Vandam@ie.edu

Trends Reshaping the Workforce

Seven primary trends are increasingly altering the way the workplace, and the world, look and operate.

Digitization

According to the World Economic Forum, technological advancements have landed us on the cusp of a fourth industrial revolution—also referred to as the digital age.[1] The pace of adoption of new technologies, including Industry 4.0, the Internet of Things, the mobile internet, artificial intelligence, machine learning, and robotization, as well as the use of big data and predictive analytics, will continue to accelerate. These technologies will disrupt existing business models, create new generations of products and services, and help organizations operate seamlessly and be more competitive globally.

Already during the pandemic, many sectors have harnessed technology to advance their business model—consider telehealth, online shopping, online education, and online advising in professional and financial services. And industry plants have learned to operate with a limited number of physically present employees.

Past industrial revolutions similarly disrupted organizations and entire industries—and had a huge impact on society and work.

Automation and Shifting Work Arrangements

Today, people perform 71 percent of processes, with machines doing the rest. A shift is imminent: the World Economic Forum predicts that by 2025, technology will perform 52 percent of current work tasks.[2] While the figures are staggering, it isn't all bleak. It is expected that, with more people on the planet and more people in emerging countries entering the middle class, the global economy will continue to grow. This growth will create new work for people. Furthermore, it is expected that people and machines will augment each other and work together more closely—for example, in robot-assisted surgery.

---

[1] K. Schwab, *The Fourth Industrial Revolution: What It Means, How to Respond*, World Economic Forum, 14 January, 2016.

[2] O. Cann, *Machines Will Do More Tasks Than Humans by 2025 but Robot Revolution Will Still Create 58 Million Net New Jobs in Next Five Years*, World Economic Forum, September 17, 2018.

The relationship between employees and employers continues to evolve as well. Not long ago, most work in organizations was done by full-time employees. Today, an organization's workforce comprises a combination of full-time employees and those with alternative work arrangements, including contractors, part-time workers, freelancers, and gig workers. This balance will continue to shift.

People should plan to have multiple careers and work for many companies, in a variety of roles and work arrangements. Indeed, rather than dwelling on how many jobs will be lost, organizations and people should focus on preparing for the jobs, and work arrangements, of the future.

Hybrid and Remote Work

Information workers have been able to work entirely remotely during the pandemic. Overall, the results have been positive: remote work has increased productivity, reduced or eliminated commute time, supported the environment, provided people with more flexibility, and, somewhat surprisingly, encouraged feelings of inclusion, with everyone working in the same virtual room. However, many employees and leaders have expressed the need for and value of spending time in person in the office. At the same time, a large majority of workers want flexible- and remote-working options to continue, and a growing number of organizations are allowing large segments of their workforce to work remotely two to three days a week, on average.[3] Indeed, in new hybrid-working models, some people might be entirely remote while others will divide their time between working remotely and in the office. Recent research suggests that 38 percent of jobs can be performed remotely in high-income countries.[4]

Companies are looking at hybrid and remote work as an opportunity to become more competitive by reducing office costs. The post pandemic corporate office, then, might become an "experience center": a place where people meet, build or reinforce strong human relationships, participate in brainstorming sessions, form networks, and live the company culture. It will be less a place where people just respond to email.

---

[3] McKinsey Global Institute, What's Next for Remote Work: An Analyses of 2,000 Tasks, 800 Jobs, and Nine Countries, November 23, 2020.
[4] K. Schwab, *The Future of Jobs Report 2020*, World Economic Forum, October 2020.

Empowerment of Teams

Organizations have experienced the power of moving away from individual activities and hierarchies toward work that is done in (virtual) teams and networks. A growing number of organizations encourage people to play various roles, contributing to and being part of multiple teams. This shift is energizing, as it harnesses people's competencies and strengths throughout the organization and provides people-development opportunities in the workplace.

Organizations are structuring themselves in ways that make them fitter, flatter, and faster in order to unlock value. And they're empowering decentralized teams to make decisions at the speed of business. A variety of organizational models along these lines have been introduced, including the "holacracy," under which power is distributed throughout the organization.[5] This model gives individuals and teams freedom while keeping the organization aligned with its purpose. It is especially suited to environments where creativity is required to develop a specific product, such as a video game.

Furthermore, leading companies will build data-rich platforms because they understand that data and predictive analytics are fueling powerful decisions that can be made independently in small teams.

Digital Transformation, with a Focus on Talent

Successful companies are well known for attracting and retaining top talent, as this is the scarcest resource. Talent pays back: talented people in highly complex jobs are seven times more productive than average performers.[6] And tackling digital transformation, leading in innovation, and gaining a competitive edge is only possible with the right quality and quantity of talent.

Many roles critical to the organization already. And demand is expected to increase for roles that support digital transformation—including data analysts and scientists, AI and machine learning specialists, software developers and big data specialists, as well as for those less directly related to transformation, such as digital marketers, project managers, fintech engineers, and strategic advisors.

---

[5] Website: https://www.holacracy.org/explore/why-practice-holacracy.
[6] S.Keller, M. Meaney, *Attracting and Retaining the Right Talent*, McKinsey, November 24, 2017.

Human Leadership

Twentieth-century leadership was based on controlling people and managing workflows. This approach needs to be replaced by human leadership, which is characterized by leaders taking a deep interest in people's well-being. Gary Nurnison, CEO of management consulting company Korn Ferry, argues that "what the world is calling for now is radically human leadership—leadership that's based on humility, on not just showing empathy but having empathy, on being vulnerable, on being authentic."[7]

Human-leadership practices include empathic listening, building positive relationships, developing trust, sharing optimism and positivity, and motiving and engaging people. These practices have their roots in positive psychology. Martin Seligman, a professor at the University of Pennsylvania who is often referred to as the cofounder of positive psychology, describes the concept as one that "helps achieve scientific understanding and effective interventions to build thriving individuals, families, communities and organizations."

Human leaders do the following, particularly during times of uncertainty, such as the COVID-19 pandemic[8]:

- show empathy, openness, honestly, and vulnerability
- communicate frequently and transparently
- practice being deliberately calm
- know how to lead virtually with impact
- support employees' emotional health
- promote work–life balance and healthy working habits

These behaviors have a huge impact on the culture of an organization. It is not surprising that companies with strong cultures achieve up to three times greater return on shareholder value than companies without a strong and values-driven culture.[9] And truly human leaders play a critical role in shaping, reinforcing, and living the culture.

As Leena Nair, chief human resources officer at Unilever said, "*As leaders we need to focus on digitization, but at the same time, we need to become more human.*"[10]

---

[7] E. Greenawald, The CEO of Management Consultancy Korn Ferry on How to Become a 'Radically Human Leader', *Insider*, March 17, 2021.

[8] N.C. Nielsen, G. D'Auria, S. Zolley, *Turning in, Turning Outward: Cultivating Compassionate Leadership in Crisis*, McKinsey, May 1, 2020.

[9] A. De Smet, C. Gagnon, E. Mygatt, *Organizing for the Future. Nine Keys to Coming a Future-Ready Company*, McKinsey, January 11, 2021.

[10] L. Naire, *The Future of Work—How to Be More Human in a Digital World?* RippleHire, 2019.

An Emphasis on Well-Being and Vitality

People have a high risk of experiencing burnout in their work, and work is a leading cause of stress. Prior to the pandemic, one study found that 94 percent of workers feel stressed and almost one-third say their stress level is high to unsustainably high.[11] And a rapidly growing number of professionals who are in their twenties are experiencing burnout—a worrisome trend.[12] In 2019, the World Health Organization classified burnout as an official work-related condition.[13]

Since the start of the pandemic, work conditions have changed for everyone, in one way or another, and this has brought significant well-being challenges as people have struggled to adapt to new ways of work fueled by progressive digitization. Only 46 percent of US adults described themselves as "thriving" in 2020, similar to the measure during the Great Recession of 2008 and 2009.[14] Of course, high stress and burnout have a negative impact on employee engagement.

One of the Sustainable Development Goals set by the United Nations focuses on good health and well-being. People's well-being within organizations is a critical factor to overall well-being. It's no surprise that well-being in the workplace has emerged as a strategic focus, as it affects such crucial factors as productivity and organizational performance. IE University has launched a Center for Health, Well-Being & Happiness to educate and support students on this important topic and help them to flourish.

The Implications of These Trends for the Workforce

These trends will have a couple of critical effects on the workforce.

---

[11] B. Denny, J. Schwartz, E. Volini, Designing Work for Well-Being: Living and Performing at Your Best, *Deloitte Insights*, May 15, 2020.

[12] L. Petersen, Burnout In Your Early 20s Is Real, No Matter What The Boomers Think, *Elite Daily*, February 3, 2020.

[13] Burn-out an "occupational phenomenon": International Classification of Diseases, World Health Organization, May 28, 2019.

[14] D. Witters, J. Harter, *Worry and Stress Fuel Record Drop in US Life Satisfaction*, Gallup, May 8, 2020.

7 The Role of Business Education in Supporting the Future of Work

Fig. 7.1 The top ten competencies by 2025 (Elaborated by the author based on sources of the World Economic Forum, 2020)

A Shift in Needed Jobs and Skills

It is expected that there will be a massive shift in needed jobs. McKinsey research suggests that an estimated one out of three current jobs will become obsolete in Europe by 2030 through a combination of the changes related to COVID-19 and digitization.[15] And the World Economic Forum estimates that by 2025, 85 million jobs may be displaced by a shift in the division of labor between humans and machines. However, even more jobs—97 million—may emerge; these will be jobs that reflect the new division of labor among humans, machines, and algorithms.[16]

Furthermore, 40 percent of current workers' "core skills" are expected to change by 2025. And most roles are likely to require different or advanced competencies. Research from organizations including The World Economic Forum and The World Bank[17] show a consistent picture regarding the skills of the future. The World Economic Forum groups these top competencies (skills) in three different clusters: cognitive, human, and digital[18] (Fig. 7.1).

---

[15] S. Smit, T. Tacke, S. Lund, J. Manyika, *The Future of Work in Europe*, McKinsey Global Institute, 2020.
[16] K. Schwab, *The Future of Jobs Report 2020*, World Economic Forum, October 2020.
[17] *Skill Development*, The World Bank, April 5, 2021.
[18] K. Whiting, *These Are the Top 10 Job Skills of Tomorrow—And How Long It Takes to Learn Them*, World Economic Forum, 21 October 2020.

Almost independent of roles, every person needs to advance their understanding and usage of technologies and software applications. In the words of Bosch CEO Volkmar Denner, "Get learning, or stay analog."[19] That is not a threat; it is a call to action meant to empower people.

In a fast-changing, highly unpredictable, and complex external environment, organizations need human leaders who have strong digital and cognitive skills and who master social and emotional skills, adaptability, and resilience.

The authors of the book *The Second Machine Age* argue that there are more opportunities available today—for those who possess the right skills—than at any time in the past 40 years, thanks to the characteristics of the new economy. But for those who lack the necessary skills, the next 10–15 years will be perilous, since they will face the constant threat of machines stealing their jobs.[20]

Indeed, Pew Research[21] suggests that automation, robotics, algorithms, and AI can do equal or better work than humans in a wide array of roles—from dermatologists and insurance claims adjusters to hiring managers and border patrol agents.

To remain employable during a career that could stretch nearly half a century and under this pressure on jobs, every single person needs to be reskilled or upskilled.

The Need for Ongoing Development and Well-Being

To successfully adapt to the pressure on jobs and skills, people need to develop mindsets of lifelong learning and make personal investments in terms of time and money.

Organizations also have a role to play. The only organizations that will be successful will have a talented workforce with the right competencies and employees who continue to learn. Therefore, companies need to embrace that every talented person needs development to make a sustainable and long-term contribution to the organization. Organizations also need to design work and

---

[19] Get Digital or Stay Analogue, *Volkmar Denne, Bosch Website.* https://www.bosch.com/stories/denners-view-digital-learning/, 18 December 2018. These are the top 10 job skills of tomorrow—and how long it takes to learn them.

[20] *Digital Leadership: The Second Machine Age: An Industrial Revolution Powered by Digital Technologies,* CapGemini Consulting, 2013.

[21] *The Future of Jobs and Jobs Training,* Pew Research Center, May 2017.

roles in a way that turns the *workplace* into a *learning place*, as most professional development can happen on-the-job. Great leaders understand that education and learning are essential in developing a learning organization.

And given that companies need individuals who perform at a consistently high level and who continue to learn and unlearn, they need to encourage vitality. Leadership practices should support people's well-being, and organizations should educate employees on how they can boost their health, well-being, and happiness.

The Essential Role of Business Education

Business education can play a significant role in supporting organizations and individuals during this time of upheaval and throughout the digital age. A few actions will be particularly important.

Provide cognitive, human, and digital competencies: Business schools need to help graduates master a mix of cognitive, human, and digital competencies to be prepared for today's jobs and a different kind of career. Human skills can be referred to as the "power skills" needed to succeed today and in the future—skills that cannot be done by machines or artificial intelligence. These skills are much harder to develop than technical skills but have a long lifespan. Examples include emotional intelligence, curiosity, creativity, empathy, problem solving, adaptability, resilience, social and emotional intelligence, ethics, and values. Furthermore, students need to know how to both learn and unlearn. Indeed, the goal of learning in the twenty-first century is not just about knowledge acquisition and memorization. It is invaluable that students develop unique human skills and mindsets. For example, an entrepreneurial mindset will foster problem solving, decision-making and innovating and will prepare students to quickly be able to adapt to changing requirements.

Rethink offerings to allow for renewal: As people will be in the workforce for 45 years or longer, they have to upskill and reskill themselves at the speed of business. Many need to become "serial masters," developing and deepening their expertise in multiple fields. Beyond traditional degrees, employers are looking for people who have earned alternative credentials—versus credentials that are based on tests and grades—that demonstrate expertise in different fields. In light of this, business schools need to stay on top of developing and renewing their offerings, including moving toward degrees earned in stackable education modules and building micro credentials as well as smaller learning nuggets that support capability development during peoples' entire careers.

Embrace technology: Educational technologies (edtech) should be used to advance the learning experience, scale its reach, and support effective learning experiences. Additionally, edtech can make learning offerings more affordable for people. This is very important, given that the growing number of people in alternative work arrangements, including part-time workers, contractors, freelancers, and gig workers, as well as owners of companies, have to fund 100 percent of their own development. Beyond edtech, students need to master technologies that are used in the workplace with regards to productivity, meetings, collaboration, projects, learning, functional applications (for example, finance, supply chain, marketing, and customer-relationship management), document management, and artificial intelligence.

Provide new learning spaces: Business schools need to deploy different, and digital, learning spaces needed to advance the learning experience and provide students with real-world experience. Examples include virtual reality, augmented reality, simulations, and games.

Work together: Many large corporations have established their own corporate universities or academies. Many of them will need to collaborate with professional education vendors or partners who can help them deliver high-quality, customized development programs and tap faculty and other subject-matter experts for unique insights.

Innovate: Business schools need to innovate and advance the learning experience. The costs for participating in programs are significant and the return on investment must be clear. Schools and faculty need to tap into the rich insights from the sciences that are at the foundation of learning and development and harness different instructional methods, including action-based learning and project-based learning (Fig. 7.2). Twenty-first century learning needs to be collaborative, active, personalized, and applied.

Employ first-rate instructors: At the heart of any excellent learning experience is faculty members or facilitators who have unique subject-matter expertise but also who have mastered the art and science of teaching. Business schools need to double down in the development of top-notch faculty who can deliver on the promise of faculty excellence.

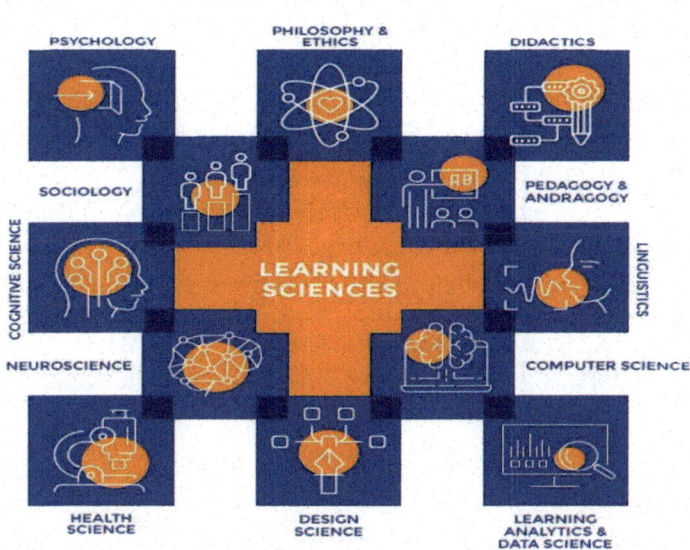

Fig. 7.2 The foundations of learning sciences (Elaborated by the Author)

Conclusion

It is very exciting to experience the future of work. Companies can use this momentum to reinvent and transform themselves and establish a values-based culture that embraces human-leadership practices that will allow talented people to flourish. These shifts will help organizations accelerate change and innovation and remain competitive. After all, success in digital transformation comes down to people's capabilities and having lifelong-learning mindsets.

An extraordinary time lays ahead for those who have the right expertise, skills, and mindsets, as they will enjoy opportunities to have an impact during the digital age. And without a doubt, business education will play an instrumental role in supporting individuals and companies in building the capabilities and culture required to thrive.

References

Books

B. Chapman, R. Sisodia, *Everybody Matters: The Extraordinary Power of Caring for Your People Like Family* (London: Penquin Books, 2016).
N.H.M. Van Dam, *Elevating Learning & Development: Insights & Practice Guidance from the Field* (Raleigh : Lulu Publishing, 2018).
C. Feser, N. Nielsen, M. Rennie, editors, *Leadership at Scale* (New York: HBG, 2018).
J. Schwartz, Riss, S. *Work Disrupted* (New Jersey: Wiley, 2021).
D. Susskind, *A World Without Work* (New York: Metropolitan books, 2020).

Articles

N.H.M. van Dam, E. Rogers, *People, Purpose and Performance at Barry-Wehmiller: Business as a Powerful Force for Good*. Madrid: IE Publishing, October 2019.
N.H.M. Van Dam, From Lifelong Learning to Lifelong Employability. *McKinsey Quarterly* 1 – 2019.
N.H.M. van Dam, N.H.M., N. Le Pertel, *The Future of Education: Everything Is Liquid*. Orlando: BizEd Magazine, October, 2020.
K. Schwab, *The Future of Jobs Report 2020*, World Economic Forum, October 2020.
A. De Smet, C. Gagnon, E. Mygatt, *Organizing for the Future. Nine Keys to Coming a Future-Ready Company*, McKinsey, January 11, 2021.

8

The Innovative Ecosystem

Michael Arena

Having one foot in the business world and another in academia offers a special vision and understanding of the world. These kind of people see business challenges from a wider perspective, connecting the pieces of the strategic puzzle, making historical sense of the issues at hand. Michael Arena is a good example of a talent manager who combines these facets. He is currently VP for Talent and Development at Amazon Web Services and was previously Chief Talent Officer at General Motors. He has also combined these responsibilities with his role as a visiting scientist at MIT, a coach at Stanford and a member of the Organizational Dynamics faculty at the University of Pennsylvania, as well as a board member of AACSB, the global association of business schools.

Arena is an observant person, who listens before he speaks. When he does, his opinions are profound and well argued. He has an innovative vision of leadership and talent management. The following comments are taken from an interview held on March 11, 2021.

M. Arena (✉)
Amazon Web Services (AWS), Seattle, WA, USA
e-mail: arenamic@amazon.com

Developing Talent in Today's Organizations

I've been in talent management for almost 20 years, and I'd say the field hasn't advanced much over the last decade. The war for talent started the idea of people management. Management practices today are still fairly similar to those of 15 years ago, but the world has changed and our management tools have not kept pace, so we are in for a giant wave of innovation in the talent management area. Additionally, the years of one-size-fits all in corporations is over and we can expect to see much more agile talent management systems.

You build *innovators* in an organization differently to how you build *operators*: it requires different emotions, different experiences, different review systems. Talent management will become much more bimodal in the years to come.

We will also see a giant shift toward social capital as well. Human capital will always be important, but it's just a starting point. Social capital is how well positioned we are to leverage what we know, and there is a lot of latent human capital in organizations today that haven't focused enough on how to connect people.

The next wave will be how we evaluate people in the flow of work. How do we get people to release the latent potential inside organizations? Organizations can be seen as a combination of supertankers and startups or speedboats. The supertanker, the traditional organization, is scalable, it's one-size-fits-all, and best-practice talent management works well there; but organizations that have to constantly reinvent themselves need speed boats as well. We're going to be far more advanced at thinking about different social arrangements to get people into speed boats, with companies like Amazon, that we call 'two-pizza teams' and can move very fast and invent the future, along with supertankers that bring the necessary degree of stability.

At the same time, our top management systems must evolve to match the emerging business management systems, which will be much more fluid. Sometimes I say that we will be much more liquid than static in the future.

There's a radical difference between how a traditional organization manages talent and how a startup does. We need to reconcile the differences because all organizations are a little bit of both. But all organizations that can adapt are a little bit of both: part startup, part supertanker.

There are a lot of entrepreneurial people even in large, static companies. They're latent though, they're deep inside the organization. We rarely suffer from a deficit of ideas in organizations. Instead, we suffer from an inability to scale those ideas up into commercialized products and solutions. We'll see a defragmenting of the organization, which I call adapting to space, as well as much more intentionality about building these entrepreneurial pockets; I call them social arrangements, small pockets of entrepreneurs. They'll be put them on the edge where they can move really fast using agile methodologies. These small teams of 8–10 people can move 10 times faster than the core of the organization.

We need to understand the nuances of creating these arrangements so we can come up with new ideas that require connections to other entities. We can build those ideas which require these small entrepreneurial pockets, and then we can quickly scale those ideas, which requires some bridging back into the operational tools. Neither is perfect. Our talent tools are going to be looking at how we can position those entrepreneurial people to do what they do so brilliantly. Because once these folks build products and build solutions, they can manage it very well. That's how traditional organizations will get around this.

For example, the General Motors approach: they have these small units on the margins that they incubate, build, and keep connected. One of the problems with incubators is they get too disconnected, and they lose the ability to later scale. General Motors has done an incredible job with groups like Cruise Automation and some other electric vehicle activities, and they keep them loosely connected so they will ultimately become the new core.

Amazon does things a little bit differently, reflecting its growth pattern. Amazon expects the same person to build and then operate what they have built. The company is like the land of a thousand startups where entrepreneurial leaders are hired to build ideas that meet the customer's needs, to build solutions and then build the team to carry them out, and they almost act like many large organizations working on their own.

Bridging Innovation and Management

We have bred operational leaders in those organizations: traditional talent management has predominantly focused on building good general managers at scale, but I think these entrepreneurial people already exist. Most of them are somewhere deep in the organization. They're usually fairly disgruntled. What we can do is cultivate them. Certainly, we want to build them, but I think more of them exist than we would generally give credit for in most organizations.

There's a third part in all this that's really important, and they are what we might call the bridge people, a rare breed who are not easy to find or build, and who need to know a little bit of both and who link those two entities together. They need to know how to be entrepreneurial, and they need an appreciation for what it takes to be entrepreneurial. But they also need to be great operators. Their job is to stand in the gap between those two entities. And while that idea is incubating, they've got to provide some protection for that entity so that the antibodies don't prematurely kill it. But later on, they're going to pull that entity into the organization so that the organization can quickly scale it, which is the benefit of a large organization. At the end of the day, our new talent management systems will have three types of people. They will have general managers, entrepreneurs, and they will also have these bridging people, who I would call integrators and protectors.

Market Focus and Global Scope

Organizations must move closer to their potential customers. Rather than calling it markets, because it's different in every part of the business, I would describe it more as localization. We're going to see a swing toward localization and the reason for that is it puts you closer to customers, that could be market, that could be segments, could be all kinds of different things: we don't have to be that prescriptive about it. I think the essence is people who are building the growth parts of the business need to be very close to their customers so that they can hear exactly what they need quickly. However, just as importantly, as you localize, you also benefit from miniaturization, from being able to move fast. And again, I already said that small, agile teams can move 10 times faster than large complex organizations. The real benefit is you get centricity to customers, you get localization where everybody is focused on the primary vision and you also get speed with that design. That's what you're going to see more and more, with some defragmentation in the organization.

The Future of Executive Education

Training and development is the area that will be most disruptive in talent management. People will learn in these new frameworks and models in a radically different way. The days of corporate universities, for the most part, are over. They will still serve a purpose, but not the entire purpose. We will see a radical localization of education and learning.

If you think about how startups learn, it's by doing. Design thinking is particularly helpful because it's an architecture that helps to force you to learn exactly what you need from your customers so that you can apply it in the moment. Large, centralized corporate universities and even business schools will become removed from customers.

We will see widespread fragmentation of learning and localization of learning. It's going to be much more about creating, more about really learning from the flow of work, about adapting quickly and working as cohorts, small groups solving problems. For example, one of the first things I did at General Motors was to shut down the corporate university, which was a very centralized, traditional, almost like an MBA program. We shut down 90% of the curriculum and we created laboratory and innovation spaces. What we ended up doing was bringing in teams to work on real customer issues using a different methodology—design thinking being a very big one. The way we changed the learning process was to learn by doing: we flipped it by bringing in teams of up to 150 people. We would give them a big business challenge to work on and they would interact with customers to learn what the customer needed. They would then come back and use design-thinking methodologies, they would do some sensemaking and prototyping, share that with the customer, and they would learn much more about the flow of work, so that there were true teaching moments. This really was a learning experience. We were providing retrospective teaching, and it would all be much more around a core issue or challenge they were trying to solve. That's not the only model, of course, but it's the model you're going to see larger corporations gravitating toward, because you get the benefit of learning and you also get the benefit of solving problems for customers and doing that as a team so that it's a collective, shared experience that has much longer lasting impacts than the more traditional classroom.

The Impact of Technology on Training and Development

Learning while dealing with the workflow is very similar to what I just described: solving real problems and bringing people together. I see two other big dimensions in the future of learning.

The first is the use of technology to do things that we would have been unable to do. When it comes to learning, we can now deliver small bits of information when you most need it. We can pick up a signal from a learner so that we know when they're struggling with something and we can push exactly the content necessary to resolve whatever core issue they're dealing with right now, either in their life cycle, their employment life cycle, the product life cycle or whatever else it may be that they're struggling with. And we're now able to provide much more real time, small snippets of information or knowledge that can help educate, but more importantly, it's part of the workflow, where people can directly apply that information or knowledge, and they're not absorbing three days' worth of content, they're absorbing three minutes' worth and it's very, very closely linked to what their next set of actions might be. That's the role technology plays. I think we're really able to use machine learning at a whole different level.

The second thing is that technology enables us to understand exactly how people come into contact with each other. If we can design solutions using machine learning techniques, it helps us to quickly diagnose through every click, every assessment, every question, to quickly diagnose the proficiency level of the learner so that we can predict mastery or predict competency sooner and not force everybody to absorb the same amount of content.

In other words, technology will soon be at the point where we may be able to determine that you have been at this much longer than I have. So, maybe you only need 30% of the time. But I'm new to this, so I need 95% of the content. And we're able to truly customize learning curriculum and the learning experience as a whole to each individual learner.

Leaders as Teachers

One thing I love about Amazon is that our leaders are consummate coaches and teachers and they don't wait until the middle of a dialog or business discussion to hit the pause button and know when they have a teaching moment. I think the role of leaders as teachers, their role as leaders and educating their broader organization is going to be important in the future.

Those leaders who are the best teachers aren't the first ones to speak. Usually, it starts with a lot of listening, allowing others to engage in a conversation. In some ways, it's a bit like a product process, only in real time.

Business schools use the Socratic model for learning. They create a case, simulate the environment, and stimulate debate. Business leaders can enable that in the real world, and the great teachers, first of all, create the conditions for people to debate with each other, so that it's not a quick decision, it's not a group think decision, but it's a true debate. So, the very first thing a great teaching leader does is enable the environment for people around them to have discussions and debates about which approach to take.

Leaders listen to that conversation and they're very attuned to the thinking processes going on. And then at the right moment they hit the pause button and say, here's how I might think about this, or here's how I remember dealing with this circumstance in the past. They are very skilled at joining up the dots and being able to share real-life cases so as to create a learning moment.

They're very good at setting boundaries and guardrails like "our customers expect more out of us than this," or "there's a better answer than this." They have very high standards and force the organization and individual leaders not to accept a short-term answer, and instead force them to look around corners and elevate their thinking in such a way that they're having a whole different third type of conversation versus the two-sided conversation that generally happens through the Socratic process.

In short, that's how great leaders do it. They are very empathetic, very good listeners. They allow organizations to engage, and only step in if they've got something insightful to say. But they don't waste those moments. They don't spend time teaching and they don't act as if they are the world's experts.

The Role of Business Schools

Business schools can play an important role in pivoting away from a focus on knowledge toward systems based on judgment. I've worked with a lot of business schools and I work with a lot of professors and a lot of business school graduates, and I find that the best students are those with judgment skills: they don't just apply theory models and frameworks or have a lot of knowledge, but they've got the judgment to be able to put what they know in context. Where I've seen universities and students struggle the most is whenever they're so fixed on the theory and they're so locked into "this is the way you do it" that they don't put it in the context to recognize that there is no single way to do something what matters is having the ability to make a call on how to apply something. These kinds of people tend to have high social quotients or social intelligence, and they also need to know how to engage the system to make the most of it.

Judgment skills and high social quotients are where universities really can help. Something like 90% of HR heads believe that most leaders fail because of their inability to do the soft skills stuff, which includes judgment. I know for a fact that most employers say it's hard to find graduates with soft skills versus the technical skills. Technical skills are almost never the challenge. At Amazon, I'll take it one step further: we spend very little time interviewing for technical skills. The way our process works—and this is public knowledge—is that the hiring manager makes an assessment based on an individual's technical abilities. And then there's a very rigorous interview process involving a group of five or six people, and 100% of that assessment is based on cultural fit and your ability to practice our leadership principles, which are much more about judgment and social skills.

Challenges for Companies in the Post-Pandemic World

I'll start big and then go very specific. First of all, we have moved work as much as five to 10 years into the future. I think what we have learned through this huge experiment of teleworking will infuse our thinking for the next generation. Many people would have resisted the notion of virtual work prior to the pandemic, although they quickly learned that productivity has remained the same or increased, especially for knowledge workers. Obviously, this doesn't apply to labor intensive work, but in almost every case involving knowledge work I have studied and evaluated internally and externally, productivity has, at minimum remained static, and, in most cases improved. It would be very easy to jump to the conclusion that we can continue to all work from home from now on, but that is wishful thinking, short-sighted. I think that productivity will also take a hit.

BCG did a great survey—and productivity is the least of my concerns—which shows that if you were satisfied with your social connections, your productivity, prior to the pandemic, your productivity increased significantly, maybe as much as threefold. In other words, those who were satisfied with their social connections experienced a threefold impact on productivity, compared to those who were dissatisfied, whose productivity fell. The good news was more people were satisfied than dissatisfied. In the long term, as we become less and less disconnected, we will see social erosion, with adverse consequences like mental stress and a consequent reduction in productivity.

The long-term issue about working virtually is how we will continue to innovate and the consequences on culture. I think there are two types of social capital: bridging and bonding.

We noticed a 30% drop in bridging social capital during the first three months of working virtually. That's one team connected to another, and that to another team. What happened in the early days is that teams continued to function, bonding social capital really, really well. But the bridge connections between and across teams soon began to erode.

That limits our ability to discover new ideas. And that could even be a connection to the customer, for example, it limits our ability to take ideas and solutions that teams develop and to quickly scale them out across the organization. If we don't think about some sort of hybrid model—which we will in the long term—there will be a radical erosion of innovation, and then on corporate culture, which is more caught than taught. I have learned about culture by watching other people in action and absorbing the way they interact with others and their model behavior. Catching social behavior in a virtual environment is incredibly challenging. If we can't find a way to get people back in touch with each other physically, then we will see a radical deterioration in innovation and shifts in cultures and organizations, with a radical set of subcultures beginning to emerge.

The future is hybrid and it will require us to think about how we work virtually and physically and how we bring people back together so that they can build bridges and learn passionately about culture.

Future Leadership Models

The premise of a one-size-fits all model for organizations is obsolete. Those organizations that apply it will soon be out of business. The S&P 500 Index illustrates that. The extinction rate is growing fast. The old model of the control and command CEO is gone.

In fact, the complexity of most organizations has surpassed human capability and those of the average CEO. Now, there are some superhuman CEOs that are brilliant at checking the pulse of their organizations. But even over time, as that organization grows, I believe it will become impossible for the top leader of any part of that organization—and certainly the CEO—to really understand everything that is going on. And this takes us back to what I was saying earlier. The new generation of CEOs are going to be far more agile. They're going to be more like enablers than dictators. They're going to be able to use high judgment to listen very closely about all the things that are happening in the organization. They're going to speak last, not first, and they're going to be the enablers of a business culture and business decisions by making sure that they're scaling the rest of their team to have these really high-level debates and conversations.

The CEOs of tomorrow will spend their time listening, watching and paying attention, shaping the future and enabling people to move in a given direction and then sometimes teaching, and sometimes making tough decisions.

The next generation of CEOs will spend their time constantly watching the market, constantly watching their organization, providing it with the opportunity for a deep, high-level dialog, and then stepping in and declaring at some point later in the process, in order to get to market sooner and satisfy customers' needs faster, more like the conductor of an orchestra than traditional managers.

Once all the information was on the table, she would pull people into the conversation and facilitate a dialog, and then make a decision and argue her position. I think that's what you're going to see in CEOs from now on.

Great leaders are also first-rate humans. And to be a great human, you've got to be a great listener and do what's right for everybody, as well as to have courage to be able to make a decision and know that you're really working for your customer. You're not working for the organization. You're not working for any individual. You're not working for yourself and your ego. You're serving a greater purpose. They're not about their own personal agenda. And they're always about what the customer needs and getting the customer what they need quickly.

9

AACSB: Paving New Ways in Business Education

Caryn L. Beck Dudley

Higher education—particularly business education—is undergoing a renaissance. The impacts of the pandemic have permanently altered the construct of education and set in motion the possibility that things can be different, perhaps even better, than before. Although immediate change was necessary at the start of the pandemic, educators around the world are realizing that long-term efforts are necessary to reshape education, to meet the demands of a new workforce, and to address issues facing our global society. AACSB International is leading the global conversation on what the future of business education could look like and questioning many of the historical notions associated with higher education.

Caryn Beck Dudley was appointed president and CEO of AACSB just a few months before the pandemic was declared in early 2020. She holds a Juris Doctor Degree and has experience as a top academic leader, having served as dean at the business schools of Utah State University, Florida State University and Santa Clara University. She combines a broad strategic vision with a marked executive orientation and the warm sociability required to run the world's largest business education network comprising more than 1700 business schools and influential

C. L. Beck Dudley (✉)
AACSB International, Tampa, FL, USA
e-mail: caryn.beckdudley@aacsb.edu

businesses worldwide. The following chapter is extracted from an interview held on April 12, 2021.

The Impact of the Pandemic on Organizations

Like most institutions, AACSB had to respond quickly over the past year, and we continue to remain agile. The biggest change has been in our accreditation processes, which are now virtual, including peer reviews for initial accreditation as well as for continuous improvement reviews. That's a big shift from the way we've conducted peer reviews in the past, and, as a result, many of our reviewers have indicated they truly miss the face-to-face interaction. Zoom fatigue became a consequence we had to overcome by getting creative, including structuring shorter visits over a longer period of days and developing and incorporating virtual campus tours as part of the review.

Another challenge we faced was transitioning all of our seminars, conferences, and meetings to a virtual setting, keeping them open and meaningful for our members. At our International Conference and Annual Meeting (ICAM) in 2020, more than 800 delegates participated virtually—which was a significant feat, given the short turnaround time we had to transition a fully planned in-person event to virtual. It also showed us just how important it was for everyone to stay connected. But I think people are ready to get back to face-to-face contact—especially for networking, which isn't as easily replicated online.

We are exploring some hybrid delivery models for events in October, but we won't be delivering fully face-to-face learning and development opportunities or accreditation visits until after January 2022. Many questions still need to be answered: Will people be able (and/or willing) to travel? What will happen with the idea of a vaccine passport? Will employees embrace the ever-evolving hybrid work environment?

With so many variables, many of our member, volunteer, and stakeholder experiences will remain hybrid, but one of the most pressing questions still to be addressed is about peer review teams. Can that process be kept hybrid when some parts have to be carried out on site? The simple truth is that hybrid experiences are very different from in-person ones. Hosting a hybrid conference, for example, isn't as simple as recording a live conference and posting it online; we have to carefully facilitate the event to ensure meaningful and valuable interaction.

One of the interesting opportunities in hybrid learning for schools is that it opens the potential for their student population to come from anywhere in the world—learners are no longer required to leave their home locations and move somewhere else for two full years. Instead, they can enter in and out of the overall program experience. Something we now understand is that a significant part of the subject matter taught in business curriculum doesn't have to be face-to-face. Instead, we must now gain a better understanding of how to spend that high-quality, very expensive face-to-face time—and what to do with that time to create an enhanced learning experience. This is one of the areas schools are now experimenting with by using a hybrid format. In other words, our schools are truly flipping the class, not just going through the motions.

The Main Challenges for Business Schools

Higher education dates back about 800 years, and business schools are roughly 125 years old. What's needed now from business schools and universities is a new level of agility and adaptability. The pandemic has shown that high-quality business education is critical because, as we've seen, we can't solve the health and societal problems we now face without addressing the business side of things. Business schools are responding to this need by reevaluating their programs and methods to best serve their learners and empower them with the skills required to lead in business.

I foresee three major challenges for business schools. The first is the growing demand for education. Many of our members didn't know whether learners would come to school this year or just stay home because of the pandemic. What we've found is that, in most places, the number of people who want education is increasing. But what they want varies and includes educational experiences that support them in their current role, help them perform in a newly assigned position, or help them prepare for a new career—or a career in an entirely new industry. There may be significant growth in the job market, which has typically been bad for business schools: when there are lots of jobs out there, people feel they don't need to go to business school. The prediction is for 6% growth, which is huge, so what does that mean for business schools generally, and for full-time programs in particular? Will the newest generation of learners be willing to quit their jobs for two years to pursue a business degree full time?

The second challenge addresses the competitive landscape. With online education, it's much easier for learners to make direct comparisons between faculty members, and that insight could inform their future decisions about where to study. A dean at one of our member schools was asked by a student why he was paying a low-quality faculty member to teach online when another popular professor was teaching the same content on YouTube for free. I think the idea of celebrity academics is going to be an interesting concept for many business schools.

The third challenge for business schools lies in admissions requirements and assessments. As a result of restrictions associated with the pandemic, a significant number of business schools waived admissions exams—calling into question their importance and relative value. The value of grading also came into question when schools began waiving traditional letter grading, instead empowering learners to choose a pass/fail option. Perhaps we need to ask ourselves what it means to be ready to undertake post-graduate education, and what does student readiness mean for the future of work? Should we be evaluating learning input, like standardized testing scores, or instead focusing on the output—a graduate's ability to lead in the workplace?

Non-Degree Offerings and Stackable Courses

Business schools are already making advances in the areas of certificates, badges, and credentials—which is especially noteworthy for executive education, where specialized credentials have traditionally been preferred. The landscape has changed, however, with businesses like Google developing their own educational programs, creating even more competition in credential badging as a more cost-effective option.

I think what we will see more of is a partnership model, especially when executive education is affiliated with a business school that has had more delineation between traditional business degrees and credentials. Most degree programs don't offer curriculum that provides skills required by an adult learner, which is where credentials can really shine. Another interesting perspective is that we could be approaching a situation where graduation doesn't matter anymore—that everyone is in a constant cycle of learning. There may be a graduation date, but the next day requires learners to continue their education or upskill because the market is changing so quickly.

AACSB's newly implemented 2020 business accreditation standards were designed with this challenge in mind. Previous iterations of the standards that may have limited how business schools could engage are gone, and interdisciplinary work and collaborating across the university is highly promoted within the current standards. As a result of this change, schools are collaborating with industry more and more to meet the needs of their lifelong learners and the ever-changing talents and skills required by employers. The standards offer a lot of flexibility for schools to vary their offerings, and to be able to stack certificates. This popular option empowers students to try shorter certificate programs and then stack them into a degree.

We have over 900 globally accredited business schools to encourage along this trajectory—and if I were still leading a business school, I'd join this trend quickly. Lagging will only create more challenges to meeting stakeholder needs down the road.

Navigating Disruptions in Education

The current disruption in education has happened because of a virus, not technology. For example, take AI: I don't think its potential has been explored enough in higher education, but we've seen a smoother transition toward virtual reality and augmented reality. Although AI can be used to assess students—by identifying specific challenges or where they need extra instruction—AI's ability to personalize education hasn't been fully explored or utilized by higher education. We are more likely to see increased use of virtual reality in study abroad programs, as well as augmented reality and virtual recruiting and internships. It's an exciting time to be a part of that movement, as we've only seen the beginnings of using that technology—who knows what else is out there! Students can learn anywhere if they have access to the appropriate technology, and I'm certain that online education models, or at least hybrid programs, are here to stay.

Experiential learning, on the other hand, has a long way to go, and we haven't mastered it by any means. How do you transfer the experiential learning that occurs in a face-to-face classroom or workplace to an online environment? It still feels clunky, but there's a lot of experimentation going on. Technology is evolving very quickly to meet demand, and the next two or three years for people who are in EdTech are going to be fruitful for them.

In this context, teachers' roles will change. Many schools have already moved away from the traditional model of the teacher who stands in front of a class as the expert while the students listen attentively and write everything down. Instead, teachers will understand how one subject interplays with others; they will be equipped to really coach students, guide them, act as mentors; they will bring teams together to work and will draw the best out of them; they will be able to access other experts the students may not know about; and they will help students decide which information is most useful.

Traditionally, faculty are not trained for those roles. This raises the question as to what doctoral education will look like in the future. What about sabbaticals within higher education? Historically, faculty have used sabbaticals to carry out research. Perhaps we'll see faculty using sabbaticals to learn new teaching methods. I think there will be a stronger emphasis on pedagogy in most universities than there has been in the past.

The Impacts on Business School Accreditation

It may sound odd given the circumstances, but our 2020 business accreditation standards could not have been launched at a better time. We want schools to deliver on their unique missions, so the standards call for the kind of increased flexibility that supports schools and empowers them to place a greater emphasis on online education—which was a critical component to learner success during the pandemic. The standards also reinforce our commitment to mission focus and peer review—and although the immediate shift from in-person to virtual school visits was effective, we will go back to face-to-face peer review visits. Their collaborative nature and the personal consultation you get from your peers is very important to our members, and it's critical that we continue to deliver that level of support.

The two most important aspects of the standards are that (1) they are principles-based and outcomes-focused, which gives schools the flexibility to pivot and meet changing stakeholder needs; and (2) they value the diversity of thought leadership in the context of a school's mission. For example, not all schools have to produce the same type of research for the same type of audience.

The other game-changer in our accreditation standards is that business schools must have a positive impact on society, which they can achieve by connecting with business, the community, and government to solve problems based on knowledge sharing and research to deliver results. We empower business school leaders to develop the vision to tackle the toughest challenges and create hubs for lifelong learning, thereby promoting prosperity and elevating economies.

I believe that business schools should be inspiring and drive innovation with the power to change the world. The theme at the World Economic Forum last year was the Great Reset, which is the commitment to build a fairer and more sustainable, more resilient future. Business schools should think of this year, and probably next, as a major reset of their programs. If schools aren't resetting, they're going to be left behind.

Looking to the Future

An interesting new development in business education, which I'm really excited about, is cross-disciplinary programs. Some business schools have become islands, isolated on their own campuses, and I don't think they can carry on like that anymore. But I'm glad that we are seeing an increasing number of cross-discipline collaborations with the sciences, engineering, and even with the arts and humanities—and I think we are going to see a lot more of these alliances in the years to come. We're also seeing greater collaboration between business schools and the world of business. We need to be asking ourselves important questions to cultivate these relationships: Which skills do employers want? What does the future of work look like? What are the skill sets learners should have to remain agile in an ever-changing business landscape?

In a broader sense, there are many areas of business operations that are changing—and I'm excited to see how they evolve. Most organizations are going to see some degree of teleworking, but we can't ignore the fact that we all miss the personal connection that comes with being together. But we clearly don't need people in an office five days a week, eight hours a day just to do that—and I've even noticed that some of our staff are more productive when they work remotely. Other people are like me—I love going into an office, I love international travel, and I love connecting with our members in person. I probably won't work remotely for too much longer—it was an interesting (and necessary) construct, but I'm done with it.

While we will continue to see people come back to the office, we're already seeing big tech companies enabling people to work from wherever they want. And in order to attract and retain talent, the rest of us are going to have to follow suit, unless someone is really needed in the office. Talent retention also opens further discussion about the future of performance appraisals, and the evolution of our current evaluation systems. Given the new hybrid and fully remote working environments, what new factors must we consider, and which ones are no longer relevant?

Mental health and well-being programs will also move into the spotlight, as well as the importance of understanding that people face many different circumstances outside of the office. There are so many scenarios to consider: those with young children at home, those who are taking care of elderly parents, or those who live in small apartments with their partner while both are trying to telework at the same time. In response, we're working hard to be cognizant of individuals' situations when they're not in the office and sensitive to the challenges they face. There are also individuals with long commutes, which means we must consider their impact on the environment, especially at scale.

It's been a very interesting experience to lead an organization during a pandemic and to identify and address the many issues needing attention. The pandemic revealed how many people, from so many different disciplines around the world, can come together to address global issues, and that no one can go it alone. We won't find solutions to big problems if we work in silos. The reason I was interested in my position at AACSB is that I really do believe business schools can change the world by working with their partners across all disciplines. And although one of AACSB's primary functions is as an accreditor, our best function is as a connector and convener, working with governments, businesses, and universities to tackle these tough global challenges. AACSB has the unique opportunity to bring various groups together for the greater good, and I look forward to serving that vision.

Purpose-Driven Leaders: The Role of Tomorrow's CEOs

A good way to describe the role of the CEO is as the conductor of an orchestra. It's all about getting the right people in the right place, all playing the right tune at the same time, allowing some to shine while others are quiet, and then allowing others to shine.

As with an orchestra, getting the right team together is key, and communicating to the orchestra to synchronize with everybody else is essential. The team must be able to work together, which means team members can't be competing. You must have people who are willing to work across the lines, so no more silos. One of the main tasks of the CEO is to ensure there are no silos and that communication flows across the organization, because there's no such thing as top-down management.

I restructured my executive team with a focus on driving member value. We have six executives leading the organization, which is the optimum number of direct reports that you can really work with effectively. That said, each individual CEO will know in their own mind how many people they need on their team. Frankly, I think CEOs need to know a lot more about what is going on throughout the entire organization than they ever have. I need to know more about the emotional well-being of my associates, my entry-level employees, so I have a lot more coffee chats and one-on-ones than I probably would have done in the past—because in this virtual environment, especially, I need to make sure everybody feels like, and knows, they are valued. The CEO is the person who makes everybody feel part of the team, regardless of where they are in the matrix.

This past year of leading an organization through a pandemic as a new CEO has been a great learning experience, and I'm excited to continue learning from others, inside and outside of my organization.

10

Traditional Corporations Going Green: Yara

Birgitte Holter

Yara is the world's leading producer of fertilizers. Recently it has announced its intent to develop fertilizers based on no CO_2 emission, making use of electricity rather than fossil fuels (but at a much higher cost). The company has also announced a commitment to develop automotive fuels from ammonia, again with significantly less CO_2 emission.

Birgitte Holter has been with Yara since 2016, initially being in the company's division to develop so-called scrubbers for ships, with significantly less emission. Before this she was with Norsk Hydro for several decades. Her professional career has always encompassed the development of new products, also accomplishing less waste and more environmentally friendly solutions.

Peter Lorange: *How do you envision the future of talent management, based on your experience?*

Birgitte Holter: I envision several fundamental changes. Above all, we must be better at continuing development of the people who are in the firm, so that we do not have to rely on hiring new needed capabilities from outside. An implication of this is that employees to a larger extent than before should be motivated to develop themselves more, so as to learn new cutting-edge things. Often, such new competences tend to be more effective when built on

---

B. Holter (✉)
Yara International, Oslo, Norway
e-mail: birgitte.holter@yara.com

what actually is in place, i.e., an evolutionary process for competence development. Importantly this might lessen a potential tendency to create "A-Teams" in the organization, those new hires with the cutting-edge competence, versus the old guard, with competences no longer so highly needed, so-called "B-Teams". To link this competence development process to emerging strategic needs is key, of course. Which competences are now needed to pursue a more digital strategy (software for farmers supporting their planting and fertilizing activities), and also for going "green" (new production processes for fertilizers; new fuels)?

PL: *Could you please describe major policies for talent management at Yara?*

BH: Our company has had general leadership development processes and training programs in place for many years, stemming all the back to the time when our company was a division of Norsk Hydro. A key dilemma now is that we are also trying to link executive education development more closely to the strategic needs our company is facing.

PL: *Yara is a major recruiter of MBAs and business school graduates. What type of talent do you search for? What are the major criticisms towards traditional business education?*

BH: Business schools have always been strong at educating its candidates when it comes to theories and concepts. The difference now is that we are also looking for practical capabilities when it comes to graduates that we are hiring. For students internships and summer exchanges programs are thus becoming increasingly important, so that their practical proficiencies may also be enhanced.

PL: *Does Yara have a corporate university of similar entity? How do you see this evolving in the future?*

BH: I do not wish to comment on this when it comes to Yara. In general, however, many big corporations are good at providing general management skills for their key people. But, as I have already touched upon, in addition there is often a need for more specific competences to support given strategies – say, technical, financial, and/or logistical. In addition, for a firm's executives to become more active in teaching others, mentoring, seems to be an increasingly critical element of what one might see in many so-called corporate university contexts.

PL: *What are the skills and attitudes that you value most in Yara's managers?*

BH: There are a lot of highly impressive competences in Yara, and much of this is truly cutting-edge in a global context. Yara's technology base is truly outstanding, and so are our trading capabilities. Yara's competence base has of course in part shifted also, since we now label ourselves as a "green" nutrition company, and not merely a more traditional producer of fertilizers. We are increasingly developing cutting-edge skills in the field(s) of nutrition. More is coming! We are building these new competences largely based on what we already know. The age of particular employees seems to have little to do with this. Rather, what matters, seems to have to do with the new contexts of their jobs. And it seems important here that one might try to avoid creating closed circles around those with emerging new competences, i.e., no "executive clubs". Rather, one might be open to diversity when it comes to gender, race and international backgrounds. It is interesting to observe how this seems to play out in several good ways at Yara:

- All of the firm's major commercial division heads are women (3)!
- All employees all over the world received similar bonuses in 2020.
- Yara's CEO has been pushing for a "green" profile since early on—highly motivating!

PL: *What are some of the most important trends in executive development today?*
BH: I have already touched upon this. Above all, to link executive development to the specific competence needs related to a given strategy seems key. To develop relevant expert competences seems key.
PL: *How has the pandemic affected the way you see talent management, the working landscape and stakeholder management? Is working remote a shared practice at Yara?*
BH: It may be useful to distinguish between office jobs versus manufacturing jobs here. When it comes to the latter, there are important health-related controls that have been put in place. But the production line remains basically as before. However, each country may cope with such health and safety regulations depending on the intensity of the pandemic. We find that in Brazil for instance, to maintain effective manufacturing has become particularly demanding. When it comes to those working in offices, the general situation might differ from manufacturing in at least two ways. On the one hand, there seems to be an increase in contacts, short meetings and sharing of information. The frequency of contacts has increased. But, on the other hand, "good workshops" may not come about so much. People may not be able to meet physically to the same extent as before. And creativity might suffer! When the pandemic is over, these cost saving considerations might regrettably also fall for a longer-term reduction of "good workshops". And the trend towards more open office landscapes might similarly make these more difficult.

PL: *What are, in your opinion, the main changes at work that will remain in a post-pandemic world, when we resume so-called "normality"?*

BH: To work more form home is likely to remain. And there shall be relatively less travel compared to pre-pandemic times. Digital meeting are likely to increase, however. And, we have seen a flourishment of competence-enhancing webinars, mostly free of charge. This is likely to continue. All these new webinar-offerings clearly add to competence building.

PL: *Yara has been a major agent for global integration. How do you envision business globalization after the pandemic?*

BH: Our "green" strategy is clearly critical now, calling for a more "global" understanding of customers as well as suppliers. Clearly there is competition, but there is also cooperation. There seems to be a clean technology tendency to "think and act" globally. But, paradoxically, the advent of the pandemic seems to have led to a trend towards the opposite, i.e., more "local" focus (in production, distribution and other activities).

PL: *What is your major dream for the future regarding Yara's executive development and training? How do you envision your company in five years?*

BH: I hope that we shall continue to "think out of the box", to "see" the future. This might perhaps be particularly key for asset-heavy firms such as ours. Our types of firms are after all the largest emitters of CO_2! My hope is that we shall be able to successfully cope with this dilemma in the future.

PL: *How would you define the role of the CEO of the future?*

Birgitte Holter: I see several key risks for the CEO of the future. Above all, he/she should be a proponent of a relatively clear and simple to comprehend program, such as "green", which might rally the organization, i.e., motivate it towards even better performance. In addition, he/she should act as the "owner/not captain", i.e., not micromanage, but leave room for others to excel. He/she should be able to bring in long-term capital, without being too short-term focused on the stock market. Above all, he/she should be a strong proponent of a visionary long-term strategy!

11

Diversity and Inclusion: Banco Santander

Chema Palomo

Banco Santander has a huge global impact and a strong presence in Europe and the Americas. Since 2014, it has been chaired by Ana Botín, one of the world's most influential women executives. Over the years, it has developed programmes that promote talent, diversity and inclusion.

Chema Palomo, as Human Resources Group Vice President, leads talent management and attraction, as well as initiatives on diversity and inclusion within a specialist area that directly reports to the Executive Chair. Still in his early forties, Chema has spent two decades working for companies on several continents. The new initiatives he helps bring about in a century-old institution, with an open mind, curiosity and networking skills, are particularly important in a sector like Financial Services that, despite the pandemic, is changing at unprecedented speed owing to globalization and innovative technology.

Interview between Chema Palomo and Santiago Íñiguez on 1 March 2021.

C. Palomo (✉)
Banco Santander, Boadilla del Monte, Spain
e-mail: josema.palomo@gruposantander.com

The Rise of a Global Talent Market

More than a bank, Santander is fast developing into an open financial services platform. Overall, platforms, like Uber, Amazon and Netflix, are large, highly integrated systems that use the same technology to offer users all over the world increasingly global products and a similar experience. Platform creation requires substantial homogenization, standardization and integration[1] regarding Human Resources and people management practices so that teams can coordinate to deliver value for the whole enterprise.

Becoming into a platform business promotes the creation of a thriving international workforce capable of pulling together as one across borders and time zones. Therefore, the advent of platforms marks a transformative trend: the rise of Global Talent market. It started a few years ago but has been propelled by the covid-19 pandemic: despite lockdowns that left many stuck in other countries for family reasons or international travel restrictions, teams still managed to stay productive and meet expectations. This experience bolsters a market where people can work overseas (even if their employer has no local footprint there) and companies are not bound to local talent but can seek out the best professionals anywhere.

The scarcity of high-qualified talent has compelled many companies to remove barriers and offer more flexibility to make themselves more attractive. This includes allowing people to work from wherever they want. Even with complex issues they need to address (such as different tax schemes and local labour regulation), companies are relentless in their pursuit of the best talent.

Furthermore, some companies have remote working embedded in their employee value proposition with the aim of differentiating themselves from competitors targeting the same profiles. Spotify, whose philosophy is "*Work isn't somewhere you go, it's something you do*", is telling employees they can work from anywhere in the world with no impact on their salaries.[2] This strategy is proving a powerful weapon to attract the best professionals in the well-known talent war drawing in all companies nowadays.

---

[1] "*Platform Revolution: How Networked Markets Are Transforming the Economy*", Geoffrey Parker, Marshall W. van Alstyne and Sangeet Paul Choudary—W.W. Norton & Company Ltd., 2017.
[2] "*Introducing Working From Anywhere*"—Spotify HR Blog, posted on February 12, 2021 https://hrblog.spotify.com/2021/02/12/introducing-working-from-anywhere/.

Pros and Cons of Teleworking

After one year with a significant headcount at home, many companies are making more long-term decisions about remote working. In Spain, it climbed from less than 4% of employees before the pandemic to 15%[3] and is expected to continue rising despite the age-old office tradition. In the coming years, working from home will be as normal as working from an office.

Hybrid models that combine office and remote working are also going to become more common. According to a recent Boston Consulting Group's survey, 75% of the employees who have transitioned to or remained remote during covid-19 say that they are at least as productive in performing their individual tasks as they were before the pandemic struck. Moreover, about 50% of them report that they are at least as productive on collaborative tasks that normally would be performed in conference or team rooms.[4]

The rationale of many companies moving to hybrid schemes is that expanding remote working has many benefits, such as a more efficient use of workspaces. Many employees also favour remote working because of many advantages they perceive for themselves and society, such as the hours it saves on weekly commutes and how it reduces traffic jams. It will also drastically cut down air pollution and, with it, the occurrence of cardiovascular and respiratory diseases in urban areas.

Notwithstanding the clear benefits, remote working poses new challenges to people managers and Human Resources departments. Some regular day-to-day processes that were very simple in the past will become more complex and will need to be revisited. For example, from a logistics standpoint, many companies have managed to on-board new hires during lock-down just as well as they did in a face-to-face setup. Many of the phases of the on-boarding processes were automated and videoconference meetings have been just as effective. However, an on-boarding programme is more than receiving your brand new corporate laptop at home on time and interacting with your new colleagues on Zoom or Microsoft Teams. At the office, introductions to team members, informal references or incidental comments occur spontaneously. New employees are in an environment where, by osmosis, they soak up the culture, meet people and get to know how company processes work. This happens in a natural way since there is a real immersion, where the physical environment is very relevant for socialization.

---

[3] "*The Pandemic Drives Teleworking in Spain: Almost Three Million Remote Employees*"—Published by El Pais on March 17, 2021. https://bit.ly/3g1LkPz.

[4] "Hybrid Work Is the New Remote Work"—Published by Boston Consulting Group on September 22, 2020. https://on.bcg.com/3dT0VhB.

Moreover, the adoption of the corporate culture is another very important issue that does not occur spontaneously when working from home. Large companies care a lot about their culture and have specific departments focused on it. The corporate culture is the personality of the company, what you breathe in your daily job. Nevertheless, when you are teleworking that culture is more difficult to understand.

As on-boarding generally sets the scene for socializing, mastering procedures and knowing whom to engage within the organization to perform well on the job, culture spreads more naturally in an office than in a remote work setting. Still, this is manageable with foresight so that processes can remain conducive to effective cultural immersion.

At Santander, we think that the best option is a hybrid setup combining office and remote working. However, the number of companies in which a significant percentage of the workforce is based remotely on a permanent scheme is surging.[5] Business leaders and Human Resources teams can (and must) come up with new ways to induct employees working remotely in a manner that ensures their loyalty, mobility and prominence within the company. We have to ensure in a proactive manner that employees working from home do not drop out, have fewer possibilities of promotion, or are unknown to the rest of the organization.

#ThePlaceToBeYourself

The pandemic has accelerated change faster than ever, taking the concept of VUCA[6] to a new dimension. As great challenges emerge, many previously effective solutions will no longer serve a purpose. It's time for new solutions that enable customers, employees, communities and shareholders to make headway in an increasingly complex world.

At Santander, we believe that each person is unique and that the things that make each of us different are the ones that allow the company to offer different solutions to the challenges that lie ahead. In order to innovate and overcome new hurdles, we must take into account the visions and experiences of everyone we work with. A diverse workforce generates fresh thinking

---

[5] *"Ford Gives 30,000 Employees The Option To Work From Home Permanently"*—Published by Forbes on March 21, 2021. https://bit.ly/3d4Xg13; *"Thousands of HSBC and JP Morgan Staff to Work at Home Regularly"*—Published by The Guardian on April 7, 2021. https://bit.ly/3256nIR.

[6] *"VUCA World 4.0 and the Covid-19 Pandemic"*—Published by Business Mirror on September 22, 2020. https://bit.ly/3wSY68X.

and ground-breaking ideas. Companies with employees from different countries and social and educational backgrounds will thrive the most in the post pandemic world.

However, diversity is not enough. Organizations will need to take further steps to create an environment where everyone can unleash their full potential. This is where inclusion comes in, where everyone can feel they count and can make a real contribution to a common goal. An inclusive environment is where employees can feel good about themselves; otherwise, they will be wasting time and energy trying to adapt to a culture that does not celebrate the fact that they are different.

At Santander, we use *#ThePlaceToBeYourself* to represent our approach to diversity and inclusion. In order to make the most of the unique capabilities of each person, we create an environment in which all our employees feel that they can be themselves, so that they are able to do more.[7] We believe that when people feel comfortable, happy and proud of their company, they channel all their energy to helping people and business prosper.

The way we speak with, listen to and interact with others plays key role in creating an inclusive environment. Thus, we must all understand how unconscious bias or micro-messages can affect others:

- Micro-messages: subtle, sometimes unconscious messages between people through conduct, looks, gestures or even tone of voice.
- Unconscious bias: unfounded prejudices or beliefs about a person, group, thing or circumstances that often lead to judgements or condition behaviour.
- Exclusion: situations where people are pulled together due to clear or less-apparent similarities they have, which can lead to the exclusion of those who do not resemble them. Also known as similarity bias, it suggests we are more likely to trust those akin to us.

However, creating a diverse and inclusive workplace goes beyond what each one of us says and does. At Santander, we are also responsible for reporting behaviour that undermines this aim through our anonymous ethical channel "*Canal Abierto*".

Santander has diversity and inclusion at the top of its list to attract, develop and retain the best employees. Our programmes and initiatives have earned us recognition from Euromoney magazine as the world's best bank for diversity

---

[7] "Estar bien para poder hacer más" (Feel good to be able to do more) is the introductory sentence of the Instagram account of Ana Botín (as of April 12, 2020).

and inclusion in 2020 as well as placement among the 10 leading companies in the world by the 2021 Bloomberg Gender-Equality Index. We have set targets for the years ahead, such as increasing female representation on the Board to between 40% and 60% by 2021. We have governance bodies overseeing corporate culture, pledges and regulations dictated by our Corporate Culture Policy, in addition to many initiatives to promote all types of diversity, both visible and invisible.

Era of Inclusive Leadership

In 2020, Santander unveiled a diversity and inclusion strategy to build and strengthen an inclusive workforce in terms of gender, LGBTIQ+, people with disabilities and cultural diversity by:

- Encouraging leaders' involvement: All people managers should commit to being open and inclusive, and be vocal and proactive about diversity.
- Increasing awareness: promoting diversity and shaping our culture through global standards, communication campaigns, diversity and inclusion training, employee networks and celebrating international days of awareness.
- Promoting balance: special focus on increasing diversity in management and on development programmes.

Of our three diversity and inclusion strategy pillars, the role of senior executives and people managers in setting an example through inclusive leadership is the most important. They need to manage diverse teams to harness each person's unique capabilities, as well as empathizing and making team members feel valued for who they are. According to a recent study by Harvard Business Review, what leaders say and do makes up to a 70% difference as to whether an individual reports feeling included. This really matters because the more people feel included, the more they speak up, go the extra mile and collaborate. All of which ultimately lifts organizational performance.[8]

Our leaders must also ensure that their teams are aware of the strategic importance of diversity and inclusion and act as ambassadors to spread key messages across the organization. They need to manage diversity in an inclusive way since this helps attract, develop and retain the most talented people

---

[8] "*The Key to Inclusive Leadership*", Juliet Bourke and Andrea Titus. Published by Harvard Business Review on March 6, 2020.

as well as attain better, sustainable results; and contribute to a better future for everyone.

Making Santander the place where everyone can be themselves is our way of helping, unique people and companies around the world prosper better and more. If we take care of everything that makes us stand out, we'll be able to rise above the new challenges the future brings.

12

Reinventing Public Service: US Postal Service

Claire Pérez-Redondo

The US Postal Service (USPS) is an independent agency of the executive branch of the US federal government, with the mission "to provide postal services to bind the Nation together through the personal, educational, literary and business correspondence of the people. It shall provide prompt, reliable and efficient services to patrons in all areas and shall render postal services to all communities."

The USPS is one of the world's largest employers, with 495,000 career employees and some 148,000 non-career employees as of 2020. If it were a private sector company it would rank 46th in the 2020 Fortune 500.

Claire Pérez-Redondo has consolidated her professional experience as a manager in the postal service industry, first at Correos, the Spanish postal company as Reengineering Process Manager and International Postal Affairs Specialist, then with USPS in 2007, rising to her current position after holding a range of executive jobs.

The contents of the following chapter are extracted from an interview with Claire on March 8, 2021.

C. Pérez-Redondo (✉)
International Civilian and Military Transportation and Networks, US Postal Service, Washington, DC, USA

The Social Mission of the USPS

One of the strengths of the USPS is that we have more than 2,000 different careers. It is a very diverse organization. I initially spent five years in global business doing strategy, bilateral negotiations and acting chief of staff for the vice president of Global Business. Then I applied for a promotion in the IT Finance portfolio as IT project manager. I was very surprised initially about the promotion because I don't have a strong technology background. I realized that my previous experience as a project manager, my work ethics and my interactions with different groups have been key.

The main purpose of the USPS is to serve American citizens and residents. We bind the nation together by providing a universal delivery service. And that has been the foundation of what we've been doing for 245 years now, which is an impressive record of continued service, to bind the nation. One of the distinctive features of our organization is our size. We are unique in terms of resources and infrastructure. It's a network which has the logistical capability to deliver mail to more than 161 million residential and business addresses.

Technically, any person who has a physical address can receive mail in the United States, as well as associate territories, overseas at US military bases, diplomatic envoys and beyond. There are no parallel last mile delivery resources at an affordable rate. Also, the USPS is at the core of the mailing industry, generating $1.6 trillion annually and employing seven million people. It's a very dynamic and competitive community. We enable retailers and small businesses, no matter where they are, to market themselves, as well as to position their products in faraway places. If you're in a rural community producing something unique, at small scale, on a craft or artisan basis, and you want to export it, you can do so at an affordable price. We deliver just about anything that you can think of.

A vital part of what we do is connect and re-connect people with each other. For example, every year we have 35 million changes of address. We process that and we make sure all mails and parcels arrive in the right location.

We have more than 230,000 delivery routes to move everything we receive.

Our mission is about moving mail and ensuring sanctity of the mail. There are more than 200 federal laws that protect the mail and its privacy. We take privacy and security of our shipments very seriously.

For example, in 2019 our postal inspectors performed more than 5000 arrests and convictions related to mail theft, mail fraud, prohibited mailing. They also carry out seizures. To give you an idea, each year, we seize assets worth more than $143 million. Some 63% are linked to illegal narcotics.

Our postal inspectors investigate potential wrongdoing; they are really at the core of protecting the mail, making sure it's not used for criminal purposes, whether through scams, or sending illegal items. Furthermore, there's not one day that you don't hear a story about a post office employee on a route that found an elderly person who was not feeling well, who noticed that the mail had not been picked up or came across small children who were lost. That is what our job is about: serve the community.

The USPS Business Model

The US Postal Service gets zero tax money. Everything we get is from the sale of products and services. We provide an essential service to the American public and we have systemic challenges. Since 2007, the USPS has recorded significant losses and its model is financially unsustainable without the investment needed to ensure the future of the network. Over the last years, the Postal Service has told Congress that fundamental changes were needed. Despite the problems, we've been able to maintain the operations by defaulting on one obligation, which is to Prefund the pension and retiree health benefit. Our focus is still to obtain legislative change and relief to ensure our organization thrives as it should.

One of the strengths of the USPS is its diversity. Forty-nine percent of the workforce would be considered as minorities. Women make up 45% of the workforce, a fact that is ingrained into the culture. A case worth mentioning is Stagecoach Mary, who was born a slave. She was freed after the Civil War and began driving, at the age of 63, a mail wagon across the country. This is just one of the many cases how USPS has embraced—as a pioneer and before any company—the integration of African American as well as Hispanic and Asian minorities. This is our richness. In retrospective, that is what is at the core of our willingness to strive, to include different persons from different backgrounds, to have "all brains in the game," to overcome issues and events—we all share a strong continuous improvement culture. Because for 200 years, we haven't continued moving mail with mules, a stage coach or a rail wagon, and instead we have always had a spirit of innovation, you could say that it is in the organization's blood. USPS was a pioneer in moving mail by air and fostered the creation of passenger air transport. We never stopped pushing the envelope: adapt to do better, faster to serve our customers.

But at the core, you need to have a resilient and diverse workforce that is able to overcome adversity and embrace change, that is sourced from young and experienced recruits from diverse backgrounds. What makes us a sustainable organization is the spirit of serving and being there for others. Maybe one of the most motivational part of my job is how USPS works with the United Nations postal agency, the Universal Postal Union, and restricted regional postal unions to support foreign postal operators' operations and performance. We are stronger together. USPS is a very strong player when it comes to cooperation for development. We've been providing technical expertise in many security, operational and logistical fields up to the point of exporting equipment. When we change equipment, we work with different postal stakeholders of developing countries to see if they could have use of it. We believe in being connected in the world with our neighbors. 40% of global mail is generated by the USPS. We are a huge exporter of mail. Our approach is simply to collaborate, to keep improving and doing the right thing for the community, even when it is tough.

A Company with a Purpose

When I think about what makes our workforce special, resilience comes first to mind. We should be attractive to a lot of young and experience people for a couple of reasons.

Firstly, sustainability is central to our business model, which reflects trends to care more for the planet and for communities. As one of the biggest entities in the country, we have committed strongly to stewardship, toward protecting the environment and leading by example. We have a lot of projects dedicated to reducing waste and to recycling. We recycle 151 million pieces of undeliverable mail each year. We have implemented solar power generation plants, like the 29,000 solar panels near our Los Angeles facility. We use renewables at our processing centers. We have reduced the energy used per square feet of our buildings by 25%. We use boxes with at least 30% recycled content. We are focusing on using alternative fuels; we have 37,000 vehicles powered by ethanol, electricity, or LPG.

Secondly, there is a wide array of careers available at USPS, accompanied by training programs, as well as potential mobility across the United States and beyond. Our workforce includes letter mail carriers up to the Postmaster General. The organization has a lot of programs to fit just about every stage of your life; your educational life, personal life, professional life. Employees who express a desire to keep moving and progressing don't just necessarily move up but sometimes progress by branching out laterally in other functions. We have people in transportation who want to understand how the processing part of the operation works, or they may decide to go to accounting, or into engineering and systems.

I am convinced this multifaceted approach makes us a richer organization. It's about how to manage a business with people who have been exposed to numerous functions and understand the business or employees who have been only one function and are not involved in say, logistics, how transportation supports processing or sales or how to support their mailing industry.

Lastly, we have strong employee engagement programs. It's not the same to engage with someone who is fresh out of university who has a different vision, is familiar with different technologies, then with someone in my age group (40+) or someone that has a 50 year-career, that has developed and grown and has been at the core of different projects and programs. In short, this intergenerational workforce provides a richness that I don't think a lot of companies can offer.

The USPS has a very robust HR department that addresses the many different needs in our organization. We have seven unions. We cater for up to 97,000 veterans, so we have that workforce with the willingness to serve, to support their nation. Working for the USPS is about understanding that you are not in a company with so much cash flow that it can do anything. We are all very conscientious and because we are entrusted with a special mission, we need to do the very best with the resources we have. I think that the feeling among many employees is that the organization is ours as citizens, so we must treat it as if it were ours.

Changes During the Pandemic

Since the USPS employs many essential workers, we knew that we would have to go above and beyond to keep moving mail, to adapt to new volume types, which included a lot of packages with medication, lavatory paper, books and many other necessities. The pandemic impacted supply chains, as well as availability of our employees, which affected staffing plans, safety and security.

The important thing is that we were able to assure continuity of operations while supporting employees during that timeframe. We worked hard to keep people safe, to keep working, to stay focused on the mission. Looking to the future, I believe more of the USPS's activities could be carried out online. We've seen a change in attitudes to telecommuting and I think it's going to allow us to reach out to talent in different locations, particularly for some of the non-operational functions. Nevertheless, we're still a very heavy human-based operation and that aspect is not going to change. The opportunities for automation, online transactions are more in the field of retail, pick up/lockers/delivery and processing streamlining. Life after the pandemic is going to be very different and will require us to be adaptable and flexible like never before.

In the international arena, for example, we move 99% of mail on passenger aircraft, which left us with no capacity. In response, I had to reach out and to create hubs and start working along multimodal lines. I had experience with multimodal in the past, but I hadn't done it that quickly, trying to think out of the box. Having developed a strong network of peers internally and with foreign postal operators, it supported the creation of this contingency planning. That is critical for a manager / executive. Keep developing your network, and reach out for help or advice. You are never too smart to receive guidance and advice and transform it into a positive output. After the pandemic is over, I don't want to go back to normal, because I don't want normal, I want better. And I think that's about the way our organization works. We've never settled for "let's get back to what it was before," because you would deny getting the fruits of what we learned from a very difficult experience. In other words, after Covid the question would be "what did we learn from having people work online?" What did they learn about telecommuting? What changes implemented should stay permanent?

We were able to absorb the increased volumes and had to deal with national and a worldwide wave of lockdown, and we did fantastically well during the US presidential elections. We were 99% on time, although there were delays over the Christmas vacation period. We're constantly looking at asking ourselves what can we do, what can we do differently to be where we want to be? Personally, the pandemic was about doing all we could for our workforce during—what was undoubtedly—an extremely stressful time. The organization raised above and beyond. There was a very supportive, liberal use of leave, we allowed people to take leave to support their families, to school their kids at home and telecommute. At the same time, we faced the challenge of making sure we had enough staff to keep the sorting centers, delivery routes and retails postal offices performing their essential tasks. The pandemic helped us to see what tasks could be done remotely.

But there is one thing that didn't change: we had to deliver and physically drive to a place to deliver mail. We looked at everything that could be potentially done to minimize human interaction. And we've been thinking about safety. Safety requires a relentless drive to evaluate each process to allow people to work safely, even together, more than ever. For example, in

Rotterdam port, during the pandemic, the Dutch worked on adding automation at the docks to avoid having people interacting. Constant innovation is driven by need of safety. We have a strong engineering group that keeps pushing automation of loads within the plants and the surface transportation group has been working with supply management on self-driven trailers. In conclusion, I believe the pandemic acted like a catalyst to drive streamlined and safer processes, because if it's not Covid, at some point it may be something else. Throughout history, we have been through different pandemics and we always learned from it. The most important thing is to be grateful to have a job, that our families are healthy and we're fulfilling our mission, and that's a lot in these times.

In-Company Training Programs

We have a numerous corporate program, and specifically leadership programs: the individual leadership program, the manager leadership program, the advanced leadership program and then the executive program. We have two centers where we train postal inspectors, the executive team and the manager team. In parallel, we have a multitude of free online classes. In my case, I took online classes first to enhance my management program skills. I wanted to do my PMP certification, so I went onto the USPS learning portal, I took all the classes that were available and then I went to my manager and asked about financial support. After that, I did a Lean Six Sigma training and now I'm thinking about doing a PhD. The USPS is supportive with each individual and funds external programs if they align with need of the organization. USPS is also growing its executive coaching group and has mentoring programs. We offer different support for each stage of an employee professional life (and personal life). We really encourage people to continue their professional development and the result is that we have a strong network of professionals at all levels.

The Future of Postal Services

We can expect legislative reform in the coming years. We cannot sustain our mission under the current financial model. We are still focusing on serving every address in the United States from the biggest city to the small hamlets. But whatever happens, I believe that we will carry the commitment of binding the nation together. We will continue to focus on improvement, consolidation, streamlining, on searching for any opportunity to do better and be more sustainable.

For example, how can we improve our fleet or how can we really meet our customers' expectations? If we tell a customer that it's a two-day delivery time, we must meet that delivery expectation. If we cannot fulfill that promise, we need to change. Change is inevitable: this organization has adapted to huge changes over the last 200 years, and it will continue. This will mean, from an engineering, from an intelligence point of view, providing more online support, automating where we can and keeping the workforce engaged and happy to serve, to be proud of what they're doing, to keep being the leaders in terms of service. For us, the focus is on seeing everything as possible: every time there's a hurricane or whatever kind of weather incident, we always come through. Sometimes we are the first on the scene of a natural disaster, with the first responders. In short, it's about keeping that culture alive of never giving up until the job is done.

We have a mission statement, which I mentioned, but even though USPS has not official motto, there is an inscription on New York City's General Post Office from 1914 "*Neither snow nor rain nor heat nor gloom of night stays these couriers from the swift completion of their appointed rounds.*" This phrase has its origins from a translation of Herodotus' Histories, when referring to the courier service that existed during the Persian Empire. Angarium, the term used for the institution of the royal mounted couriers in ancient Persia, was composed of riders (messengers) who would use the networks between Susa and Sardis (a nine-day journey) to deliver a message on behalf of the king of Persia. King Darius was the one who perfected it half a century later.

For me, the quote also expresses the resilience through events, the commitment of those been chosen to perform that mission and belief that life continues evolving. We know that markets and technology are going to evolve, but the need for postal deliveries is going to remain. And we will have to evolve, as always. Ours is a very simple but also a very difficult mission, and I don't see that changing anytime soon.

Part II

The Renaissance of Business Schools

13

Abracadabra: How Technology-Enhanced Education Personalizes Learning

Diego del Alcázar Benjumea and Santiago Iñiguez

The New Liquid Education

We live in a liquid world, where the conventional dimensions of space and time have blurred, and where the impact of technology has inexorably transformed our behavior and our vision of the world.[1] This liquid modernity was announced by Polish philosopher Zygmunt Bauman,[2] who explained that the way we conceptualize time has been transformed from linear to pointillist. Bauman criticized the impatience that characterizes contemporary generations—they prefer juice to peeling an orange—and also questioned the view that education is a product and not a process or path.

---

[1] S. Riis, *Philosophy of Technology: Oxford Bibliographies Online Research Guide* (Oxford Bibliographies Online Research Guides) (Oxford: Oxford University Press, 2011); A. Ede, *Technology and Society. A World History* (Cambridge, UK: Cambridge University Press, 2019), Ch. 11.

[2] Z. Bauman, *Liquid Life* (Cambridge, UK: Polity Press, 2005); and Z. Bauman, *On Education: Conversations with Ricardo Mazzeo* (Cambridge, UK: Polity Press, 2012).

D. del Alcázar Benjumea (✉)
IE University, Madrid, Spain
e-mail: secretaria.presidencia@ie.edu

S. Iñiguez
Madrid, Spain
e-mail: santiago.iniguez@ie.edu

In this context, work, education and social relations have also acquired a liquid nature. The pandemic that began in March 2020 has speeded up this phenomenon irreversibly.[3] Forced by lockdown in much of the world, many companies and universities moved their activities from the physical to the virtual environment. At first, many institutions were slow to react to the pandemic,[4] but in the following months most universities and business schools moved their programs to online or videoconference formats, implementing educational changes at unprecedented speeds.[5]

In this sense, the generalization of access to digital platforms in all types of organizations has promoted teleworking,[6] while Learning Management Systems (LMS) and multiple applications facilitate teaching in hybrid formats, allowing students and teachers to interact both face-to-face and remotely.[7] The digital environment also enables diachronic interaction, so that students can participate in forums or do exercises and simulations at their convenience, stretching the educational momentum beyond synchronous class time.

This concept of liquid education extends beyond the conventional didactic framework, the face-to-face class with the teacher. Moreover, it extends learning in a multifaceted way, expanding the sources of knowledge or training beyond teachers to include the role played by students, professional colleagues, or peers on social networks.[8]

---

[3] F. Diep, "The Pandemic May Have Permanently Altered Campuses. Here's How. Trends Accelerated by Covid-19 May Make More Sense Than Ever in the Future, Experts Say", *Chronicle of Higher Education*, March 15, 2021. https://www.chronicle.com/article/the-pandemic-may-have-permanently-altered-campuses-heres-how; S. Gallagher and J. Palmer, "The Pandemic Pushed Universities Online: The Change Was Long Overdue", *Harvard Business Review*, September 29, 2020.

[4] M. Korn, D. Belking and J. Chung, "Coronavirus Pushes Colleges to the Breaking Point, Forcing 'Hard Choices' About Education. Forecast Declines in Enrollment and Revenue Triggers Spending Cuts and Salary Freezes", *The Wall Street Journal*, April 30, 2020.

[5] V. Govindarajan and A. Srivastava, "What the Shift to Virtual Learning Could Mean for the Future of Higher Ed", *Harvard Business Review*, March 31, 2020.

[6] The Financial Times opened a new section on teleworking: https://www.ft.com/stream/aeabd6cf-28bb-40e1-9e73-feb05eef090a; J.M. Barrero, N. Bloom and S.J. Davis, "Why Working from Home Will Stick", *Financial Times*, January 21, 2021. https://static1.squarespace.com/static/5cfdf6cb8acf860 0012f8920/t/600ba00a0210533f9f0d31c2/1611374608159/WFH_Will_Stick+January+21+2020.pdf.

[7] B. McMurtrie and B. Supiano, "Teaching: Making Hybrid Learning Teaching for You", *The Chronicle of Higher Education*, July 30, 2020. https://www.chronicle.com/newsletter/teaching/2020-07-30; E. Dorn, F. Panier, N. Probst, and J. Sarakatsannis, "Back to School: A Framework for Remote and Hybrid Learning Amid COVID-19", *McKinsey*, article August 31, 2020. https://www.mckinsey.com/industries/public-and-social-sector/our-insights/back-to-school-a-framework-for-remote-and-hybrid-learning-amid-covid-19.

[8] Social networks as platforms were a basic component of operations for MOOCs and other previous initiatives like *The Personal MBA*, launched in the 2000s. Vid. S. Iñiguez de Onzoño, *The Learning Curve. How Business Schools Are Re-Inventing Education* (London: Palgrave MacMillan, 2011), p. 62.

In reality, technology has been disrupting education for two decades. Clayton Christensen, the father of disruption, explained that this phenomenon does not occur quickly, as happens, for example, with the so-called breakout technologies, which have an immediate impact on the consumption of a product or service,[9] and instead it takes place slowly, over time, first affecting certain activities in the educational value chain, resolving essential learning processes more efficiently or less expensively, and affecting the least-differentiated or worst-positioned universities.

The Stages of Technological Disruption in Higher Education

As said, disruption in the field of business schools and executive education, accelerated by the pandemic, has been taking place over the past two decades, and can be classified into three distinct phases.

The first phase of "e-learning" began with the appearance of the big education retailers (e.g. Apollo, Laureate or Corynthian), to which various business schools reacted by creating consortiums and developing content platforms (the best known being UNext, whose partners included the universities of Columbia, Stanford and Chicago).[10] Companies entering e-learning by combining face-to-face and online training are investing huge resources in the development of technological platforms and expect rapid growth in non-degree executive education with these formats. During this phase, it was believed that the competitive advantage was conferred by the platform, so consortia of business schools were created around large technological projects. In addition, there was also a boom in corporate universities created by the companies themselves.[11] Bachelor's and Master's degrees in business administration are consolidating their position as the most sought-after in the

---

[9] C. Christensen, *The Innovator's Dilemma: When New Technologies Cause Great Firms to Fail* (Cambridge, MA: Harvard University Press, 2016); and C. Christensen and H.E. Eyring, *The Innovative University. Changing the DNA of Higher Education from the Inside Out* (New York, NY: Jossey Bass, 2011).

[10] S. Iñiguez de Onzoño, op. cit., Ch. 9.2: "The Dream of Icarus: UNext".

[11] Networks of corporate universities have been set up across continents with the aim of sharing expertise, identifying new tendencies, and developing joint knowledge. The best known is Corporate University Exchange, an association headquartered in the US and with members around the world, along with the corporate division of EFMD, the European Foundation for Management Development, which has developed its own system of accreditation for CUs, known as CLIP, the Corporate Learning Improvement Process, which has already recognized more than 25 institutions, all of them European. See J. Boone, "Corporate Universities: Boardroom to mortarboard", *Financial Times*, November 10, 2006. https://www.ft.com/content/54b9700e-70c6-11db-8e0b-0000779e2340.

market,[12] which, far from generating competition between new entrants and established business schools, is driving the appearance and development of new educational centers, especially in emerging countries.[13]

During this first stage of e-learning, business schools found that the development of Learning Management System (LMS) platforms for online education is not necessarily an activity in which they have expertise or competitive advantages. In fact, it is difficult to capitalize on the investment required to develop such platforms, unless they are used by large numbers of students and institutions. That said, universities are often reluctant to use platforms developed by competing institutions, especially if they have to pay for them. In fact, most of the educational platforms or LMSs in use at the moment do not belong to traditional education institutions.

The second phase began with the creation of the big MOOC providers. Udemy was created in 2010, Udacity and Coursera in 2011 and edx in 2012.[14] These content platforms produced surprisingly high expectations. The courses were expected to eventually replace degree programs, drastically reduce the cost of education, be recognized by employers and offer universal access to higher education.[15] The key competitive advantage of MOOC platforms was not only the technology that supported the design, marketing and delivery, but also the ability to create a large library of content that attracted traffic and generated a stable consumer base. The passage of time has shown the conclusive impact of these platforms, especially for complementing formal education with self-learning programs, as well as for operating the phenomenon known as flipping the class. However, the expectations that were raised at their launch have not been fulfilled. Neither have they enjoyed universal access, given that MOOC consumers are mostly graduates from developed countries, nor have they replaced formal training, nor do they guarantee access to the labor market.

---

[12] As reflected in GMAC annual reports: "Demand for MBA and Business Mster's Programs. Insights and Candidates Decision Making", April 2019. https://www.gmac.com/-/media/files/gmac/research/admissions-and-application-trends/demand-for-mba-and-business-masters-programsinsights-on-candidate-decision-making-summary-reportmbac.pdf.

[13] On the one hand, online programs provide opportunities to internationalize operations for all business schools: J. Moules, "Digital Platforms Give Business Schools Global Reach", *Financial Times*, March 21, 2021. On the other hand, the number of new business schools, as well as those entering the international rankings and achieving global accreditation has increased, as reported by of AACSB. https://www.aacsb.edu/newsroom/2021/2/confirming-global-quality-and-distinction-in-business-education.

[14] S. Porter, To MOOC or Not to MOOC. *How Can Online Learning Help to Build the Future of Higher Education* (Waltham, MA: Chandos, Elsevier, 2015).

[15] D. Bradshaw, "What Moocs Mean for Executive Education," *Financial Times*, May 11, 2014; S. Iñiguez de Onzoño, *Cosmopolitan Managers. Executive Education that Works* (London: Palgrave Macmillan, 2017), Ch. 4.6: "Taking MOOCs seriously".

The third phase, liquid education and hybrid formats, is beginning precisely now. In this last stage, all the lessons learned in the previous stages are being applied, and it is the educational institutions themselves—universities and business schools—which, on their own initiative or driven by market realities, are leading the change. The key to developing competitive advantages at this stage is no longer technology, which has become a commodity, nor content, which is similarly accessible to all universities, but the experience. Faced with the classic question, also posed by the media, as to which is king, platform or content, the answer is that experience trumps both.[16] The advantage lies in how business schools involve their professors in the new hybrid formats, use the latest educational applications, integrate innovative solutions tailored to each student, promote alternative ways to achieve degrees—like micro credentials and stackable courses—and turn the educational experience into something differential.

Micro credentials are highly intensive online courses that provide a set of skills that are worth certifying in their own right. With these certificates it's possible to offer scalable access to a top learning academic experience online, and in addition those that have been the top performers of the program could be offered access to a face-to-face experience on campus. These courses could also serve as the primary admissions criteria for the face-to-face experience on campus. In addition, the hidden beneficiaries of this formula are the online-only micro credentials students, as they could have the rubber stamp credit of the leading university offering the program in an accessible and flexible form.[17]

The New Liquid Environment Boosts the Personalization of Education

Technology, in parallel with developments in cognitive psychology and the educational sciences, has produced a formidable paradigm shift in the learning process and in the mission of educators. Traditionally, the goal of education has been to transfer fundamental, relatively standardized knowledge and to prepare students for joining the professional world. That said, the future of education is increasingly seen as an opportunity to develop and strengthen the individual qualities of the learner. The Copernican shift in education brought about by technology means moving from standardization

---

[16] Ibid., Chs. 4.3.
[17] S. Sarma and L. Yoquinto, *Grasp, The Science Transforming How We Learn* (London: Robinson, Little Brown, 2020).

to personalization. Thanks to technology, education will no longer consist of acquiring the knowledge and skills to perform a job, but will also allow us to enhance students' personality, focus on their strengths and regulate efforts to achieve individual learning objectives, measuring the results and deciding which educational tools are the most appropriate.

Furthermore, technology can emphasize the humanization of education and managerial development. We sometimes think of technology as an obstacle to personalization, proximity, sociability or humanity, but this is a fallacy rooted in the age-old belief among many people that technology is a threat to humanity: the destruction of jobs by automation and, ultimately, that machines will eventually control the world. But integrating technology and teaching can help humanize the learning process as never before. In addition to adapting to personal circumstances, it establishes closer ties between teachers and students, as well as between students themselves, or in the case of in-company training, a greater sense of belonging to the organization.

It also helps teachers with repetitive tasks such as assessing academic performance, conveying basic information and answering frequently asked questions. With all this, technology can free up teachers' time to allow them to focus on more value-added activities for students.

Flexible, adaptable, intensive, intuitive and even entertaining: these are the hallmarks of hybrid formats, which combine online learning with face-to-face classes. The advantage of e-learning is that it is more flexible and focused, as it adapts to the learner's circumstances, and allows for more interactivity among participants. In short, hybrid formats in both higher education and corporate training are here to stay. That said, there are still some analysts out there who underestimate the importance of the impact of hybrid formats, because they associate them with massive online self-study training, or because they believe that nothing can ever replace face-to-face teaching.[18] At this point it is important to underline that only high-quality blended programs work, whereby online modules are taught by the same teachers who participate in the face-to-face sessions and limited to small groups of highly motivated students.

There is also a widespread belief that senior management is averse to internal online training. This is true, to a large extent, but we must ask ourselves whether this is a generational problem and whether the next batch of CEOs—who will be more accustomed to the virtual environment and communication via mobile platforms—will be more receptive to these new

---

[18] P. Fain, "Takedown of Online Education", Inside Higher Education, January 16, 2019. https://www.insidehighered.com/digital-learning/article/2019/01/16/online-learning-fails-deliver-finds-report-aimed-discouraging.

methodologies.[19] We need only bring to mind the board meetings of a century ago, in rooms with vast desks, lots of marble, mahogany and leather, and compare them with today's, often carried out via digital platforms, videoconferencing and other technologies that allow directors to communicate with each other, anytime.

It is worth noting that 80% of teachers with no experience of virtual education say that it is less effective than its face-to-face counterpart, while most educators with experience in this area say that the results are just as good, if not better.[20] We should also add that many academics mistakenly think that they will literally be made redundant. These prejudices also extend to other professionals, especially senior managers who have been traditionally educated and tend to associate quality education with face-to-face teaching. However, the forced hybrid formats run at most business schools over lockdowns have changed views among teachers significantly, for the positive.[21]

Whatever the arguments, there has been a rapid increase in the number of educational institutions offering blended courses, combining quality online training with traditional classroom instruction. For example, *Grade Level: Tracking Online Education in the United States* shows that 70.8% of academic leaders believe that online education is a critical part of their long-term strategies, up from 48.8% in 2002.[22] At the same time, 77% think that online training products deliver equal or better results than traditional training. Only 28% admit that their staff of educators accept the value and legitimacy of virtual training.

Another corporate training survey, this time conducted by Roland Berger, estimated that 77% of U.S. companies used e-learning to develop their professional programs, while in Europe more than 3000 companies used these methods. The same survey estimated that 90% of companies would use digital platforms in the coming years.[23] Thus, it is clear that hybrid formats are going to play an increasingly important role in executive training for

---

[19] See Chapters 22 and 23 of this same book.

[20] L. Redpath, "Confronting the Bias against On-Line Learning in Management Education." *Academy of Management Learning & Education*, Vol. 11, No. 1, 2012, pp. 125–140.

[21] D. Lederman, "Faculty Confidence in Online Learning Grows", *Inside Higher Education*, October 6, 2020. https://www.insidehighered.com/digital-learning/article/2020/10/06/covid-era-experience-strengthens-faculty-belief-value-online.

[22] I.E. Allen and J. Seaman, "Grade Level: Tracking Online Education in the United States," February 2015. https://eric.ed.gov/?id=ED572778.

[23] Roland Berger, "Corporate Learning Goes Digital: How Companies Can Benefit from Online Education," May 2014. https://www.google.com/search?client=safari&rls=en&q=Roland+Berger,+%E2%80%9CCorporate+Learning+Goes+Digital:+How+Companies+Can+Benefit+from+Online+Education,%E2%80%9D&ie=UTF-8&oe=UTF-8.

those participants who cannot attend face-to-face sessions. The question is not, therefore, whether these formats are the future or whether face-to-face training is more effective, but rather, what is the optimal or blended mode for a given learning situation. Obviously, striking the balance between virtual and face-to-face training will depend on the objectives of the program, the profile of the participants, the content to be taught, the skills and competencies to be developed, and even the costs, infrastructure and capacity of trainers and educators to deliver their teachings online.

What Makes Hybrid Formats Different?

With the expected return to normality after the pandemic, several experts, including those interviewed in this book, believe that some of the initiatives developed over the last decade and widely implemented during the last year, are here to stay. In our experience, the majority of students in full time programs prefer value face-to-face interaction over remote interaction via digital media. However, convenience, the growing demands of sustainability in any social activity, including education, but above all the advantages they offer, will most likely make hybrid formats and liquid education the preferred configuration for most business schools and executive education centers.

Which parts of this approach should be retained and improved? I would suggest the following:

- *Learning analytics:* this allows for personalized monitoring of students' individual performance and, based on the experience and models developed from big data, to design better educational experiences to achieve learning objectives, guide the performance of the teacher or tutor, reduce academic failure and better integrate all the components of a program.[24]
- *Delivery:* in the past, real-time classroom in presence was the basic—and almost exclusive—teaching format. Technology-enhanced forms of learning and new applications permit the development of a huge variety of new formats. For example, hybrid classes with remote and face-to-face attendees, overcoming the barriers imposed by distance, international mobility or other circumstances. Also, asynchronous sessions, which can, for example, take place over several days, such as forums, interactive team or individual exercises carried out online and supervised by the teacher,

---

[24] C. Hall, J.R. Cristina, J.R. Mattox and P. Parskey. *Learning Analytics. Using Talent Data to Improve Business Outcomes* (London: Kogan Page, 2011).

simulations, self-learning content, tests, educational games and a wide plethora already in development.
- *Multimedia learning materials*: smart books and smart learning materials will allow students to learn at own pace, emphasizing or clarifying areas of greater difficulty, or advancing more quickly and expanding complementary areas, using examples and cases related to personal preferences, without relaxing the demands of learning. They will promote the acquisition of knowledge, but also the development of a decisive innovation such as curiosity, as well as critical faculties and other basic skills for personal development.
- *Assessment methods and proctoring systems*: in contrast to traditional exams, which are basically about memory skills, new approaches assess learning capabilities based on a wide range of factors, helping teachers to evaluate their students in a creative and constructive way, as well as to provide vital feedback. They also allow for assessment to be carried out safely and reliably at a distance, guaranteeing the identity and continuity of the student.
- *From teacher to educational team*: the role of the teacher is still central in the new hybrid formats, but it is only possible through collaboration with other teams that provide technical support, student coordination, content preparation and design the sessions. Although the new hybrid formats foster a closer, deeper and improved student–teacher experience, support teams are more necessary than in a traditional face-to-face environment in order to deliver and scale classes.
- *Peer interaction and feedback*: the new hybrid formats are characteristically immersive and interactive, promoting relationships and exchanges between participants in a program. Digitally based social mechanisms and applications allow for rapid and simultaneous communication, which, if well managed, can integrate class members, strengthen group and institutional identity, resolve difficulties and unify messages. In addition, the feedback provided by students, who can sometimes exercise influence over their peers, can be enormously useful for learning, confirming strengths or identifying areas for improvement.
- *Applied projects, internships and exchanges:* the potential delocalization of students' hybrid formats offer can facilitate the combination of internships or international stays with attendance on courses taught at the business school, both in synchronous and particularly asynchronous formats. The new formats also encourage the participation of guest lecturers or corporate representatives from anywhere in the world, without the need for travel. On the other hand, the use of devices, software and other augmented

reality developments makes it possible to travel to remote locations without moving: for example, to virtually visit the Airbus factory, or to attend a board meeting in the same virtual room with participants from different continents.

Learning to Survive in the Artificial Intelligence Age

Artificial Intelligence is the ability of a computer to perform tasks that are usually performed by humans with no need of human discernment. So why should it be so important what we learn when a machine already knows everything that we need to know? As you can imagine, we don't aim to have a dystopic situation in which machines are able to take control over how humans should live, and for that not to happen, it is essential to establish the limits that artificial intelligence has in contrast to human intelligence.

Machines and humans' intelligences have something in common, cognition, that is the process of thought from which we are able to create our knowledge and understanding from the world. The result of cognition is what many AI systems deliver through their algorithmic minds. To differentiate artificial form human intelligence, we now need to understand how humans can look beyond the knowledge and understanding of the world, by developing knowledge of themselves and of their own cognition. Metacognition (big subject of discussion since Aristotle) is composed of the basic assumptions that lie behind the way we know and think, the conceptual framework that helps understanding what knowledge is.[25]

Having this differentiation in mind, we now should aim to understand what things we should take into account, so we don't make the mistake of allowing the limited intelligence of machines disrupt human control, and for this, education plays a key role. Obviously, having technological skills will be key for our coexistence with AI, although it's even more important not only to learn what technology can do for us, but also what it can't, and will never will. One of the most unique human capacities (beyond metacognition) is actually the one that machines will never be able to replicate, although it's also one of the hardest to teach. I'm referring to creativity and how we can learn to be creative in a world of AI.[26]

---

[25] R. Luckin, *Machine Learning and Human Intelligence: The Future of Education for the 21st Century* (London: UCL Institute of Education Press, 2018).

[26] J.E. Aoun, Robot—Proof: Higher Education in the Age of Artificial Intelligence (Cambridge, MA: MIT Press, 2017).

Creativity happens when we are knowledgeable of the matter that we are facing. Generating that knowledge happens through education. For example, at IE University we believe that in order to enhance our creativity in the world of AI we should master certain skills and reinforce certain attitudes:

1. **Tech and data skills**: if we aim to control AI we should at least understand and speak the language of technology. Although we intuitively navigate with no problem through different websites and apps, we don't necessarily understand what is behind those apps. As coding is the language of technology, we should at least be literate of this language.

    In addition to technology, in the digital age we have realized data is the new gold. Although what is really gold is our ability to find a meaning of the tons of information pouring to our devices. This is why big data is so important to survive in a world of AI, to be able to read the digital record when it's necessary and to look to another place when it's dispensable (fake news).
2. **Diversity**: this human attitude will be essential in a world dominated by AI as we will enhance our understanding of other cultures and perspectives (including the ones of the machines if we are fluent in tech) having a broader understanding of the world, enriching our minds and broadening our thinking. Education is the key to connecting people around the world in multiple ways.
3. **Entrepreneurial mindset**: in a world where everything is changing so fast, governments, corporations and individuals will increasingly struggle to adapt. Therefore, we most convey an entrepreneurial spirit to our students so they can have the flexibility that allows them to adjust in a creative manner. Having an entrepreneurial spirit will be essential to survive in an ever-changing world. In addition, in a world dominated by AI we need to enable the existence of talented and innovative leaders that peoples' lives.
4. **Humanities**: as in The Odyssey of Homer, every journey starts with an individual. If we can truly understand what makes us who we are—our passions, talents and aspirations—then we can create greater meaning in a world dominated by AI. It is only through the study and critique of literature, history, art and philosophy that individuals and societies will be able to navigate the complex questions raised by technological, societal and environmental change.

The Role of the Teacher Is Pivotal

In this context of increasing integration between technology and teaching, the role of teachers becomes more decisive than before, as they move from a unidirectional approach to orchestrating the entire learning process and even the platform. Attracting professors to this new environment will not be easy, in part because the boards of most business schools require high quorums to approve major changes in the educational curriculum. This collegial approach, which is deeply rooted in academia, could hinder a transformation process that requires a rapid response to the changes taking place or slow down the adaptation of the role of academics to the new needs of education. This gives a certain advantage to executive education centers and consulting firms with business-oriented outlook and decision-making systems.

The other convention that could delay the adoption of new teaching methods and the integration of technology in education is tenure, the life-long nature of some teaching positions in universities, regardless of performance or an academic's commitment to innovation. Only those with a clear academic vocation and a firm commitment to teaching will be motivated to effect change. At times, institutional resistance from faculty senates, along with the collegial governance prevalent in traditional universities, are driving other entities to attempt to bring change through the creation of independent businesses, as happened at one time with Duke CE, although it has since returned to being part of the university, or by hiring faculty who are outside the system, as has happened at Cornell University's New York campus. One of the factors that most delayed the adoption of hybrid formats at the beginning of the pandemic, for example, was the reluctance of faculty to either teach their classes online or return to campus.[27]

On the other hand, it must be recognized that teaching in hybrid formats is potentially more stressful for teachers. It is no longer enough to teach a class from the podium; teachers have to manage a platform, interact with students in person and/or remotely, control the visual support mechanisms—cameras—and sound, and perhaps a digital whiteboard, in addition to being logically entertaining to keep their audience engaged. However, sometimes this effort is truncated by connectivity and network failures and even student apathy, factors that may be addressed in advance.

---

[27] M.D. Miller, "A Year of Remote Teaching: The Good, the Bad and the Next Steps", *Chronicle of Higher Education*, March 17, 2021. https://www.chronicle.com/article/a-year-of-remote-teaching-the-good-the-bad-and-the-next-steps.

In order to implement hybrid formats, the following initiatives may be helpful:

- Create financial and other incentives to encourage teachers to incorporate new educational methodologies. As a general rule, hybrid formats require more preparation than face-to-face sessions, especially at the beginning. This can be compensated for by making one blended session equivalent to two or more traditional sessions.
- Preparation and training in the use of asynchronous methods such as forums or digital content supervised by the teacher, which are necessary to become familiar with the technology and the new approach to teaching. This is where technology companies can play a fundamental role, as they already invest in training. This would be in their own interest, since they will gain an important ally in the process.
- Encourage new teaching methods. Face-to-face and virtual sessions can become interactive experiences that can transcend traditional educational formats. This process will elicit better evaluations from participants and enhance the reputation of teachers, which in turn will lead to better salaries.
- Improve the role of academics as teachers. In general, teaching has been undervalued in recent years in favor of research. Instead, these two important aspects should go hand in hand. With this in mind, it would be worthwhile to review the incentive system in universities and to recognize and value the increase in teaching, especially in the new virtual context. This is something that could be addressed from the outset, for example, during doctoral programs studied by the academics of the future with the aim of raising awareness and providing them with new skills they will need to be good teachers.
- Combining technology with teaching continues to create new approaches to enhancing the educational experience. Much research has been conducted on the benefits and drawbacks of hybrid formats and more is needed if we are to better understand the transition from classroom to integrating technology.

Conclusion: Education Must Remain a Journey

There has been speculation as to whether in the future it will be possible to install a chip in the brain that would allow us to instantly acquire knowledge on the scale of the Encyclopaedia Britannica. This may still be some time away, if it ever happens at all, although reality always trumps fiction. Nevertheless, there are two drawbacks to the approach. The first was highlighted recently when Chris Anderson, editor in chief of Wired magazine, argued that Big Data, will make obsolete the traditional method used by scientists of hypothesis, model, test.[28] Luciano Floridi, an Oxford academic, countered with a reference to Plato, who explained that knowledge is more than the mere accumulation of information or data. Floridi explained that data does not speak for itself and needs what he calls smart questioners.[29] Even if we had that chip installed in our brains with the entire Encyclopedia Britannica, and we could answer the question as to who Plato was, we would still need the Humanities and education to explain why he remains so important to the world of ideas.

At the same time, the idea that technology can replace essential parts of learning such as careful reading, the association of ideas or understanding complex issues, overlooks the fact that the most enjoyable part of education is the journey, not the destination. As one of the central works of literature, Homer's Odyssey, teaches us, the meaning of education becomes clear as we travel through life, which both teaches and changes us.[30] Liquid education will facilitate the permanent change which, as Heraclitus explained,[31] we all experience on a daily basis.

---

[28] C. Anderson, "The End of Theory: The Data Deluge Makes the Scientific Method Obsolete" Wired, June 23, 2008. https://www.wired.com/2008/06/pb-theory/.
[29] L. Fioridi, *The Fourth Revolution: How the Infosphere Is Reshaping Human Reality* (Oxford: Oxford University Press, 2014), 129–130.
[30] Homer, *The Odyssey* (London: Penguin, 2003).
[31] D.W., Graham, "Heraclitus", *The Stanford Encyclopedia of Philosophy* (Fall 2019 Edition), Edward N. Zalta (ed.). https://plato.stanford.edu/cgi-bin/encyclopedia/archinfo.cgi?entry=heraclitus&archive=fall2019.

14

The MBA Is Dead: Long Live the MBA

Gabriela Alvarado Cabrera and Santiago Iñiguez

In Search of the Perfect MBA

Over recent decades, the MBA has been one of the most in-demand post-graduate qualifications, despite periodic economic crises.[1] Unlike other specialist programs, which have evolved more elastically or cyclically, demand for MBAs has remained steady, with the exception of some periods marked by special circumstances, like student VISA restrictions,[2] or during the period

---

[1] As reflected in GMAC annual reports: "Demand for MBA and Business Master's Programs. Insights and Candidates Decision Making," April 2019. https://www.gmac.com/-/media/files/gmac/research/admissions-and-application-trends/demand-for-mba-and-business-masters-programsinsights-on-candidate-decision-making-summary-reportmbac.pdf.

[2] J. Moules, "Demand for MBAs Falls for the First Time. Applications for Places in Courses Drops Nearly 7% in the US," *Financial Times*, February 2, 2021, following international students' VISA restrictions imposed by the Trump administration. https://www.ft.com/content/e5c07830-1eb0-40bb-b0a0-f657252ea8ab.

G. A. Cabrera (✉)
IPADE Business School, Mexico City, Mexico
e-mail: malvarado@ipade.mx

S. Iñiguez
IE University, Madrid, Spain
e-mail: santiago.iniguez@ie.edu

marked by the COVID-19 pandemic, although the information at the time of writing points to a recovery.[3]

Any number of prophets have predicted the death of the MBA over the years, but the qualification has proved resilient. In the wake of the financial crisis of 2008, a debate raged about the role business schools had played in creating the situation, characterized by media coverage such as Businessweek's open forum entitled *Business Schools Are Largely Responsible for The US Financial Crisis. Pro or Con?*,[4] an article in *The New York Times* asking "if the way business students are taught has contributed to the most serious economic crisis in decades",[5] as well as the acknowledgement by the then Dean of Harvard Business School, Jay O. Light, that "business schools should shoulder some of the blame."[6]

In short, for a few years, business schools and MBA graduates became a popular target, with criticism falling into three main categories.

- First, that MBAs produce overly ambitious, arrogant individuals whose knowledge is based on theories and perceptions that have little to do with entrepreneurialism or the dedication required of business leaders. Writing in the wake of the financial crash, The Guardian's Peter Walker argued: "Too many MBA programmes, the simplified version goes, draw in young, greedy types with little business experience and indoctrinate them with half-baked management and finance theories, along with an unshakeable belief in their own talents, before sending them out to earn ill-deserved fortunes in investment banking and consulting."[7] Bob Sutton, Professor of Management Science at Stanford Graduate School of Business, sums up the approach of many of his colleagues: "Most of the models and assumptions they pass on to their students reflect a fundamental belief about human beings: We are hard-wired to be selfish. They assume that it's a dog-eat-dog world, and that humans want and take as much for themselves as possible and to stomp on others along the way."[8]

---

[3] J. Moules, "MBAs Rebound as Prospective Students Flee Worsening Economy. Surge in Applications for Business Schools after Pandemic Hits Employment," *Financial Times*, June 21, 2020. https://www.ft.com/content/3284265f-993c-4f4d-80c9-419e4f58f2a5.

[4] The Debate Room, "Financial Crisis: Blame B-schools. Business Schools Are Largely Responsible for the U. S. Financial Crisis. Pro or Con?" *Businessweek*, November 24, 2008.

[5] K. Holland, "Is It Time to Retrain B-Schools?" *The New York Times*, March 14, 2009.

[6] J. O. Light: "Change Is in the Offing," *HBR Blog Network*, May 7, 2009. https://hbr.org/2009/05/change-is-in-the-offing.

[7] P. Walker, "Who Taught Them Greed Is Good? To What Extent Are Business Schools' MBA Courses Responsible for the Global Financial Crash?" *The Observer*, March 8, 2009.

[8] R. Sutton, "Do Economists Breed Greed and Guile?" in "How to Fix Business Schools," *Harvard Business Review Blogs*, April 5, 2009.

That said, there is a much wider range of MBA programs available now, compared to the days of the masters of the universe caricatured in movies from the greed is good era of the 1980s. At the same time, many innovative companies with leadership cultures far removed from the model of the ambitious executive are actively recruiting at business schools. In addition, a growing number of MBA programs have become benchmarks for training entrepreneurs.

- Second, the salaries once offered to MBA graduates were criticized as counterproductive and excessive, when in reality they simply reflected the market value of MBA degrees.[9] On the other hand, given the diversity of MBA programs and the breadth of latitudes in which they are offered, as well as the multiple career opportunities they offer, merely focusing on the salaries reflected in the rankings of the best schools can be misleading.
- The third fundamental criticism is the lack of ethics in management education, which is supposedly reflected in the attitudes of MBA graduates.[10] Again, MBA programs have evolved over the last three decades. The majority of them have introduced content related to business ethics and professional deontology into their syllabi. Under the influence of accreditation agencies, rankings and employers, responsibility and sustainability are now included in many subjects, while academic research in these areas has flourished.

There is a strong populist undertone in much of the criticism of MBAs, which contradicts the thriving demand sustained over time, and perhaps should be seen as part of a broader questioning of the usefulness of education. In-company or on-the-job training, it has been argued, is more useful when it comes to finding a job and is much cheaper. This approach forgets that the purpose of the education and training at the core of an MBA is not just to transfer knowledge or develop skills; it is not just about access to employment. It is also about cultivating good global citizens, providing a comprehensive transformative experience, cultivating a worldview

---

[9] K. Starkey, "Business Schools- Look at History to Broaden Your Intellectual Horizons," *Financial Times*, October 20, 2008.

[10] Thomas Piper argued that the best way to teach business ethics is not just through a specific course looking at leadership and social responsibility, but by addressing these questions throughout the whole MBA program. First, he says, because "ethical dilemmas arise in all functional areas and at all levels of the organization." Second, because when teachers avoid the subject, "we send an unintended but powerful signal that they are not a priority." Effective business ethics teaching depends in large part on its inclusion across the board as an integral part of acquiring a business education. See T. Piper, M.C. Gentile, and S. Daloz Parks, *Can Ethics Be Taught? Perspectives, Challenges and Approaches at Harvard Business School* (Cambridge, MA: Harvard Business School Press, 1993), p. 127.

in students, instilling the entrepreneurial verve and good management habits. The MBA program can be characterized, as has been said, as the "Grand Tour of the twenty-first century."[11]

The Full Value Proposition of the Learning Process and of an MBA Program

Business schools can be characterized as "learning hubs," institutions that combine physical and virtual space thanks to educational technologies, and that offer educational and training services, together with the development of global research.

Sometimes, when evaluating MBA programs, the focus is mainly on content: the subjects that make up the program, the courses, and credits. The next section reviews this aspect, and the interesting and little-known conclusion is that it tends to be very similar in all business schools.

Beyond content, there are other key elements in MBA programs that can be decisive or add more value from the point of view of the student, the employer, or other stakeholders. These other key elements may include the experience at the program, access to networks provided by the school, as well as the variety of formats and modalities for taking the program. All these factors offer business schools opportunities for differentiation, particularly in our post-pandemic times, when the risk of commoditization is greater and the adoption of hybrid formats has become widespread overnight.

Regardless of the degree students receive at the end of their MBA or master in management, we would argue that what really makes study at a business school worthwhile is the overall learning experience itself, from forming friendships with fellow students, extracurricular activities, or coming to understand and appreciate the values of the institution; these are what set candidates apart in the eyes of potential employers. Needless to say, the type of campus, urban or rural, is also a key factor in how students experience their studies.

In our experience, among the most common reasons candidates mention when applying to business school is access to a network of alumni, headhunters, in-company contacts, and other institutions. With this in mind, business schools now have teams tasked with maintaining contact with graduates over the course of their careers, wherever they live and work. At the same time as this boosts a school's cache through association with business leaders,

---

[11] S. Iñiguez de Onzoño, *The Learning Curve. How Business Schools Are Re-inventing Education* (London: Palgrave Macmillan, 2011), p. 150.

it serves another purpose: successful graduates are a school's best way to attract new students. In turn, graduates are likely to contribute financially to their former alma mater. US business schools have been particularly successful in developing alumni networks, building on the long-established tradition of fundraising in the United States. In contrast, European schools' focus on education has meant they often overlook the importance of maintaining contact over the years with their alumni.

The work carried out over the years by careers and alumni departments is now being further developed thanks to the internet and social networks. Business schools are now active on Facebook, Twitter, LinkedIn, and WhatsApp, among others, which they use to organize frequent social events and reunions.

MBA Content and Learning Goals Prior to the COVID-19 Pandemic

Based on the Association of MBAs accreditation criteria, an MBA is "a generalist, postgraduate, post-experience degree designed to develop holistic, innovative, and socially responsible business leaders for high performance organizations in the global market, through the development of knowledge, skills and values required to succeed in complex environments."[12]

The accreditation body stresses the importance of MBA graduates' acquisition of the following skill sets:

- Critical thinking and analysis of complex data
- Decision-making based on complex information
- Acting with integrity and commitment to lifelong learning
- Leadership and people management
- Cross-cultural abilities and mindset
- Functional knowledge integration and strategic management skills

In October 2020, as part of the Jobs Reset Summit, the World Economic Forum (WEF) presented its *Future of Jobs Report*, identifying the top 10 skills for 2025 and grouping them into four major categories[13]:

---

[12] AMBA, *MBA Accreditation Criteria*, 2016.
[13] World Economic Forum, *The Future of Jobs Report 2020*.

1. Problem-solving:
   - Analytical thinking and innovation
   - Complex problem-solving
   - Critical thinking and analysis
   - Creativity, originality, and initiative
   - Reasoning, problem-solving, and ideation
2. Self-management:
   - Active learning and learning strategies
   - Resilience, stress tolerance, and flexibility
3. Working with people:
   - Leadership and social influence
4. Technology use and development:
   - Technology use, monitoring, and control
   - Technology design and programming

In a post-pandemic context, the report further highlighted the value of critical thinking and problem-solving, which top the list of abilities expected by employers in the next five years, along with new skills in self-management such as active learning, resilience, stress tolerance, and flexibility.

When comparing the findings of the WEF's study with the abilities MBA programs are required to develop, it becomes apparent that skills related to technology use and development, resilience, and flexibility are not among the most important. Since such skills are not clearly specified, it should lead MBA associate deans to rethink the core set of abilities their graduates need to acquire for the next normal. Further, the program conventional focus on business administration will need to expand to also emphasize business transformation.

Prevailing Body of Knowledge

As said before, taking an MBA is not only about skills acquisition, but also about developing a broad base of management knowledge as well as a full transformative experience. To identify best practices on curriculum, we have

Table 14.1 Top 10 full-time MBA

Core course	% of programs
Corporate Finance	100
Financial Accounting	100
Marketing	100
Operations Management	100
Strategy	100
Microeconomics	90
Macroeconomics	90
Organizational Behavior	80
Statistics	70
Leadership	60
Business Ethics	60
Managerial Accounting	40
Data Analytics	40
Communication skills	30
Entrepreneurship	20

Sources Financial Times (2020) and schools' websites

analyzed the top 10 full-time MBA programs, as well as the top 10 executive MBA programs according to the FT global MBA and executive MBA rankings, respectively.[14]

Tables 14.1 and 14.2 show the percentage of leading full-time and executive MBA programs, separately, which include a certain course in its core curriculum.

As can be seen, whether full-time or executive, the established body of knowledge defining an MBA involves five courses: Corporate Finance, Financial Accounting, Marketing, Operations Management, and Strategy. This is consistent with the conventional focus on integrating functional knowledge and developing strategic thinking that MBA programs have stressed for decades. Still, such subjects are also connected to the problem-solving group of skills for 2025 identified by the World Economic Forum report.

However, when looking at the core courses in both tables, interesting differences between full-time and executive MBAs emerge. While quantitative and theoretical courses are more prevalent in full-time programs, courses on managerial and entrepreneurial skills (leadership, entrepreneurship, talent

---

[14] Financial Times, *Executive MBA Ranking 2020*. http://rankings.ft.com/businessschoolrankings/executive-mba-ranking-2020; Financial Times, *Global MBA Ranking 2020*. http://rankings.ft.com/businessschoolrankings/global-mba-ranking-2020.

Table 14.2 Top 10 executive MBA

Core course	% of programs
Corporate Finance	100
Financial Accounting	100
Marketing	100
Operations Management / Supply Chain Management	100
Strategy	100
Leadership	90
Macroeconomics	80
Microeconomics	70
Innovation and Entrepreneurship	70
Managerial Accounting	60
Organizational Behavior	50
Talent Management	50
Business Ethics	40
Statistics	40
Digital Transformation	40
Negotiation	30
Entrepreneurial Finance and FinTech	30
Data Analytics	20
International Political Analysis	20
International Business	20

management) and current relevant topics for business (digital transformation, entrepreneurial finance, and fintech) have become the standard in the executive ones.

The above-mentioned differences might be easily explained by the fact that the people take one or the other for different reasons. Full-time MBA students are typically looking for a career change, whereas participants in an executive MBA want to strengthen their abilities and acquire new knowledge to expand their businesses and for personal growth.

Even though full-time programs usually include a broader portfolio of electives, if we look deeper into the curriculum of the top 10 MBAs, we find that most focus on traditional entrepreneurial and functional subjects and skills, and only half the programs offer electives on technology or digital topics. At the same time, seven out of the top 10 EMBAs offer various elective courses covering issues that include technological innovation, digital strategy, big data analytics, AI, and machine learning, to mention a few.

EMBA programs are addressing the knowledge updating required by their participants, which will have repercussions. The COVID-19 crisis encouraged the adoption of digital technology in short order, with organizations and workforces embracing digital transformation as the world looks ahead to a new normal. Even before the crisis, organizations that were digitally and analytically mature outperformed competitors without strong digital and analytics capabilities; the pandemic only widened the gap.

After the pandemic, professionals and firms that adapt quickly embrace new ways of working, and make digital and analytics a core element of their strategy will be better positioned for the future. Some leading business schools have already introduced elective courses on tech, digital, and data science skills. It's now time to consider including them as part of their required curriculum.

In short, the moment to embrace change, flexibility, innovation, and purpose has arrived, and a few MBA programs have started to offer courses that explore leading in times of ambiguity, strategic agility, and the future of talent and work, in line with the WEF's self-management set of skills. The COVID-19 pandemic has provided the opportunity to enter into the list of core courses of the next normal MBA.

How Mature Is the MBA as a Program?

The traditional business maturity theory establishes that sectors evolve through the stages of introduction, growth, maturity, and decline.[15] This is essentially an anthropomorphic approach based on the assumption that companies and industries resemble humans, a frequent comparison in strategic analysis. While this approach is easy to understand and intuitive, it also has its drawbacks.

Consider, for example, the maxim of John Stopford, creator of the London Business School's strategy department, who refutes this comparison by showing how innovation occurs even in supposedly mature industries, which can often give rise to new businesses: "There are no mature industries; there are only mature companies."[16]

Stopford's words are pertinent when we consider the supposed maturity of MBA programs, based on the intense competition between business schools, stable GMAT applications in recent years, the slowdown in the growth of applications in the U.S. market, and the threat of other substitute programs, particularly in new areas related to technology and data sciences.

---

[15] T. Levitt, "Exploit the Product Life Cycle," *Harvard Business Review*, November 1965. https://hbr.org/1965/11/exploit-the-product-life-cycle.

[16] C. Baden-Fuller and J. Stopford, *Rejuvenating the Mature Business: The Competitive Challenge* (Boston, MA: Harvard Business School Press, 1994), p. 3.

The truth, in our view, is not that MBA programs are mature, but simply that there are some mature business schools that have not innovated sufficiently in recent years. In this sense, the pandemic has acted as a catalyst for new programs, content, formats, and learning experiences. There are several reasons to support this view.

- First, if we look at the broad family of MBA programs, which includes executive MBAs, those specializing in particular sectors or disciplines (such as finance or marketing), in traditional or online formats, or even masters in management, we can see that the aggregate market for graduate management programs has grown over the past decade and that the outlook is positive. In addition, new business schools and executive education centers continue to be created, especially in emerging regions.
- Second, there is still plenty of room for growth in mature markets if schools do more to attract women to MBA programs. This is still an issue in many schools, where the percentage of women is still below the average for other equally demanding degrees such as law or medicine. The average percentage of women with MBAs is still very low, although it has grown in recent years (still below 50% in many top schools) compared to other degrees.[17]
- Third, there are still great opportunities to internationalize the student body at many business schools. The pandemic has temporarily suspended international student mobility and this has had a significant impact on applications to MBA programs around the world. In addition, social distancing restrictions, lockdowns, and curfews deterred many potential students from pursuing MBA programs abroad during the 2020–2021 academic year, given that they would not meet the expectations described above.
- Fourth, some of the statistics we use can be misleading. Although there has been modest growth in the number of GMAT applications in recent years, many schools around the world use alternative mechanisms to screen applicants, including their own tests, especially in executive MBA programs where experience is more important than analytical skills. In addition, some elite schools have started to accept tests waivers.
- Fifth, the growth of lifelong learning can be expected to generate new forms of MBA programs, multi-modal, with stackable offerings and pathways that build up to a graduate degree. This, together with the impact

---

[17] Vid. FT rankings, quoted on (14).

of new educational platforms and applications, as well as technology-enhanced learning, will lead to multiple solutions adapted to the personal circumstances of time and place of future participants throughout their careers.

Internationalization Amid the New Normality

According to the model developed by EQUIS, internationalization encompasses four major dimensions[18]:

1. Policy issues influencing the whole school, such as having a well-defined strategy for internationalization, the international reputation the school enjoys, and having international representatives in its governance system.
2. Content aspects of the learning and development process as reflected in an international curriculum, learning resources, and publications.
3. Context issues resulting from the experience of the various stakeholders. This includes the intercultural mix of the core, adjunct, and visiting faculty, and the intercultural composition of the students, exchange students, alumni, and staff.
4. Elements of the wider network to which the school belongs including international connections with practice, academic partners, and professional networks, as well as activities abroad.

Clearly, the COVID-19 crisis has not affected the accessibility and teaching of international content in the MBA curriculum, while its impact on policy issues has mainly prompted certain adjustments to business schools' internationalization strategy. On the other hand, the dimensions of context and network have been certainly affected, especially as regards international and exchange students, along with activities abroad. As mentioned in the previous section, the pandemic has put international student mobility on hold in the short-term and this situation might extend to the mid-term.[19] Meanwhile, business schools have set out virtual mobility programs making use of distance learning tools.

---

[18] EFMD Global, *2020 EQUIS—Standards & Criteria*.
[19] C. Bremner, *Travel 2040. Climate Emergency to Force a Revolution in the Industry* (Euromonitor International, 2020).

Internationalizing the classroom through distance education can be done under different schemes, ranging from a basic level to one providing a more complete international experience, as described below.[20]

(a) Synchronous remote teaching in which an international professor teaches local students by means of a virtual platform and collaboration tools.
(b) In-house internationalization, where an international professor teaches simultaneously various groups of students located in different regions of the world through synchronous remote teaching.
(c) Cross-internationalization in which faculty members of schools located in different countries co-teach students from the schools where they belong via synchronous remote teaching.

While the cross-internationalization approach offers a more comprehensive international experience, it also involves additional challenges in terms of logistics and mutual recognition between institutions. In any case, distance education has not only enabled business schools in general, and MBA programs in particular, to deal with the issues of international context and network posed by COVID-19, but also democratized access to international education to students who otherwise could not afford it.[21]

Before COVID-19, the world was already hybrid. After the pandemic, it will be even more. Hence, the next normal "traditional MBA" will no longer be 100% in-person, but one that enriches students experience through technology-enhanced learning.

The World Economic Forum has placed resilience and flexibility among the top 10 skills for the future. As noted earlier, the MBA has proved flexible and resilient. Maybe, we should look closer at its evolution and learn from it.

---

[20] M. López S., "Rethinking Internationalization," *EFMD Global*, August 14, 2020.
[21] G. Alvarado, H. Thomas, L. Thomas, and A. Wilson, *Latin America: Management Education's Growth and Future Pathways* (Bingley, UK: Emerald Publishing, 2018).

15

Covid-19: Organizational Responses to Societal and Business Challenges

Salvador Carmona

The SARS-Cov-2, widely known as COVID-19, is a worldwide, health crisis that exerts severe effects on the economy, industries and firms. In the case of tourism industry, for example, the global spread of the pandemic imposes major problems on its prospects of financial recovery. As noted by Škare et al. (2021) the tourism industry has traditionally experienced local crises but once the specific crises were over, both local and international tourists used to visit the affected jurisdictions and this brought about timely, financial recoveries. In contrast to the local character of past crises, the worldwide character of COVID-19 provided a significantly different scenario; it requires a global end of the pandemic as a prerequisite for international traveling. Therefore, the worldwide recovery of the tourism industry will take longer than the usual; 10 months that are expected in the case of local crises. Furthermore, the impact of COVID-19 is harsh for many other industries; in Western countries (e.g., Europe), the airline industry is enforcing major job cuts (www.flightglobal.com). At the micro-level the situation is not significantly different and well-known firms such as Hertz experience most important layoffs. De Vito and Gómez (2020) examined how the coronavirus crisis could affect the liquidity of listed firms across 26 countries; they found that companies

S. Carmona (✉)
IE University, Segovia, Spain
e-mail: salvador.carmona@ie.edu

would significantly increase their short-term liabilities and, as consequence of the crisis, 1/10th of all sample firms could become illiquid within six months.

The effects of COVID-19 on the economy are dramatic at both the macro- and micro-levels. However, markets are dynamic and have responded both reactively and proactively to the challenges and threats posed by the pandemic. In turn, I argue, this provides some learning opportunities on successful management practices in periods of crisis. In this chapter, I address organizational responses to social and business challenges accelerated by the pandemic. According to WWF (2020), the earth has lost over 68 per cent of its biodiversity in just the last 50 years. As we will see, this environmental degradation is related to the emergence of pandemics and, hence, I examine organizational responses to climate change as well as the extent to which such responses have been accelerated in the context of the COVID-19 crisis. At the micro, organizational level, I focus on how innovative firms changed their business models and work organization to cope with the uncertainty coming from an increasingly complex environment. Furthermore, the pandemic has severely affected family-owned firms and, given their overwhelming role in the global economy, I explore some of their critical challenges under the pandemic. Finally, I provide some concluding remarks.

Societal Values

In an article published in *The New England Journal of Medicine*, Bill Gates (2018) elaborated on the risk and innovations to implement in cases of pandemic. In 2020, the outbreak of COVID-19 demonstrated the high value of Gates' reflections and the well-taken initiatives raised in Gates' article would have been worth of enforcement. In 2021, amidst the peak of the COVID-19 crisis, Gates warned about an upcoming disaster; the devastating effects of climate change. As in 2018, Gates made specific suggestions to address this global issue. However, and despite the effects of environmental catastrophes in February 2021, such as the Texas snowfall and episodes of cold weather in the Middle East that signal a situation of global warning (www.washington.com), some people are reluctant to admit this critical situation (e.g., deniers of climate change; the Trump Administration). Fortunately, there is an increasing, global awareness of the devastating effects of climate change, as noted by the new U.S. administration, which has re-joined the Paris-Agreement. Furthermore, an increasing number of companies are enforcing ambitious, environmental protection projects; for example, G.M. announced that it will only sell zero-emission vehicles by 2035 (www.nytimes.com). In a similar vein, Amazon, noting that the transportation sector accounts for 28% of the U.S.' CO2 emissions (www.forbes.com), plans to invest in firms that ratchet down the heat-trapping emissions and to consume their products. However, which are the financial implications of these projects?

For some, these environmental protection projects are costly and compromise firms' financial performance. In contrast to this intuition, chief financial officers are now promoting sustainability measures in their firms to attract new investors, lower their companies' borrowing costs and cut operating expenses (www.wsj.com). As noted by Tzouvanas et al. (2020), who used a sample of 288 European manufacturing firms over a period of 11 years, firms with superior environmental performance tend to be more profitable. Furthermore, 20 companies in the S&P 500 Index mentioned the acronym ESG (Environment, Society, and Government) between October 1 and December 31, 2020, while just six firms did this three years before. From a global perspective, the term ESG was mentioned by 205 times on investors calls during the fourth quarter of 2020. Importantly also, chief financial officers at South Korean LG Electronics, Chinese utility provider CLP Holdings, and French electric equipment Schneider Electric all said that they consider sustainability metrics a priority. Overall, this evidence suggests that there is no compromise between environmental protection actions and financial performance. On the other hand, stock markets and financial stakeholders increasingly value organizational activities addressing climate change.

Management Challenges and Business Opportunities

The COVID-19 pandemic is changing a significant number of management practices and processes. Addressing these changes constitutes a *must* to ensure the long-term survival of firms. At the same time, some of these challenges bring about interesting business opportunities.

Business Models

In response to the pandemic, many firms introduce changes in their business models. For example, Coca-Cola (www.coca-colacompany.com), is using its manufacturing facilities and logistics to make and deliver medical supplies to the COVID-19 front lines. Bottling and concentrate plants engaged in this process are shifting production to make hand sanitizer for donation to hospitals, clinics, and nursing homes. Similarly, Chevron provides medical supplies to communities as well as protection and equipment to essential workers (e.g., medical workers, police, and firefighters), in addition to provide them with fuel discounts and gift cards (www.chevron.com).

Firms responding to the challenges raised by the COVID-19 pandemic also used coopetition, the intertwine of cooperation and competition, to change their business models (Crick and Crick, 2020). COVID-19 vaccines are in high demand by jurisdictions from around the world and, sometimes, supply shortages result in controversial situations such as local and national authorities competing for vaccines. To increase the supply of vaccines, pharmaceutical firms are engaging in coopetition. For example, Pfizer's manufacturing facilities cannot meet the increasing demand for its vaccine, whose effectiveness is very high as it drops symptomatic COVID-19 by 94%. On the other hand, Sanofi's project to develop a COVID-19 vaccine with GlaxoSmithKline showed an insufficient immune response in older people, delaying its launch to late 2021 (www.cnn.com). Under these circumstances, Pfizer and Sanofi, regular competitors in the pharma industry, are conducting a coopetition project, which results in Sanofi filling and packing millions of doses of Pfizer's COVID-19 vaccine. Furthermore, coopetition should also be critical to address issues experienced by firm's supply chains whose global character makes them severely affected by confinements, lockdowns and restrictions to international transportation. A substantial proportion of air freight transportation relied on passenger planes, which the pandemic has significantly reduced, especially at the international level. In turn, this increases firms' trading costs as well as impose disruptions in their supply chains. Furthermore, the pandemic has made regulators to enact major restrictions on international trade, especially for products related to sensitive industries (e.g., health care). Therefore, coopetition among firms established in different jurisdictions would ensure reliable supply chains and result in valuable partnerships.

Coopetition may also have beneficial effects for non-profit organizations. As shown by the Voluntary Sector Impact Barometer in its October 2020 report, two in five (39%) charities and community groups in the UK experience a deteriorating financial situation (www.phys.org). To address this critical situation, charities are implementing innovative projects such as accelerating their digital transformation, increasing the delivery of their online services, and engaging in coopetition. For example, in Chicago, the Homelessness and Health Response Group for Equity leads a multidisciplinary group of more than 100 members, including *inter alia* hospitals and housing advocates, to ensure quarantine and isolation for people with unsafe home environments as well as acquiring and providing self-insolate personal equipment to group settings across the city (www.cdc.gov).

The Future of Work

The outbreak of the pandemic raised issues about the workplace (e.g., physical distance). Furthermore, the confinements and lockdowns brought about significant changes in the organization of work; since March 2020, we have witnessed a widespread move to working from home. According to data gathered from 22,500 Americans over several waves, Barrero, Bloom and Davis (2021) showed that nearly half of all paid hours were provided from home between May and December 2020. Furthermore, Barrero et al. (2021) also collected data about the extent to which working from home will remain as an organizational practice and their findings are robust; homework is here to stay. Whereas just 5% of total workdays were supplied from home before the pandemic, Barrero et al. found 22% of all full workdays will be supplied from home once the pandemic ends. Additionally, they provide data on the mechanisms behind this persistent move to working from home as well as the implications of this shift. Concerning the mechanisms, they identified better-than-expected experiences for working from home, investments in physical and human capital, diminished stigma, reluctance to return to pre-pandemic activities, and innovation supporting this working shift. With respect to the implications, Barrero et al. (2021) noted that working from home does not only appeal to low/middle-level income workers but also to high-income workers. Additionally, in-remote working has other beneficial effects for employees, such as a 5–10% cost reduction in worker spending in major city centres. At the organizational level, they also identified that post-pandemic work from home would result in productivity improvements around 2.7%.

During the initial confinements in March 2020, the move to working from home featured improvisation in work organization. However, the upcoming, long-term changes in the workplace require from companies careful planning and organization (www.ft.com). Employees working from home should be provided with a good and healthy setting, which will require from firms' additional investments in technology (e.g., computers, connectivity) and work environment (e.g., ergonomic chairs). Such infrastructure constitutes a major matter of concern, as extensive working from home also has its downside; extant evidence shows that in-remote working requires managing too many details and everything is a mix (www.nytimes.com). Such multitasking has negative effects on the memory and verbal abilities of people and, hence, it requires strict planning of the work environment (e.g., avoid multitasking) to avoid parental burnout. Finally, from the standpoint of the organization of work, human resource departments should ensure that in-remote working does not bring about any kind of discrimination for employees assigned to working from home for significantly longer periods than the firm's average.

Family-Owned Firms

Gomez and Mironov (2021) gathered data from 4000 publicly listed firms, located in 167 regions in 10 European countries. They examined the extent to which markets discount the value of CEOs for shareholders. That is, do markets react to the eventual threat to shareholder value derived from the likelihood of CEOs catching the virus, falling sick and, eventually, dying? In doing this, they focused on the age of the CEOs, in the understanding that older CEOs have higher risks of being harshly affected by the COVID-19 than their younger counterparts. In this respect, Gómez and Mironov found that stock abnormal returns in March and April 2020 for firms managed by CEOs older than the median sample (59.5 years) are 6% lower vis-à-vis companies managed by younger CEOs and operating in the same region where the firm is headquartered. Consistent with decreases in the threat to CEO health and life, stock returns from firms ran by older CEOs experienced an almost symmetric rebound in May 2020, after the first virus wave receded in Europe. On the other hand, stocks from firms ran by younger CEOs experienced no change in returns. Therefore, this evidence indicates that markets discount CEO value for shareholders. Furthermore, should this be important for publicly listed firms, we suggest that a very similar pattern may apply to family-owned firms, where the leader plays a prominent role. Therefore, successions in family-owned firms represent a critical event.

As consequence of the COVID-19 pandemic, De Massis and Rondi (2020) noted that a vast cohort of senior family-business leaders have suddenly passed away or are leaving the business earlier than expected. In turn, such disruptions require families in business to consider alternatives to intra-family succession, such as external successions, business sale, or business closure. Therefore, the COVID-19 pandemic stresses such an important process in family-business as the leadership succession, especially in view of Gomez and Mironov's (2021) findings on the extent to which the markets discount CEO value for shareholders. Therefore, and as De Massis and Rondi (2020) noted, we still have much to learn about how does planned succession unfold in family-owned firms. Under what circumstances is succession planning beneficial? How does the sale or the closure of the family business in the "new normal" differ from its failure? The succession in family-owned firms constitutes a major process and some of the effects of the pandemic will likely stay after getting back to the 'new normal'.

Concluding Remarks

In this chapter, I have examined organizational responses to some of the societal and business challenges raised by the COVID-19 pandemic. Although the degradation of the natural environment is well known, the enforcement of corrective measures provides some very good opportunities for improvement. The COVID-19 crisis as well as future pandemics are related to environmental degradation and we have observed how major industries (e.g., car-makers, online shopping) commit to zero-emission in the mid-term. Furthermore, in contrast to the understanding that environmental protection policies compromise financial performance, the empirical data show that financial investors highly value organizational projects addressing climate change and that firms with superior environmental performance tend to be more profitable.

At the micro, organizational level, the health crisis has brought about significant changes in such critical aspects as business models and the organization of work. Concerning business models, we have observed how firms have used the idle capacity caused by the decreasing demand on their regular products to engage in the production and delivery of health care goods. Furthermore, many firms and non-profit organizations develop partnerships that intertwine competition and cooperation (e.g., coopetition) to satisfy the upcoming, market demands. With respect to the future of work, extant evidence shows that a substantial portion of all full working days will be supplied from home once the pandemic is over. Although this situation has significant benefits for employees (e.g., expenditures reductions in major city centres) and firms (e.g., productivity improvements), organizations should also be aware of downsides such as health and discrimination issues for employees working longer from home than the firm's average. At this micro-level, we have also examined the effects of the COVID-19 crisis on family-owned firms, which are dominant in the global economy. In particular, I examined the impact of the pandemic on the usual, intra-family successions and how financial markets discount the value of such potential transitions. Overall, this review suggests that the challenges raised by the COVID-19 crisis trigger innovative organizational responses as well as business opportunities for firms, and many of these practices and processes will stick after the end of the pandemic.

References

Links

https://www.cdc.gov/pcd/issues/2020/20_0250.htm.
https://www.chevron.com/stories/supporting-communities-during-the-covid-19-crisis.
https://edition.cnn.com/2021/01/27/europe/sanofi-vaccine-doses-intl/index.html.
https://www.coca-colacompany.com/news/coca-cola-supply-chain-pivots-to-produce-hand-sanitizer.
https://www.flightglobal.com/strategy/how-many-jobs-have-europes-airlines-cut-in-2020/141746.article.
https://www.forbes.com/sites/kensilverstein/2021/02/18/amazons-restless-nights-center-on-achieving-net-zero-by-2040/?sh=2fc333526dac.
https://www.nytimes.com/2021/01/28/business/gm-zero-emission-vehicles.html.
https://www.nytimes.com/2021/02/24/parenting/quarantine-brain-memory.html?searchResultPosition=1.
https://phys.org/news/2020-10-largest-voluntary-organisations-reveals-devastating.html.
https://www.washingtonpost.com/world/2021/02/18/texas-cold-global-climate-change/.
https://www.wsj.com/articles/esg-metrics-help-cfos-attract-new-investors-reduce-costs-11612780321.

Bibliography

Barrero, J. M., Bloom, N., & Davis, S. J. (2021). *Why Working From Home Will Stick*. University of Chicago, Becker Friedman Institute for Economics Working Paper (2020-174).

Crick, J. M., & Crick, D. (2020). Coopetition and COVID-19: Collaborative Business-to-Business Marketing Strategies in a Pandemic Crisis. *Industrial Marketing Management*, 88, 206–213.

De Massis, A., & Rondi, E. (2020). COVID-19 and the future of family business research. *Journal of Management Studies*, 57(8), 1727–1731.

De Vito, A., & Gómez, J. P. (2020). Estimating the COVID-19 Cash Crunch: Global Evidence and Policy. *Journal of Accounting and Public Policy*, 39(2), 106741.

Gates, B. (2018). Innovation for Pandemic. *New England Journal of Medicine*, 378(22), 2057–2060.

Gates, B. (2021). *How to Avoid a Climate Disaster: The Solutions We Have and the Breakthroughs We Need*. Knopf.

Gomez, J. P., & Mironov, M. (2021). COVID-19 and the Value of CEOs: The Unintended Effect of Soccer Games across European stocks. Available at SSRN 3645401.

Škare, M., Soriano, D. R., & Porada-Rochón, M. (2021). Impact of COVID-19 on the travel and tourism industry. *Technological Forecasting and Social Change*, 163.

Tzouvanas, P., Kizys, R., Chatziantoniou, I., & Sagitova, R. (2020). Environmental and Financial Performance in the European Manufacturing Sector: An Analysis of Extreme Tail Dependency. *The British Accounting Review*, 52(6), 100863.

WWF. (2020). Living Planet Report 2020—Bending the Curve of Biodiversity Loss. Available at: https://livingplanet.panda.org/.

16

Reimagine Executive Education

Jerry Wind

My basic premise is that Executive Education must change. The current approaches to Exec Ed are inappropriate for the new reality we face now and will face post-pandemic. The reinvented Exec Ed programs should challenge and ideally change what we know and do today. This chapter outlines 10 challenges that effective Exec Ed programs have to address. The guidelines to address the challenges suggest the need for reimagining our current mental models and approaches to Exec Ed. Six examples of innovative programs are briefly discussed to inspire the reader to start experimenting with these challenges. Such experiments are a must if we are to assure that our Exec Ed programs add value to the participants, their sponsors, the offering organizations and society.

Intro

Since March 2020, all universities shifted successfully to online learning. Work from home for most firms and organizations has been successful. eCommerce had replaced much of traditional retailing. Telemedicine which

---

J. Wind (✉)
The Wharton School, University of Pennsylvania, Philadelphia, PA, USA
e-mail: windj@wharton.upenn.edu

is gaining acceptance and communication via Zoom and other platforms has replaced most of traditional face to face communication and even selling. Ignoring the lessons of these transformations and just going back to our pre-pandemic models and behavior is unthinkable.

Executive Education is no exception and requires a fresh look and challenging our current approaches. This should reflect not only the lessons from the current crisis but also the implications of the long-term trends that have been accelerated significantly during the multifaceted crisis of the pandemic, the associated economic crisis and unemployment, the urgency in addressing the call for social justice, the threats of the continued climate change and more recently in the US the ideological divide.

The disruptive and uncertain environment calls for challenging and changing our mental models of education in general and of Exec Ed in particular. This requires that our focus be truly on our customers and their current and future needs (which most Exec Ed programs are not doing) and realize that almost everything we now do may have to change and that times of crisis create opportunities (see for example, my recent book *Transformation in Times of Crisis*).[1]

In challenging the current approaches of Exec Ed programs, I briefly outlined 10 needed guidelines for change:

1. Expand the target audience and consider changing the name
2. Design for lifelong learning
3. Challenge the unit of learning
4. Reimagine the objectives and content
5. Employ innovative pedagogical approaches
6. Don't take the schedule for granted
7. Create and orchestrate a community of learners
8. Leverage the technology
9. Design the needed integration with the future of work initiatives and the offering of innovative agile and diverse programs and experiences
10. Develop new business and revenue models.

---

[1] Nitin and Wind, *Transformations in Times of Crisis*, Notion Press (Nov 2020).

The Challenges for the Next Gen Exec Ed Programs

1. <u>Expand the target audience and consider changing the name.</u> How many of the people who can benefit from post graduate education which is often defined as "Executive Education" actually perceive themselves as "executives"? Should we broaden our target audience to include the close to 1/3 of the US workforce who are now part of the gig economy, as well as the leaders and managers of non-business organizations such as not-for-profits and governments? It is obvious that the graduates of all disciplines whether architecture, nursing, engineering, liberal arts, communication and any of the sciences can benefit from a postgraduate education. And especially the high school and college dropouts who could benefit from a boost to their education and the need to upgrade their skills and competencies to meet the employability requirements of the twenty-first century. If we agree with the need to expand the audience beyond "executives" we may also consider whether the name "Executive Education" is the right name and whether the offering of such programs should be limited for business schools or expanded for all disciplines.
2. <u>Design for lifelong learning.</u> Today most Exec Ed programs are designed as postgraduate programs of short duration of five days or so, with the exception of advanced management education programs, which are typically four weeks or occasionally longer and serve for many as a substitute for an MBA degree. In today's environment upgrading the skills of all workers is a must! Consider for example, the advances in science and technology and especially the enormous advances in AI and cloud computing, and the other changes brought about by the current crises such as work from home, reliance on Zoom and other communication platforms. The acceleration of other trends such as eLearning and eCommerce that are changing the nature of work. In this context Exec Ed has to be much broader and reconceived as part of lifelong education, especially with the realization that in the future the traditional undergraduate and graduate degree programs will have to change to accommodate the new reality of the need for lifelong education. This may mean that the foundation of college and even masters degrees will be shorter and will have to rely on follow up continuing lifelong education. Given that traditional universities, and especially the elite research universities, are historically slow to adopt and innovate, it offers great opportunity to innovative Exec Ed type programs which can offer not a one-time five day course, but lifelong offerings spread over years with just in time

needed educational offerings. This can also be accompanied by innovative lifetime subscription type revenue models. Given that the need for lifelong learning for all (and not only executives) is inevitable reimagining the current lifelong education offering is a must. An intriguing and most appropriate vision for this area is offered by Wilfried Vanhonacker, who sees it as "co-learning ecosystem (involving students, faculty and others) governed by an intelligent backbone that tracks the development and honing of unique capabilities and that suggests fully adopted opportunities to enhance those capabilities[2]".

3. <u>Challenge the unit of learning</u>. Most current Exec Ed programs are focused on individuals. Yet with the advances in AI, one can easily imagine a world in which each decision-maker has his or her personal digital assistant to help diagnose any problem and find the right solution. Today we see this in an increasing number of Watson applications. Consider for example the Sloan Kettering initiative in which Watson works with the physicians on diagnosing the patients and prescribing the treatments. With the advances in AI and the emergence of what Satya Nadella calls "ambient intelligence", we can expect within a few years that every decision maker will have in his or her pocket a smartphone powered by AI. Exec Ed should, therefore, be ready to accommodate these "person-machine" units of learning and changing the role of each.[3] Furthermore, since many of today's challenges require group interaction both for the design of the strategy and its implementation, innovative Exec Ed programs should be able to accommodate such a reality. This can be done either by having customized programs for teams of executives or having each executive communicate with his or her support team in real time. The rethinking of the unit of learning has significant implication to the overall design of the relationship among the individual learner, his or her team, and overall organization, the faculty and other participants. In addition, should we experiment with having Watson or other Deep Mind machines be one of the participants in our Exec Ed progress?

4. <u>Reimagine the objectives and content</u>. The objectives and content of the new lifelong education have to reflect not only the needed leadership

---

[2] Private communication.
[3] As an example, for the growing literature on Human–Machine Interaction in the Age of AI, see Paul R. Daughtery and H. James Wilson, *Human + Machine: Reimagining Work in the Age of AI*, Harvard Business Review Press (2018); and Garry Kasparov, *Deep Thinking: Where Machine Intelligence Ends and Human Creativity Begins*, PublicAffairs (2017).

and management skills required today and in the unknown and disruptive future, but also the increasing demand for ethical consideration and values and the shift from shareholder orientation to a stakeholder orientation. In addition to building the learner's creativity and critical judgement skills, it should also stress the importance of truth, science and democracy. And as we prepare for the world of ambient intelligence let's not forget the importance of including in the content of our educational programs the fundamentals of how algorithms work, how AI learns, what the capabilities and shortcomings are and what ethical considerations should we have. Most challenges facing organizations and society require bridging the internal disciplinary silos as well as linking the organization to its ecosystem and external resources. This requires the ability to orchestrate the various internal and external networks and adopting a new leadership style that highlights co-creation and "win–win" to all involved. While the focus is likely to continue to be on upgrading the needed skills and competencies to address the twenty-first century employability needs, let's not forget the value of balancing it with a broader liberal arts perspective and the enhancement of personal and organizational wellness. Some of the guiding principles in determining the objectives and content of any program are the ability to (a) customize the content and approach to the needs of the learners and their unique context, (b) continuously experiment and learn, (c) adapt and change as needed and (d) ability to scale and have meaningful impact.

5. <u>Employ innovative pedagogical approaches.</u> The traditional focus of Exec Ed on classroom-based education has to change to a hybrid model, reflecting the lessons from the adoption of eLearning during the current crises. Furthermore, in designing the pedagogical approaches of the Exec Ed programs of the future let's leverage the fact that we have fewer constraints than the ones imposed by the traditional degree programs and experiment with insights from the neuroscience of learning, gaming and gamification and other advances in learning theories and findings that advance learning science. It is well established that experiential learning is more effective than passive lecture style education. Yet most current Exec Ed programs still rely on lectures, whether in the classroom or online. With the exception of the use of simulations,[4] little attention has been given to applying the learned knowledge in the real world. Even less attention is often given to the integration of the various lectures and helping the learners design strategies for implementing the

---

[4] For an example of effective simulation, see Wharton Interactive | Game Changing Learning: https://interactive.wharton.upenn.edu/.

acquired knowledge. Given that most participants in Exec Ed programs are concurrently employed it should be relatively easy to design innovative programs that link the academic content with the participants daily activities. Imagine a world in which the successful completion of a program, and its coveted certificate, will be only after proof of successful application of the learnings in a real-world experiment. The added benefit of such an approach is enhancing the value of experimentation, which is key to success in a turbulent environment. The need for continuous experimentation is both critical for any learner and equally important to the designers of the Exec Ed programs. The design of innovative pedagogical approaches should include all aspects of learning—the content and its delivery, the level and form of personalization of the learning experience, the way of providing feedback and assessment and by whom, the context of the learning, the extracurricular activities and the design of the physical and digital architecture etc.

6. Don't take the schedule for granted. Innovative pedagogical approaches, and the constraints on the available time of the participants, suggest the need for flexible schedules. Flipped classroom design frees the "lecture" part of the program to be taken any time and any place. The group application of the material can be done in pre-scheduled times either in physical spaces (with social distancing) or virtually. Ideally flexible schedules will allow time to implement the learning in a real-world environment by experimenting and reporting back on the results of the experiment and the lessons learned. In designing future schedules, it is important to remember that current schedules have often been designed for the convenience of the scheduler and not driven by consideration of enhanced learning effectiveness.

7. Create and orchestrate a community of learners. Today most short-term Exec Ed programs are designed as a one-time event. A major benefit of any program is the interaction among the members and ideally over time interaction in which they can share what works and doesn't work and the lessons they gain from trying to implement the material they learned. Imagine future programs designed to create and sustain a community of learners with the commitment to share their experiences and the lessons from their experiments. Having such a network will generate the data on what works and doesn't work and allow for continuous meta-analysis and the development of useful empirical generalizations for the benefit of all. The challenge of course is how to motivate the learners to actively participate in and contribute to the network. And how to make it attractive to others to aspire to join. In this respect finding the right user-friendly

collaboration platform is a must[5] and equally important is the creation of incentives for participation including the inclusion of attractive anchor participants and at least one effective orchestrator. Remember that participants learn from each other as much as they learn from the faculty. In this respect much can be learned from games and gamification and the use of gaming platforms as well as from lessons from the creation and operations of effective networks. Effective community of learners would ideally include the faculty as participants in the "co-learning ecosystem" that Vanhonacker envision. This will lead to a fundamental and welcome change in the role of the faculty. It will also encourage the engagement of other stakeholders including open talent experts.

8. Leverage the technology. The recent shift of all universities to eLearning has sped up significantly the digital transformation of all providers of Exec Ed programs and of the learners. Communicating via Zoom or other platforms is as common as phone calls were before the crisis. And the use of Zoom rooms allows for more intimate group interactions. While future Exec Ed programs will reflect this change, they should be alert to the continuous advances in science and technology and incorporate them in their program design and offering. We mentioned above the likely impact of AI and gaming platforms but designers of Exec Ed program should be open to explore and experiment with new technologies such as AR/VR/XR, GPT-3 and other large language models especially as they are expanding beyond text to visuals, and advances in facial recognition and AI as used, for example, in the WOW room (at the IE Business School) to monitor the learner's engagements. The EdTech area is one of the most active technology investment areas and innovative EdTech startups are continuously seeking solutions to enhance the effectiveness of learning. See, for example, the many entries by EdTech startups to the Reimagine Education global competition and consider the findings of HolonIQ that VC investments in EdTech startups in 2019 exceeded $6 billion. In leveraging technology in the new lifelong learning programs let's consider how it can improve and change all aspects of learning, including:

(a) The learning process such as experiential simulations, games, and other ways (such as AR/VR/XR) that can engage the learner and enhance the learning

---

[5] An example for such a platform is Hive: https://hive.com/ that is used, for example, by Wharton Exec Ed to manage all aspects of the Advanced Management Program (AMP), including their Alumni network.

(b) The engine that allows personalization and continues real-time adaptability
(c) The real-time unobtrusive monitoring of learning—taking the WOW room technology to the next level
(d) The learning assessment (both by peers and by AI) and real-time feedback.

9. <u>Design the needed integration with the future of work initiatives and the offering of innovative agile and diverse programs and experiences.</u> The successful shift to digital work from home has led most organizations to question whether the old paradigm of work and workplace is still valid and start exploring new models of work. This has also led to the founding of the *Center for the Transformation of Work*. An integral part of the future of work should be the assurance of real-time educational options that offer all workers, including those working as open talent, the needed resources to upgrade their skills and competencies to performs their job from any place. HolonIQ predicts by 2030 a global skill deficit of over 85 million workers. While no one can accurately predict the needed skills 10 or even five years from now, we do know that there will be continuous demand to update our skills and to assure that we have the motivation and curiosity for continued lifelong learning. This has significant implications to the designers and providers of the lifelong learning programs of the future who have to be ready for continuous innovation and experimentation with wide range of programs and experiences. Thus, agility is key and one size fits all is dead!

10. <u>Develop new business and revenue models.</u> The above and especially the need to expand the scope of Exec Ed programs beyond the traditional market of Exec Ed and broaden the accessibility for lifelong education for all has major implications for the business and revenue models of Exec Ed. Too many universities have looked at Exec Ed as a cash cow that requires limited investment and provides small incremental income to their faculty and large income stream to them. The proliferation of free or close to free excellent educational material on any topic on Coursera, EDX, other platforms, and from an increasing number of universities (which are putting their lectures online) challenges the traditional business and revenue models of Exec Ed. Those who would like to participate and thrive in the new lifelong education market have to create new business models that accommodate the above guidelines. At the same time, they also have to reinvent their revenue models and capitalize on the growing global demand for accessible lifelong education programs. This requires reimaging new cost and revenue models for affordable lifelong

learning. It cannot be achieved by occasional cost cutting initiatives and require the creation of new mental, business and revenue models. Let's start by explorin what can we learn from innovative revenue models of innovators such as Minerva, Georgia Tech MS in computer science, the African Leadership University and Duolingo. Rethinking the business and revenue models can result not only in more affordable education but by creative use of intelligent technology one can both reduce the cost and increase the effectiveness of the learning process.

Toward Implementation

Can some of these ideas be implemented? I believe they can! And experimenting with them is a must! I encourage every reader to (a) search for innovative educational programs that incorporate these and related guidelines, (b) enjoy the process of discovery that can start with a Google search, (c) read the excellent books of Wilfried Vanhonacker[6] and Peter Lorange[7] and (d) enjoy the many innovative educational entries to the Reimagine Education competition. In addition, let's consider the following examples: the Wharton Fellows program The Slalom Fellows, the educational programs of the ICAA, the Barnes Foundation's offerings, TUMO Center for Creative Technology and the tGELF innovative, *Entrepreneurial Sports Generation Competition*.

1. The Wharton Fellows. This program for senior executives ran for 20 years on an innovative educational model. it offered a select group of senior executives three unique programs a year typically between 3–5 days in one and at times two or three locations around the world. A common theme was "The Next Big Thing" with trips to Silicon Valley, Las Vegas, Seattle, Dallas/Austin, Singapore and other locations. In each location we picked a contemporary theme and then several organizations leading the way. The Fellows selected the sessions they wanted to attend. The program content centered on visits to leading businesses and organizations and learning by interacting with the presenters who were the senior executives of the host organization. These 3–5 visits a day concluded with reflection sessions and the encouragement to identify experiments they can undertake upon their return to their organizations. While the efforts to develop a close network

---

[6] Wilfried R. Vanhonacker, *Rough Diamonds: Rethinking How We Educate Future Generations*, Houndstooth Press (2021).
[7] Peter Lorange, *The Business School of the Future*, Cambridge University Press (2019).

among the participants did not succeed due to lack of the right platform, informal groups of participants did emerge and continue interacting until today.
2. The Slalom Fellows. One of the participants in the Wharton Fellows program, Brad Jackson, the CEO of Slalom, decided to take the Wharton fellows experience to the next level as part of the Slalom value proposition focusing on continuous experimentation with innovative educational programs (but with the long-term goal of impacting not only his own executives and those of his clients but expanding it to hundreds of thousands of learners around the world). An initial effort earlier this year focused on *The Leader's Brain: Lessons from Neuroscience to Enhance your Leadership, Build Stronger Teams, Make Better Decisions, Inspire Greater Innovation, and Improve Learning and Performance*. The program was structured in four parts: (i) a preprogram introductory session and homework assignment a few weeks before the start of the program, (ii) four weekly virtual sessions of two hours each led by Prof. Michael Pratt,[8] (iii) A three-week time to apply the material learned by conducting experiments focusing on insights from neuroscience for the future of work with mentoring support by Prof. Platt and his team and (iv) a final 2½ hour virtual meeting reporting on the ten experiments conducted by the participants and reflecting on the lessons from the program. The participants—a mixture of Slalom executives and clients or prospects they invited—found the program to be very valuable and most indicated interest in joining other such programs on different topics.
3. The ICAA. The Institute of Classical Architecture and Art has a rich portfolio of continuing educational offerings for its members offered by each of the 16 chapters and central operations. Their programs range from a number of short (around 1–2 hours) member generated webinars, through 1–2 day workshops, one week intensives and four week summer studios to learning tours abroad. They run an education forum to facilitate dialogue among ICAA instructors and education leaders from their chapters and other. In addition, they offer a rich library of videos. The events are heavily attended by their members who find these lifelong educational offerings of enormous value. Many of their webinars are open to non-members and in addition they offer programs for middle school students to develop an appreciation of the practice of classical architecture—an amazing range of valuable programs that assure that their members are up to date in their knowledge and practices.

---

[8] Michael L. Platt, James S. Riepe University Professor, University of Pennsylvania, the author of *The Leader's Brain*, Wharton School Press (2020).

4. The Barnes Foundation offers a wide range of educational offerings for members and the public. These include private (virtual and in-person) tours of the collection, endless number of digital programs ranging from an hour to a series of three one-hour sessions spread over three weeks, to certificate programs. During the pandemic they added daily *Barnes Takeout*—art talks by their curators each focusing on the story of a painting, a sculpture, or an art object. While not a conventional Exec Ed program, the rich set of offerings with a global reach provide a great example of an organization focused on engaging their current and new audiences by offering meaningful lifelong education (in this case for art lovers and those who seek inspiration from art to enhance their way of seeing and creativity).
5. TUMO Center for Creative Technologies. The Armenian learning centers which expanded to Paris, Moscow, Beirut and other cities is based on a creative learning programs for teens. The programs are composed of self-learning activities (supported by coaches who advise and provide encouragement), workshops (that range from beginners to advanced) and project labs (with technology and design professional from around the world who run the project labs, which last from a couple of weeks to several months). All workshops and labs are around 14 learning targets, such as animation, game development, web development, 3D modeling, robotics, motion graphics, programming, new media and related fields. At the core of the TUMO programs are individualized continuously evolving learning plans, managed by an intelligent system with no faculty involved. As teens progress through the program completing projects, they build up a portfolio of their work that becomes their living diploma. This innovative and most successful model can easily be adopted to the new Exec Ed area.
6. tGELF: The Global Education and Leadership Foundation was founded by Shiv Khemka to cultivate ethical, altruistic leadership aimed at improving the overall standards of the world. While their achievements are remarkable, connecting over million students, to increase their impact Shiv launched the *Entrepreneurial Sports Generation* using sport metaphor to recruit ethical entrepreneurs from around the world to solve the critical challenges of the world. The sports inspired model organizes local, regional, national and global competition among entrepreneurs. In its first year they recruited over 300,000 entrepreneurs who received over $300 million in prize money. Shiv's plans are even more ambitious, and he is aiming this year for a million entrepreneurs and billion dollars in prize money. This model using large-scale competition is a creative way

of stimulating creative solutions to the world most pressing challenges. The preparation of the entries for the competition, the feedback from the judges and the interaction among the competitors are effective ways of educating the participants. While not a typical Exec Ed program its innovative approach achieves the intended results.

Conclusions

Given the dramatic changes since March of 2020 and the unprecedented acceleration of the forces of change, Executive Education programs have to change. In this paper I proposed 10 guidelines for change and encourage the reader to search for examples and innovative practices that capture the spirit of my guidelines and start experimenting with any combination of these suggestions. I also offered six innovative examples of lifelong education initiatives that would ideally inspire the reader to be bold and experiment with truly innovative approaches for the benefit of the learners, their sponsors, the offering organization and society. As part of these changes, I hope you would consider changing the name of your program from Executive Education to a name that suggests continuous lifelong learning for all audiences. But most importantly, have the courage to change your current mental models of and approach to Exec Ed and innovate. Can you design and launch a breakthrough, lifelong Exec Ed program that changes the paradigm as Minerva did for college education[9]?

Websites

https://www.ie.edu/madeofchange/
https://www.reimagine-education.com/
https://www.holoniq.com/
https://transformationofwork.org/
https://www.cc.gatech.edu/future/masters/mscs
https://www.alueducation.com/
https://www.duolingo.com/
https://www.reimagine-education.com/
https://www.slalom.com/home
https://www.classicist.org/

---

[9] For the amazing Minerva story, see Ben Nelson, *Building the Intentional University: Minerva and the Future of Higher Education*, MIT Press (2017) and https://www.minerva.kgi.edu/.

https://www.barnesfoundation.org/
https://tumo.org/
http://www.tgelf.org/
https://www.minerva.kgi.edu/

17

Bridging Academia and Business: Mazars

Laurent Choain

Laurent Choain is an unusual person, who thinks and behaves differently and possesses a personal charm that appeals to all kinds of people. Under his name on his LinkedIn profile is "titles are free of charge." For the past 10 years he has led talent, education and culture at Mazars,[1] a global audit and corporate services company, where he has co-led CEO transitions and held various roles, as well as transforming its corporate university. In addition, Choain serves on several boards, and seats on the Peter Drucker Society.[2]

Over the course of our conversation, Choain covers many areas, notably his views on management and executive development: I began by asking him about Mazars' focus on Generation Y.

---

[1] Mazars is a global audit, accounting and consulting company, with strong European roots, headquartered in France, with over 26,000 employees and €1.9 billion revenues generated in 2019.
[2] https://www.druckerforum.org/about-layout/.

Interview held between Laurent Choain and Santiago Iñiguez on January 20, 2021.

L. Choain (✉)
Chief Leadership, Education and Culture at Mazars, Paris, France
e-mail: laurent.choain@mazars.fr

Focusing on the Young Generations

Allow me to begin by sharing with you a piece of advice from my wife, a psychologist, which undoubtedly influenced my decision to join Mazars. While I was deciding which sector to go into, she reminded me that my circle of friends was composed of people in their 60s, if not in their 70s, and soon to retire; her advice was to reconnect to my generation, not to the previous generation. I decided to go a step further and connect to the next generations.

When I joined Mazars in 2010 I focused on what we call Generation Y, then a promising young generation. I started to see Mazars as an employer of young people and orientated my HR strategy in this direction. I was given a free hand to organize things and to develop my vision of what Mazars should be.

To me it was very clear that the issue was not about retaining talent, it was about the employability of people, and I was only interested in the flow of our people, who anyway were not expected to stay. Let's be honest, this is the industry anyhow: 95% of people do not stay in the audit or consulting business. So, if what matters is employability, then we should align our HR policies, our employer branding, our recruitment campaigns, our management style, which we did. Mazars is a challenger in its sector, which means that the best way to differentiate is as an organization. In other words, what matters is not what you do, it's who you are.

The fact is our strategy of employing Generation Y people made us pioneers. We are prototyping what other companies will do, which is how I developed this vision of what Generation Y should be. Instead of telling them what they should be, I listened to them about what we should be. Basically, the vision was that of a disrupter, if you want. When I did so, nobody was interested in Generation Y, but now everybody's focused on the youngest generations.

So, some people would say, oh, you're so visionary because you're anticipating moves and so on. The thing is that as soon as something becomes conventional, I will switch to something else, because again, we are challengers. We need to be at the forefront of thinking and practice in my field. We need to focus on two things. One is linked to the overall environment of companies. The other is linked to the evolution of management techniques.

Two decades ago, CSR was basically greenwashing. Then it became less fashionable and suddenly again, it has become not only very fashionable, but is now a must for these giant, mission-led corporations.

Then, the question we raised ourselves was: What is Mazars' CSR? And then I could immediately see that everybody was focusing on the same things, such as their carbon footprint which, in my view, is not the ideal way to proceed.

Elaborating on Mazars' DNA

I Took advantage of the new strategic review to start thinking of it from a more people-centric standpoint. Because if you ask me what is the purpose of Mazars, I was not going to expand off-the-shelf concepts about carbon footprint. I asked if the world be better with or without Mazars, why is the world better because Mazars exists, or would the world be a worse place if Mazars weren't around?

First element of social responsibility: we have to remember that our job is not only, primarily to serve clients. It is about securing and bettering financial markets and more globally the economic and business ecosystem, which not only apply to our audit line of work but to our consulting services as well.

At the same time, we have to remember that other professional service firms have disappeared for not respecting this founding value. Why is audit and accounting now on the high wire? Our profession, which is meant to serve not the clients and the shareholders, but actually the market and the people, is under scrutiny, if not in danger.

Why are we in danger today? Because there are too few players in this market, to be honest. And this is the second differentiating and purposeful constituency of our social responsibility. The concentration is too high, with only four major, dominant players in a complex and increasingly regulated field, and four other second-tier players with a global reach. This situation leads to potential conflicts of interest as the market is too huge to serve. In our industry, seven in the eight leading players are organized exactly the same, with Anglo-Saxon-dominated governance, if not American governance and organized as networks, not as one firm like McKinsey would be, for example. In short, we need to remain different. We need to stay the element of diversity in a too look-alike world.

Last component of our purpose, most of our thousands of recruits are fresh grads, which is not something that many organizations can claim. We are the first employers of these young people, and we are the first to confront them with what work means. We familiarize them with the discipline of work, with the ethics behind it and how they are going to have a relationship with work for the rest of their professional lives.

So, we have a big, initial responsibility, which is to educate these young people about work, we have to instill a work *habitus*, as we would say in sociology. But it's not enough, because at the same time, we know that 90% of these young people will stay with us for between three and ten years. They will then leave us, not for our competitors, but to populate the executive and managerial ranks of all kinds of companies in all kinds of industries. It means that not only do we have to turn them into brilliant professionals, but moreover we also need to expose them to the right kind of modern management models and practice, otherwise, they integrate in their cognitive patterns old-fashioned ways of managing people, and this trickles down to the entire economy for generations.

That's a responsibility that is less obvious, because we tend to focus the technicaltraining of these people on their job. But I believe that we need also to educate them for the world of work beyond our company, and that what is going to make a positive difference is their constructive scepticism and distinctive personal conduct. Of course, we will need good managers and ultimately partners who will stay with us, between 2 and 5%, maybe, maximum, of the people who come to work for us. But we should educate the 95% of people that are going to leave us to manage in the best possible way wherever they will be afterward.

What Is Good Management?

In short, the whole thing is about saving capitalism through promoting better management. I will stick to what Roger Martin and Fred Kofman[3] have described better than me. Martin explains the danger of managers who aim to optimize the price of the stock rather than the performance of the company with an analogy of football players betting on their own games. If the players focus on winning the game, all of their incentives align with excellent performance. However, if they are rewarded based on the betting pool, they begin to worry about managing the odds.

About 20 years ago, a growing number of people started to point out that this model was doing a lot of harm. So, from I would say 2010, let's say more or less from the Drucker Forum, some voices started to question the overall thinking in management, arguing that the shareholder value concept did more harm than good, and that we need to reinvent management.

---

[3] R. Martin, *When More Is Not Better: Overcoming America's Obsession with Economic Efficiency* (Cambridge, MA: Harvard Business Review Press, 2021).

It's the Gary Hamel thing: Hamel contends that if management does not reinvent itself by using these ideas, companies cannot survive.[4] If we are to move to a different management paradigm, two key issues will need to be addressed. First, the measurement of management performance. Secondly, the design of incentives. As long as performance is measured as short-term shareholder wealth maximization and management incentives are linked to this objective, there isn't much hope for change.

The goal that Hamel puts at the very top of his list is that management should serve a higher purpose than shareholder wealth maximization. Similarly, Peter Drucker says the only alternative to bad management is tyranny. If we want to have democratic societies, we need to pay attention to the quality of intermediary management. To put it simply, what we would have called modern management over the past 10–15 years means actually taking a more collaborative, open way of managing people and paying more attention to people, being more people-centric.

Let me phrase it differently, turning to coaching rather than command and control. You have all these people with emotional intelligence and all of these people that were moving toward this new approach. Then came COVID. Looking at the question of management in terms of Kondratieff and Juglar cycles,[5] there has been a larger cycle toward a more human-centric management based on a coaching approach. But now COVID has forced us to rethink many aspects in a much more transactional way of practising management—on distance. In the late vision, the role of the manager was to secure the transaction between capital and the workforce. It was a very transactional and hence a very efficient way of addressing management. Peter Drucker's MBO [Management by Objectives] approach measures the performance of employees as compared to typical standards for the job. But when coining the concept of knowledge workers, Drucker later stated that if employees help determine those standards, they will be more likely to fulfill them. In other words, you cannot direct the knowledge worker's productivity as it proved successful in the second half of the twentieth century with workers and clerks.

We thought that transactional management was history, but then came COVID. And suddenly, instead of having people around you, instead of wasting time at the coffee machine and socialize, we had this curious situation whereby we all had to adapt to working through screens. People who used to be managers in physical places and with some kind of human and permanent interaction, suddenly were having to operate via a screen. And

---

[4] G. Hamel and M. Zanini, *Humanocracy: Creating Organizations as Amazing as the People Inside* (Cambridge, MA: Harvard Business Review Press, 2020).
[5] https://www.kondratieff.net/kondratieffcycles.

how do you work when you work with a screen like this? You start on time, you finish on time, you tend to stick to the content. You tend not to waste time chatting with your colleagues at the coffee machine and so on. The social relationship becomes more distant. This means that at the end of the day, because of COVID, and even though we weren't aware of it, suddenly we had given up all this relation-based management to go back to transaction-based management.

Overnight, I think that COVID has revived something that in my view was dead, which was this transactional approach to management and suddenly it has popped back up again.

At the same time, the question of the productivity of knowledge workers has become more about organizing this and trying to go for more transactions between humans, which has meant that the workplace is not so important because there is no social interaction. So why should I go to the office? The day I return to the office, I will have seen my manager in a not particularly flattering light. And my level of belief in what a company is will have diminished.

I think we're living through a moment where we've lost an enormous amount of belief in relationship management, even if everybody says we will need to reconnect to it. And this will not be easy because the overall cycle remains the same: modernizing management. But modern management, in my view, is really about relationship management, not about transactional management, but that's not where we are today.

So, when I speak about a modern vision and a modern approach to management for Mazars and maybe the wider profession, and maybe beyond that, the idea is to reconnect with an overall purpose we thought was the right one, which was to go for a more relationship-based approach or even the manager-coach. At the same time, there are many antagonistic forces at work. So, in my view, in the next four to five years, and especially after COVID, we will have to strengthen this vision we had of modern management. And this will raise issues about the workplace. This will question the nature of management. This is something on which I'm going to focus very much in the next five years.

How to Encourage Younger Generations to Engage with Their Company

In 2013, we extensively researched Generation Y, and by 2018 we were looking at Generation Z, asking more or less the same set of 62 questions. That's an extensive questionnaire, and across 92 countries. If you look at the issue from a management angle, first of all, Generation Y is bigger than Generation Z in many countries. Baby boomers and Ys make up 28% each of the population in most western economies, while X and Z are 17%, respectively.

If you ask the Ys if they want to be a manager, most open studies show they don't want to be managed, and they don't want to be managers. We looked into this more closely, and we came to the conclusion that not only do they want to be a manager, but they are in a hurry. Some 83% of the people who were not yet in a position of management said they wanted to be a manager. They were also asked why they wanted to join a company? The answer for the Ys is: change the companies.

Zs don't want to be managers. Why do they join companies? Well, a company is just a stopover and it has to provide some fun and some education, but in three to four years they will move on.

In short, there seems to be a very large Generation Y who clearly wants to run the show, doesn't want to be told what to do and isn't interested in the older generation's values and guidance. They want the freedom to invent their own codes. But the younger generation, which, by the way, is less numerous, says they don't want to take the burden of the lead, and just want to consume and enjoy the company they work partly and shortly for.

In other words, for the next 15 years, the Ys will lead the Zs, and the road won't be paved with roses. How are we going to prepare the Ys to lead the Zs? And how can we make sure it's not a total disaster? Don't worry about it and keep out, would the Yers say.

Nobody seems interested in the fact that Gen Y is now entering into its forties, and are taking over senior management roles, while the Zs aren't and couldn't care less about it so far.

In 2018, we conducted a survey of 7000 Ys from 64 different nationalities. Mazars is a multidisciplinary and multicultural group. We are now present in 92 countries and diversity is an extremely variable reality. We recruit more than 5000 young people worldwide each year, therefore, Mazars is young by nature. Understanding the motivations of this generation is essential for us.

Subsequently, we are a company that provides services, with collective intelligence being the founding principle and it is necessary to be knowledgeable about the expectations of this generation.

When asked about their life goals, 28.5% of Ys give priority to the balance between their private and professional life and 27.3% want to live life to the fullest. But at Mazars, what they first want is fun, learn and feedback. Ys believe that human qualities (57.5%), the capacity to learn throughout life (55%) and ambition (51%) are the keys to professional success. This is followed by networking (46.4%) and technical skills (45.9%). According to 77% of young people asked, gender equality is a major challenge for companies: a challenge which was particularly significant for the women who participated, as 83.3% think that it is necessary for companies to work on the subject, men are also not far behind with a positive response of 66.4%. However, to the question: do you think Mazars will give you an equal and fair chance to advance in your career? up to 98% of the members of our worldwide talent pool would answer positively.

Before we carried out the survey, we were absolutely convinced that we would have totally different answers, depending on the country. And that was really a big surprise. One of the things the Generation Y survey shows is that in the modern world, I have more commonalities, for instance, with my colleague in South Africa than I have with my own son. For example, if I talk about Colombo, the detective, to my colleagues in South Africa they know who I mean. But my son, who is Generation Z, doesn't have a clue, or at best thinks it's the capital of Sri Lanka.

In other words, my generation and Generation Z don't share the same subculture. The second characteristic that emerged is that for my generation, our subculture is very national. For instance, you have plenty of heroes in Spain that we don't know in France, and vice versa. Today, subcultures are totally globalized, transnational. Generation Z's heroes are from Game of Thrones, or any other global television series.

Can We Change the Attitudes of Generation Z?

Generation Z gives the impression that they are here to consume and not to lead. That's partly because they are conventional, and they are not willing to take over responsibility for the sake of taking over responsibility. They do it when they have to. At the same time, they are resilient, they learn quickly. But fundamentally, we don't see them taking a proactive role. They are largely passive, they are consumers, not transformers.

When we created Mazars University back in 2008, we had one simple question in mind that proves useful with them now: why stop learning once you graduate? In a talent-intensive industry, we very much rely on the quality of our people. Education at all stages of the professional journey is what increasingly makes the difference.

We didn't set up a Mazars University to become a school of excellence. We want Mazars as a whole to become a school of excellence. The project I'm launching here is about building, first of all, a worldwide platform where education goes along with career progression. And of course, the question becomes, who is going to be the faculty? And so, we are not going to outsource it. We are going to totally insource it. In turning our partners, or let's say a significant part of them, into faculty.

Which means that the question becomes, first of all, what is the job of this faculty? And there is a misunderstanding here because many people think that the job of the faculty is simply to deliver courses. This is maybe 10% of the job. The job consists, first of all, of learning, searching, designing, curating, administrating exams and so on. This is part of our stewardship, which is passing the company to the next generation in a better shape. So, then the know-how for us as a university becomes being able to turn people into full-fledged faculty.

What Makes a Great CEO?

The biggest challenge for a CEO is being an inclusive leader. I have coached so many CEOs and executives over the years, and what I've concluded is, like Marshall Goldsmith said,[6] *what got you here won't get you there*. These people want to be recognized as leaders, they need to make decisions and they need to win. As a result, they are always torn between the need to show that they are the right individual for the job and at the same time can delegate, but when I talk about an inclusive approach to leading, I don't just mean delegating, I mean trusting people to say "I know less than you, so you make the decision." If we stick to Peter Drucker's definition of a knowledge worker, it's someone who knows better than the boss in their field of competence. Everybody says that Steve Jobs said this, but I have written proof that Robert Mazars said in 1971: "if you hire smart people, it's not in order to tell them what to do, it's to ask them what to do."

---

[6] M. Goldsmith, What got you here won't get you there (Lonodn: Profile Books, 2009).

The difficulty leaders in the future will face is that first of all, people will not believe in the spirit of the firm. This entrepreneurial shared spirit between people who effectively own the company and the executives who are just the workforce, except they are paid more and we make them believe that they are the company and the company is theirs. We're seeing the end of this. We cannot postulate that the initial reflex of people will be to believe in the firm, to believe in the company spirit. This, in my view, will disappear. This means that the role of the leader will be to find ways to align individual commitment with collective commitment, so that everyone has a sense of purpose. And if they are not able to do so, if they just think that it is a given, like this is the case today, then they will end up in trouble.

18

Executive Education in Southeast Asia: Asian Institute of Management

Jikyeong Kang

Located in Manila, the Asian Institute of Management was founded in 1968 by Harvard Business School Advisory Board with two local universities, gaining rapid momentum as a reference for executive education in Southeast Asia at a time when there were few international business schools in this continent.

Jikyeong Kang has chaired and served on the boards of different international networks and companies and held professorship positions at leading business schools in Europe and Asia. Her cosmopolitan experience and background provide her with a privileged perspective to talk about the future of business education. The following questionnaire was completed in May 2021.

1. *How has the pandemic affected the activity at AIM?*

The Institute has been on lockdown since March 2020, and our faculty and staff have been working from home, and all our courses, including non-degree short courses have been delivered online via Zoom platform. Some support staff, such as ICT, Finance, HR, etc., go to the Institute as needed and spend a few hours at a time in office. We have maintained what I call

---

J. Kang (✉)
Asian Institute of Management, Makati, Philippines
e-mail: JKang@AIM.EDU

"MOODs" very well—Minimally Operational Offices and Dorms. Social distancing, face covering, and more recently face shields and allied practices are strictly enforced. We also have made emergency and routine medical help available on campus, and there is a nurse and a doctor on duty. We have not had any casualties for the first 12 months, but during the last months, we lost two students to Covid.

Faculty have pivoted exceptionally well. All teaching migrated fast to Zoom with one week transition time. Faculty have customized and curated content for online delivery. We have heavily adapted Blackboard. We ran different kinds of workshops and tutorials for online teaching since AIM did not have any online programs before the pandemic by inviting experts. Given the circumstances we are in, the experience has been good and definitely much better than what we initially expected.

During the last year, we have completely and permanently changed our structure and pedagogy for the prestigious Master in Development Program, to a blended program with synchronous and asynchronous sessions, mixed with lots of other learning aides. Student reviews and satisfaction so far have been encouraging and inspiring.

One program has decided to make a permanent shift to a hybrid model (some in the classroom and some joining via online connection) even when the lockdown is over. Two other programs are in the process of shifting to a blended learning model.

Unlike degree programs, it took two months of transition time for us to start offering non-degree programs on Zoom platforms due to client's hesitation/reluctance. However, we have had more positive outcomes (including revenue) than we have ever imagined. Roughly eight out of ten custom programs clients have eventually agreed to push through with online delivery of what was originally contracted as face-to-face programs.

All in all, the pandemic has created a lot of unexpected challenges but it also has given a big push to our much needed adoption of online/blended learning approaches.

We have done well so far. We certainly could have done better.

2. *What are, in your opinion, the main challenges for business schools after the pandemic?*

COVID19 has delivered a nasty shock to the academe, with institutions of learning around the world going through disruptions, affecting the plans of millions of students. Business schools are suffering along with the rest, but the pandemic has occurred when we are already facing a host of problems. A survey of the deans of American business schools found that almost all thought that the pandemic would lead to permanent closures of many schools. Fortunately, that has not happened. In other words, there are certain things the business schools did well and did strategically. Christoph Loch (Dean, Judge Business School, Cambridge) rightly put, "If we do this right, if we do this strategically, this is going to stay beyond Covid." He is right. We have pivoted and delivered in ways the circumstances demanded. This has been a strategic shift. I would not like to consider this a temporary shift. The cost, time, efforts, and adaptations we implemented and practiced for the past one year cannot go waste. So we cannot and will not go back to a business school system where in-person exchanges are not combined with online and technology-oriented teaching and learning. Maintaining this to our strategic advantage is the greatest challenge we will face.

The second challenge we will face is something we have already been facing, but the pandemic has accentuated it. That is of getting the "value versus fee" equation right for the students. Given that many of our flagship teaching activity is going to be blended, we should get the value proposition right. Schools of prestige, which have charged enormous fees for the "in-person, campus experience in a plush, *'branded'* campus," will have to figure out ways of justifying the cost for online or blended equivalents.

We will also have to tackle Working-From-Home (WFH) policies. I know many of my colleagues around the world has changed their views almost 180 degrees and now think it is very possible to operate with flexible schedules and WFH policies, because the pandemic forced us to experience these. If we don't proactively and strategically tackle this subject, we may have to prepare ourselves to lose a lot of our faculty and staff.

Apart from these, business schools will face challenges arising from decreased revenue, dwindling student enrollments, employability opportunities.

Coming to think of these, none of these challenges are exclusive to the situation the pandemic created. We have been going through and tackling these for quite some years now, with varying degrees of success. These have grown exponential because of the pandemic.

The greatest of all challenges is that of our business models—what business models will sustain and what will not, is a critical issue we have to tackle. How do schools maintain balance in this environment is going to be a great challenge for all of us.

3. ***Do you believe that courses leading to certificates, badges, stackable degrees, or related recognitions may progressively replace formal degrees in the future?***

We are living in an era of micro-credentials. While experts in the field have different interpretations, many agree that the concept has emerged in response to the skills gap triggered by new technologies. Or triggered by the cost-value mismatch of degree programs. Essentially, micro-credentials are bite-sized chunks of training, whether an online course, bootcamp certificate, or apprenticeship from a traditional university, specialty provider or online learning platform. I do not see these micro-credentials entirely replacing formal degree programs or diplomas offered by traditional educational institutions. Instead, I see them as an interesting, a "must-have," and an essential disruptive force. But over time, I believe they will be gaining more and more prominence.

Many of our students will (even as they are enrolled in our schools) pick up skills and certifications by enrolling in such stackable programs. So, we will have an MBA student who studies in a top-ranking business school, who also in parallel enrolls in a bunch (up to six in the current circumstances) of ala carte programs and stack them. These could be on highly technical themes, emerging new-age topics, coding bootcamps, or even divergent topics. Collectively, the "stack of micro-credentials" will be a good supplement to the degree s/he is about to earn from the business school.

Some micro-credentials might have been developed to fill the gaps universities cannot, and in turn might be perceived in relevant sectors as good alternatives to traditional degrees. But according to research by Sean Gallagher and team (Northeastern University, 2018) that does not mean university degrees do not have significant value. For now, I will not think that these stackable credentials will replace a degree earned from an institution of eminence.

4. ***The pandemic has accelerated the adoption of hybrid formats at all educational institutions, including those reactive towards technology or more traditional. Which elements of this hybridization will remain after the pandemic?***

The education sector has changed, and there is no going back. A new global survey by the World Economic Forum reveals that seven out of ten adults worldwide (72%) think that, in five years, higher education will be done online at least as much as on-site. Specifically, almost a quarter of adults worldwide (23%) believe that in five years, higher education in their country will be carried out entirely or mostly online. The other half (49%) believe it will take place both online and on-site.

The survey's results reflect that some things will not probably be the same again. Priorities will change: while a year ago the main challenge was to guarantee the continuity of learning processes through different "non-classroom" methodologies, today there is the additional challenge of implementing a hybrid model that includes a combination of face-to-face and non-face-to-face learning (*eLearning*) schemes.

It is very important to think about students of all types and ages, as we will all be *lifelong learners*. From the universities' point of view, the fact of being able to attract students who can follow their classes from anywhere in the world can be a real revolution. I think a "BLENDED, REACTIVE TO TECHNOLOGY MODEL" will stay. The future of learning will be a blended learning ecosystem, infused with technology in a classroom (virtual or physical) made possible by AI and immersive technologies.

The implications are far reaching. How to meet students' expectations for perfect digital experience? How to compete in the digital space? How to move from a face-to-face student model to a new digital context? Not to mention the classroom's digitalization, the digital transformation of educational content, assessment processes, etc.

5. *What will be in your opinion the next major contributions of technology to education?*

In a recent talk I gave, I conjured up a story, which I will try to recall here:

> *It is a fine morning in September 2025. Freshman John arrived on campus quite early. He had received a text message on his phone, along with a push notification on the University app — it said, "Hello, Welcome." The message contained a map that guided him to the registration point. Ten minutes later, John completed the facial ID registration and admission process, and he officially became a freshman.*

> *In the days that followed, John's smartphone acted as his personal guide to the university. His smartphone sent him a map guiding him to his dormitory and, when he got in, he immediately received a personalized message welcoming him. When he went out for lunch, he saw a push notification containing information about the surrounding canteens and restaurants. As he wandered around the campus in the afternoon, he received a message providing information about nearby historical buildings, and listing activities that he might be interested in.*

"I had just joined, but I felt like I was meeting an old friend," John said, all thrilled. "Everything you want to know about the university, you can find on the mobile app."

Classes began very soon.

John is an early bird. He would arrive in the classroom building quite early. Walking past the cafeteria on his way to class, he receives the day's menu on an app – he pre-orders lunch via the app.

He would approach the classroom building – the RFID chip in his ID would recognize him and unlock the automated doors. As he enters and settles down in his seat, the climate control kicks on and adjusts the temperature at 75 F. His classmates start arriving.

The professor walks in, shares slides instantly with the class via WiFi. He runs his session – he uses AI controls, bots, and a smart board.

Done with the session, John picks his hot lunch that was waiting for him at the cafeteria counter.

This story was about the arrival of "SMART UNIVERSITIES." This is going to be a reality very soon. Apart from what the story tells, I have the following to speculate:

Student Recruitment Technologies: The campus visit is a rite of passage for many college students, both at the undergraduate and graduate level. However, these tours can be costly and time-consuming—especially for international students. In an effort to remove this barrier, more universities are turning to virtual reality (VR) tours to attract tuition-paying international students.

Classroom Simulations and Gamification: The potential of VR for higher education is enormous. It has applications when incorporated into the curricula. VR has the ability to create a learning environment in which students can obtain authentic, but low-stakes, hands-on experience. Schools like MIT Sloan are already using VR role-playing games to enhance student learning and engagement.

5G: As the fifth generation of wireless technology, 5G offers many advantages—more powerful networks, faster downloads, and dramatically accelerated transfer of information. These have enormous benefits to classroom learning. A 5G-enabled classroom can perhaps include a holographic teacher who can beam in to lead discussions on specialized topics; seamless virtual reality experiences that can help students better engage; or connected devices that could help close gaps in education for international students.

6. ***What areas of the learning process may be more affected by AI—artificial intelligence and AR—augmented reality in the future?***

This question is intimately connected to the previous.

Virtual reality (VR), Augmented Reality (AR), and Artificial Intelligence (AI) have the potential to reinvent education in the future classroom from a culture of teaching to "learning through experiences." AI, VR, and AR will enhance the learning experience.

These programs can also help learners work on soft skills. At Penn State University, researchers have built an immersive augmented reality program called "FIRST CLASS" in which future teachers can engage with simulated students in a virtual classroom setting. And—just like real students—they may get bored or act out, providing teachers the opportunity to practice handling difficult or novel situations.

By working together, VR, AR, and AI can produce content for whole curriculums and lesson plans—the AI aspect would account for the technical, nuts, and bolts while the VR and AR aspect would formulate the virtual experiences and simulations. The costs of VR / AR headsets powered by mobile phones and compatible computers have been declining—offering a more affordable adoption of VR technology in the classroom. The simulations provided by VR, AR, and AI make it easier and more accessible to engage in hands-on learning without the hassle of expensive costs or getting resources.

AI can be used for easing out the logistics—to help create courses, assemble readings, and automate quiz and test production.

7. ***How do you envision the impact of online education and hybrid formats in executive education and corporate learning?***

Blended learning is currently transforming the delivery of executive programs through the innovative use of technology. Corporate learning officers have begun to use online learning more regularly in leadership development programs. As a result, blended programs are now common in most corporate academies.

Online learning was once promoted as a more accessible yet lesser version of its in-person counterpart. Since then, educators have realized that digital offerings can bring unique value to education. More than just a measure of convenience or a supplement to the "real" course, it is an innovation that can renew engagement and motivation for the educational experience in today's technology-driven society.

Blended learning can be the merging of face-to-face teaching and e-learning in a way that maximizes the strengths of both formats. In an executive program, the online portion can be interspersed with in-person modules where participants and instructors meet and collaborate. It allows the program to be spread out over a longer time frame, allowing for more in-depth personal reflection and analysis. Participants do independent work as well as participate in live chats and webinars, give and receive feedback, exchange ideas and share experiences directly related to their daily work. It is the perfect combination of self-guided learning and group participation.

8. *How will all the above changes affect the accreditation of business schools?*

I think the current "light touch" treatment of mode of delivery, executive education, badges/certificates/stackable credentials, etc. will have to be looked at more closely. As The topic of how we maintain the quality of education using non-traditional delivery methods, platforms, etc., while keeping our curriculum relevant will become important.

Compared to our non-traditional competitors, such as corporate universities, EdTech companies, we business schools and our professional associations have a long tradition of certifying knowledge and learning. But, we will have to be more inclusive and clearer about what is included in the accreditation of business schools and which elements of a business schools is being accredited.

9. *What is your major dream for the future of AIM?*

Asian Institute of Management was founded in 1968 by a group of visionaries with support from Harvard Business School Advisory Board. The Institute has had a great legacy, it has had a strong brand value. The school is committed to Management and Leadership development. We are an Asia-focused school, committed to creating and disseminating contextualized knowledge. For that the Institute continues to produce original content and knowledge.

My dream for AIM would be to further develop this Asia Leadership and Asia Knowledge Focus and acquire preeminence, even as we compete robustly on conventional metrics with new-age schools elsewhere in the continent, especially in Singapore, China, Hong Kong, and India. It is my wish that AIM is among the top ten schools in the consideration set of potential graduate students who are interested in learning more about how businesses are done in Asia. I also nurture the dream that AIM emerges an academic powerhouse in Asia in Data Science, Artificial Intelligence, and Innovative Technology, by connecting these new age disciplines to Management and Business. More importantly, we have always held on to our conviction and commitment to Sustainable Management Practices, and I would like the Institute to be reckoned worldwide for its knowledge and expertise on sustainable management.

10. *How would you define the role of the CEO of the future?*

The most inspiring CEO of the future will be one who can change the present and recast the future. The CEO should not be merely a Corporate Leader; s/he must be a Social Leader. Such a CEO is the one who will place purposeful and societal leadership center-stage, so as to build strong and sustainable businesses. Such CEOs will find themselves in the role of meaning makers and geopolitical influencers advocating for conditions that allow their businesses, employees, customers, stakeholders, and above all, the larger society, to thrive long term. Also, my role-model CEO will demonstrate inquisitiveness, agility, and an insatiable appetite for learning like nobody did, even as staying grounded in humanity and values.

19

Learning to Learn: PWC

Blair Sheppard

Blair Sheppard has become a leading reference in the world of executive education over the last three decades. Prior to becoming Dean of Fuqua Business School, he founded Duke Corporate Education, which is among the organizations that best embodies the customized education model for companies, anticipating blended learning by combining online and face-to-face modules. With a distinctive vision for talent and leadership development in companies, for the last nine years Sheppard has driven PWC's global strategies and leadership development.

In his latest book, Ten Years to Midnight: Four Urgent Global Crises and Their Strategic Solutions, *published in 2020, Sheppard addresses what he sees as the four crises facing contemporary society, which he summarizes with the acronym ADAPT. A crisis of social Asymmetry reflected in the erosion of the middle classes and income disparity: Disruption caused by technology; an Ageing population impacting on companies, institutions and the economy; Polarization*

Interview held between Blair Sheppard and Santiago Iñiguez on March 1, 2021.

B. Sheppard (✉)
Global Leader Strategy and Leadership for the PWC Network, London, UK
e-mail: blair.h.sheppard@pwc.com

of the world, manifested in the breakdown of global consensus, the rise of nationalism and populism; and a crisis of Trust, with widespread skepticism about the basic institutions of our society [1].

The Main Challenges Facing Big Corporations

The biggest issue for large professional service firms is keeping up with changing requirements at the technical, operational and leadership level: delivering services is completely different now than it was three years ago and will continue to change. This means they will have to work with much bigger and more diverse teams, and requiring a new set of competencies and involves managing a completely different set of people.

On the technical side, there is the question of the dynamics of what's required. For example, if you are a supply chain expert, you now have to understand where climate change comes into the supply chain. And then you have to understand which platforms are part of the supply chain, which changes the dynamic. Thus, even if you have a domain of expertise that you know well you're providing for a specific client, you've got to continuously update that expertise to be relevant in different contexts at the same time.

The result is a much more organic, dynamic system that people need to be able to read, where the pressures on the system are significantly greater than ever before and the number of stakeholders who have to be kept happy is greater, while the changes required to make the business successful are more acute and coming at an ever faster pace.

The Experience at Duke CE

There were three basic ideas behind the creation of Duke CE. The first is that most business schools operated on an inside out basis rather than outside in. The inside out approach is guided by the belief that the inner strengths and capabilities of the organization will produce a sustainable future, whereas outside in is guided by the belief that customer value creation is the key to success.

In other words, you talk to a client and identify their issues. You then try to do a capability mapping of the client's issues to your existing faculty. The problem is that the fit is imperfect. Client issues are typically more integrated, more complex, more dynamic, than most business school faculty can map onto. As a result the problem gets narrowed to meet the capability of the faculty. To be outside in means starting with the following questions: what's the nature of the problem? Is it educational or is some other kind of solution needed? If educational, what is the full range of the need if the problem or opportunity is to be accurately addressed. In short, it's all about outside in versus inside out.

The second issue is that you have to remember that most executive education operations are constrained by the size of their faculty and the mix of that faculty's capabilities. This led us to understand that we had to create a much larger talent pool. So, we created a black book of 2500 experts around the world.

And then the third question was how to link education, technology and experience in ways we'd never done before, in order to create the best possible solution.

What it came down to was that we were trying to create the best custom experience for students; a truly tailored experience, rather than simply the best open enrollment. Nevertheless, there is still a need for open programs to change. But on the company-specific education side, I think the core idea of starting a new company in order to build the optimum design offered a more versatile, client-focused solution, compared to the conventional approach. And there are other schools and firms that are following that same approach.

What's different since we created DukeCE is the need to provide solutions as massive scale, being more technology based, while providing some elements of certification. But returning to business education more generally, I think we're starting to see a different world. Take, for example, the MBA. They are designed for people who have been in work for three or four or five years and who want to accelerate their career. We say to them, return to education and we will put you back in the system so you can improve your career prospects. I have now come to believe that it doesn't matter what age you are—whether you are 28 or 68, you have a similar need. And the point is that no one is offering a solution to the needs of those with much more experience in the workforce.

There's badging, acknowledging the successful completion of a program or course with a verifiable description of the specific knowledge, skills and criteria required to earn the badge. Representing skills as a badge gives learners a way to share their abilities online in a way that is simple and trusted—and can be easily verified in real time. But we need to ask if someone who has a set of capabilities that were once relevant to a world which has disappeared can still apply them to a new world, reconfigured and supplemented and then placed in the world. There are missing elements today in any of the solutions that typically come with an MBA, such as a placement office. I don't see that happening. In fact, companies are beginning to build their own badging processes. The risk is that the education system gets left behind. I think that's a need that no one anticipated and is not being met. And it's huge.

I'll give you two quick examples. Firstly, imagine you're a Ph.D. geologist in an oil and gas company today. You're really, really smart, you're incredibly well-trained, but you're increasingly irrelevant. I don't want the world to lose such a resource, and I don't want that person to have to take a job that's beneath their talent. But unless we find a way to help people like that retool in the same way we're doing with a 28-year-old here on the MBA program, we're going to have a growing number of people who find themselves surplus to requirements, highly valuable, but stranded assets.

A second example: imagine you're a partner in a company and you have a particular kind of expertise, but clients do not have problems that requires that expertise anymore, and instead need different types of knowledge. This is going to happen increasingly, which means there is going to be an urgent need to anticipate where the world is going, to preparing people for that at any stage in their life and then helping place them in a new job somewhere else in the world. But I just don't see the answer emerging.

The Role of Universities in Executive Education

If this need for career development isn't met by universities it will be met by somebody else. If enough other schools hadn't done something like we did with Duke CE, the consulting companies would have taken over the executive education business. If the universities and business schools don't take the lead, then the market will find a way to meet it.

My concern is that it will take the market a while to catch up, and then a lot of very sad things will have occurred in the meantime. I think we also need to dramatically enhance our trade education as well. Because a lot of the jobs of the future are going to be in the trades—in part because of university fees—so there will be a need to go back and understand the trade associated with the thing you're learning. But if you ask me whether this is happening at the speed it needs to, I'd say no.

After the Pandemic

The effects of the current crisis are going to vary across sectors. But I think every single company in the world is rethinking the optimum combination of people, technology and real estate. I don't think there's a generic answer to that question. For example, I think that we will still need high streets and towns. I think they'll look different, but people will still want to go out and meet friends and family. We will come up with new ideas, new models and to some extent this will be influenced by new delivery models, but we're still going to have high streets. I think you might see people living closer to where they work and living in smaller spaces. For example, you might see employees living in the same building as their office. In other words, there isn't going to be one size fits all. I think companies will undertake a complete rethink of people, real estate and technology, and that will mean taking into account different interests.

The presence of technology across educational programs is irreversible. The single best program I think I've ever delivered, we designed in three weeks and delivered 100% of it online. This program was with some of the most senior people we have in our firm, I mean, our most critical assets. And it worked really well. We're all learning to do stuff online. That said, the danger is that we could go too far. Although Duke CE is a good solution for customized programs, there are times when what you need is a good generic program. You want people to interact with people in other parts of the company, other parts of the world. You want them to interact with the best colleagues and faculty and to get the best education possible on a given topic. And when you want exposure and the single best thing you can get on a given topic, this is the right thing to do. When you are trying to move a company in a particular direction and you want educational support, customized programs are the right thing to focus on. Schools need to remember what they are good at though, I think the danger is you push too far and lose where you're good and therefore you harm the whole entity in the process.

Also, if you take technology to the extreme, you end up doing more harm than good. If people have a bad experience of online learning, then they won't try it again. That doesn't help us.

I feel very proud of many programs we've created at PwC: as I said, with just three weeks, conceived, designed and executed it, 100% online. And the people who were on it were very happy with the experience. So, I think that the notion that you can't deliver a world class educational experience online is just wrong. But I also think we still need face-to-face programs for other reasons.

But we need to step back. We need to recognize that there's lots of stuff you can do with technology that is good if you just adapt it. You can achieve scale and speed in a way that's not possible face-to-face. And the world is moving so fast that scale and speed really matter. You know, it is possible to come up with an idea for a program for 25,000 people, design it in a couple of weeks and deliver it in a month. That's unheard of in the world I came from, but welcome to life in the twenty-first century. Speed and scale matter so much, which means that it would make no sense to go back solely to face-to-face education.

Of course, face-to-face education will continue to exist, but we also need to ask ourselves two questions: what are the things best done face-to-face? And what are the things that can actually be done brilliantly through electronically mediated learning? I would say that the answer is tipped more and more toward electronically mediated education, but without getting rid of face-to-face. I think orientation—bringing people on board the organization—for example, is a really hard not to do face-to-face. The point is that there are some things that you should do face-to-face, but there's fewer than we think.

The Role of CLOs

If I think of potential advice to CLOs, I'd say five things.

- The first is to understand your organization's strategy really well and don't do anything that doesn't support it. Because if you do things that are not relevant to what the firm is trying to do, you're both wasting money and putting yourself at risk. And I think not enough people spend time learning to understand their strategy.
- The second thing is to understand that there's a lot of really good stuff out there. A good third of your job is doing routine and standard things. Don't try to do something that is better done by somebody else, curate the best out there and leave the really specific stuff for your team to do.
- Thirdly, think about scale in everything you do. Do it quickly and do it to scale; if it's a good thing, it should be done for a lot of people.
- Fourth, recognize that we need a much better and more dynamic model of capabilities than we now have and that you've got to make sure that what you're doing is relevant when it comes to teaching those capability sets. You need to be able to be a generalist and a specialist, when the need arises.
- And the fifth is about balancing the paradoxes of leadership, a topic I discussed at length in my last book. There are six paradoxes which are becoming increasingly important for leaders to navigate. These are not the only paradoxes leaders face, but the ones most urgent in today's context and will remain important in the future. The paradoxes should be considered as a system; they impact each other and all need to be balanced

simultaneously. To truly differentiate yourself as a leader, learning how to comfortably inhabit both elements of each paradox will be critical to your success.

In the CLO's job I think understanding these paradoxes is really relevant. For example, you have to be a technology savvy humanist, as a CLO, if you don't understand technology you are irrelevant, if you don't understand how people work and human systems work and how technology plays into them, then you are likely to do something really bad, you're going to cause harm.

At the same time, if you're not politically capable, you won't get a thing approved, nor navigate the many constituencies required to get things done day to day, but you need to do so with integrity, lest you forget the reason you started a project in the first place or lose the trust essential to operate effectively today. The paradox is that traditionally those with a deep understanding of technology often did not also acquire the skills required to understand people's needs or how to lead them. As a result, many people who are driving technological advancement aren't equipped to consider the human implications of their work. This is also true in reverse as those who have responsibility for people haven't always understood the impact technology will have on their business and workforce. The leader's role is to nurture the success of the business and, in doing so, offer a better future for their people. That means balancing being technically savvy with a focus on humanity.

Similarly, if you don't have integrity, you'll get the wrong thing approved. In a deeply political environment, people can lose their integrity. Much time is spent meeting the needs of other people and managing the politics of getting plans to happen. Driving change is a constant state of being for leaders, but change affects the balance of power and creates a scenario in which some parties feel like they are losing. In order to keep all people engaged on the optimal outcome for the organization during times of change the integrity of the leader is even more critical.

And If you're not strategic, you will create programs that aren't relevant to the future, but if you can't execute them, it won't matter anyway.

These paradoxes also apply to CEOs. I always highlight the temptation for CEOs to continue to execute the things they do really well, while missing the opportunities that will help them remain relevant. It requires the ability to respect the past and decide what needs to be brought forward into the future, while also having the courage to try new things. Too often innovation is considered a wholly greenfield experiment, rather than something that is incremental and builds on what already exists. It needs to be both and leaders should define when to preserve the past in moving to the future and when to create completely fresh.

The danger for CEOs is failing to diagnose what's essential to who they are and therefore they throw away the baby with the bathwater. On the other hand, the danger of not innovating around everything but your core is that you will not respond to the dynamism in the market.

Three Pieces of Strategic Advice

Let me also add three further pieces of advice.

One: you have to recognize that the transformation required of companies is multiplex, and you have to figure out how to do them all at the same time in a way that works as a system. So, you've got to get to net zero and you've got to mitigate the risks of climate. You've got to figure out how to compete in a platform-based world. You've got to figure out how to be an organization that survives in an increasingly fractured world. You've got to be an organization that isn't seen as part of the problem of our increasingly difficult societal challenges. All of those have to tumble over each other and be interdependent. It is not possible to do things in sequence, I'm going to solve climate change, then I'm going to solve the technology challenge, then I'm going to solve the fractured world problem. Instead, you've got to solve them simultaneously. And that's a really hard strategy. That's a tough process.

Two: there is no perfectly right answer. It's very hard to come up with a strategy when you can't be sure what the outcome is going to be, but doing nothing is worse. In other words, when you're making an analysis of what you should do strategically, don't use zero as your baseline. Because the world's coming at you so fast that the assets you think you may have are less and less valuable every year. Doing nothing in today's world means your balance sheet is depreciating at an accelerated rate. What it comes down to is that we're doing the wrong kind of math.

My final piece of advice relates to the stakeholder versus shareholder debate. The important point here is that the danger of a stakeholder model is you focus on things that aren't material and therefore you're wasting resources and you're not helping make the world a better place. The danger of a shareholder model is that you're not focusing on the intangibles. The solution is to find a way to take the intangible elements of your strategy and make them as concrete as you can so you can evaluate them effectively; at the same time, you have to deal with the intangibles happening in the world today. And that's hard.

Reference

1. Sheppard, Blair H. *Ten Years to Midnight* (New York, NY: Berrett-Koehler Publishers, 2020), p. 2.

20

International Campuses Abroad: The University of Southampton Malaysia

Rebecca Taylor

Among the strategies for establishing a presence in international markets, the alternatives, ranked from lowest to highest risk, range from establishing strategic alliances with other universities, developing online programs, creating franchises or opening campuses in other countries. This last involves the greatest investment of resources and commitment to the target market, but also greater risks. The University of Southampton is one of the few Western universities that has implemented this type of strategy in Malaysia, which supports their recruitment and partnership engagement across the Asia market. At the helm of the University of Southampton Malaysia is CEO Rebecca Taylor, who is also the Pro-Vice-Chancellor (ASEAN) at the University of Southampton UK. Taylor began her professional career in banking, subsequently completed a Ph.D. and has since combined her academic activity with management in the university world, previously serving as the Executive Dean of the Open University Business School in the UK. In addition to her current responsibilities at the University of Southampton, she is Vice Chair of the Board of EFMD, the organisation that represents and supports the global network of business schools and that runs the internationally recognised EQUIS accreditation. The comments in this chapter are taken from an interview held on April 23, 2021.

R. Taylor (✉)
University of Southampton Malaysia, Iskandar Puteri, Johor, Malaysia
e-mail: Rebecca.Taylor@soton.ac.uk

The Impact of the Pandemic on South Asian Universities

There are some common themes.

The University of Southampton Malaysia had always intended to embrace online teaching as part of its portfolio of teaching methods but the pandemic certainly accelerated this shift. Some universities have been incorporating online delivery for many years, especially those like the Open University whose core offer has always been rooted in online distance learning. Others were embracing online delivery in different ways and at different rates in order to balance new delivery modes with their more traditional face-to-face engagement.

Prior to the pandemic, the adoption of online learning/delivery was relatively uncommon across Asia. There are a few online universities but this mode of delivery has struggled to secure the confidence of prospective students/families and regulatory bodies that is afforded the more traditional face-to-face delivery models. As such, the development of wider online offers has been relatively slow across this region. The pandemic changed all of that. In an effort to continue to teach and support students through a strict and prolonged period of lockdown, universities had to make a shift to online delivery quickly and efficiently. Despite a short initial closure of most institutions, the shift to online across the university sector happened within days and showed enormous creativity and commitment from staff and students. In this sense, the pandemic not only forced institutions to function very differently, but also promoted stronger working relationships with governments that were having to address a similar shift in their understanding and approval of the delivery modes related to different higher education institutions and their associated offers.

Overall the pandemic has resulted in a positive, sustainable shift in higher education across Asia. It has promoted greater support for creativity in delivery and offers. It has encouraged greater understanding of the value and quality of online provision, whether that is a full degree, a module or just elements of a module. It has also encouraged much stronger collaboration across the higher education sector, ministries and regulatory bodies which has been valuable in shifting public confidence in different modes of delivery and learning.

The University of Southampton Malaysia has always been a very creative institution so has often explored innovative ways to engage students in different aspects of learning. As a result, its shift to online following the first lockdown in March 2020 was relatively easy.

Few universities across Asia will reflect on this period and say that the shift was easy, but having had the experience most are now likely to say that it has resulted in some positive change for their institution. Overall there is no doubt that it has created a major shift in the mind-set of all involved—universities, prospective students, governments, regulatory and accreditation bodies—and it has changed the wider perception of quality and standards in higher education across the region.

Although quality and standards in higher education remain of utmost importance, there is a much more open dialogue and acceptance that online learning or online components within a face-to-face model can not only be of equally high quality, but they can actually improve the quality of the student learning experience and the opportunities offered to students during their studies.

The length of the pandemic also resulted in some positive outcomes; it gave universities time to demonstrate the quality and value of online offers and to work with governments and regulatory bodies to show the impact on students of a range of creative learning experiences including blended options, hybrid and flexible learning models, online exchanges and international masterclasses delivered via Zoom/Teams. This has developed a level of trust across the network that will inevitably improve the opportunities for future students and encourage more students to engage in higher education.

Challenges for Business Schools After the Pandemic

There will now be greater willingness to do new things and to allow universities to do things differently. There's going to be an appetite in universities to create a range of new offers, some of which will include online and hybrid which will be integrated with the more traditional face-to-face offerings.

An interesting finding from the University of Southampton Malaysia was that student engagement changed and in some cases improved once we offered the online components. We realised this was the result of this generation's comfort and confidence with social media. Students were more likely to ask questions in chat boxes that they had been to raise a question in a face-to-face lecture, and the more relaxed environment of Zoom and chat boxes created an additional level of rapport among the staff and students that had a positive impact on learning. In many cases the academics found that the discussion and engagement was more in-depth and robust as a result of the online learning environment.

Online teaching allowed us to respond to and support students in ways we had not been able to prior to the pandemic; with them asking more questions in an online classroom environment (that they would previously have asked the lecturer individually after the session in the face-to-face environment), the rest of the cohort was able to benefit from that broader engagement, explanation and understanding. This enabled lecturers to gain a better understanding of where students were struggling and to provide additional understanding and support to the whole group.

The University of Southampton Malaysia is now looking to incorporate some of these methods of student engagement into their teaching even as they move back to face-to-face delivery. Several online components will be retained because we know that they will help us to support students.

Over the longer term, the University recognises that people have different circumstances and reasons for engaging in a university degree programme; they might come to higher education later or they might need to balance their degree with other commitments. There have previously been fewer options for this kind of flexible learning across Asia but the experience during the pandemic has certainly prompted a change in the way learning is viewed and it is likely that more flexible models will be considered accepted and respected alternatives to the more traditional models of learning. As a result, more universities will now be focussed on creating and offering more flexible delivery models for students that want to or need to engage in different ways. And they will also be using these new models to reach new audiences—students who were not able to engage in more rigid models of higher education but who can join a university and study for a degree if there are more flexible ways of learning on offer.

Certificates, Badges and Stackable Courses

The Open University has done a lot of advanced work on stackable degrees, badging, certificates, etc. The Open University's FutureLearn platform also allows students to accumulate badges and certificates that can count towards part of a formal degree.

There is less available in Asia in relation to the 'stackable degree' but there is some very interesting discussion now taking place about micro-credentials and this is gaining momentum across the region.

There is great enthusiasm in Asia for short courses and certificates that confirm the acquisition of new skills. People often present portfolios of certificates at interviews to demonstrate their engagement in different short courses that have supported their broader learning and development. Universities are now engaging more actively in discussions about short courses, executive education and micro-credentials in order to create portfolios that meet this emerging demand. This may lend itself in future to formal, stackable degree programmes but for now the focus is on upskilling in small chucks of learning that provide flexibility and opportunity across a range of different discipline and skill areas.

The EFMD is a global organisation that leads and supports the international network or business schools. It offers a range of workshops, training and advice to individuals and institutions. An interesting step for the EFMD would be to create a series of workshops tailored to the Asia market that specifically addressed the employability and upskilling needs of staff and students. These short development courses could earn participants a certificate of achievement which would be respected across the wider employment market given the international credibility of the EFMD.

Future Technological Advances in Education

Technological advances impact the higher education sector in different ways, and rarely lead to the type of change, or speed of change that is initially anticipated. The MOOC revolution was a very interesting example of this. Initially there was a view that MOOCS would see the end of the higher education model that we know—mode of delivery, formal degrees, international engagement, etc. But this didn't happen. What MOOCs did was add a new aspect of learning to the portfolios of universities and they promoted more creativity in aspects of learning and learning offers. Interestingly they also supported university marketing and communication teams by showcasing core strengths of different institutions and helping universities develop an informal pipeline of learners who could potentially be converted from informal to formal learners.

The MOOC experience is only one example but what it illustrates is that almost without exception, technological advances in education do not replace traditional models of education, they add to them and enhance them in ways that offer current and prospective students more choice, more opportunity and more interesting learning experiences.

The Evolution of Executive Education

The pandemic has created a new dialogue around online learning and in most cases the realisation is consistent across institutions; staff and students don't want to move entirely online as they gain enormous value from the face-to-face learning model; however, some online components, or the use of online to create more choice and opportunity, through hybrid models of learning, are something that they want to embrace. The biggest shift to online is likely to be in the field of executive education. Executive education often involves the engagement of professionals across a range of roles and geographical locations. Time is precious and the ability to dedicate a number of days to a course including travel time (and expense) often prohibits participation. The post-pandemic delivery of more executive education online is likely to be embraced by an increasing number of business schools globally. This mode of delivery for executive education also offers the opportunity for business schools to offer more practice-based approaches that are universally popular. Learning units, sandwiched between applications of learning in the workplace, almost always leads to a better understanding of concepts and more valuable sharing of best practice.

Another advantage of online executive education is the ability to internationalise more easily, and therefore to provide participants with a more international experience. Cohorts that can, without having to travel, engage in an international workshop with a range of others from different companies, roles, locations, etc., often provide broader engagement and the sharing of a wider range of experience and expertise.

Equally, international advisory boards through the pandemic became more international rather than less. With the acceptance that boards could meet just as—if not more—effectively online, business schools quickly reached out to international colleagues who previously couldn't spend the time out of their roles to travel for board meetings. This has been a significant, sustainable and positive shift resulting from the pandemic, promoting more international engagement and input in the strategic planning of business schools, supporting stronger collaborations across institutions, and engaging more international colleagues in the wider learning experiences of students.

Overall, the online engagement in Boards, Executive Education and other learning experiences increased as a necessity due to the pandemic but has become a desirable aspect of future business school strategies and plans in an effort to further internationalise and engage future students in a wider range of learning opportunities.

How Accreditation Agencies Can Help Drive Innovation

The EFMD offers the opportunity for business schools to gain certification for online offers through EOCCS. Increasingly the group is seeing more engagement from institutions in Asia, and the experience of the pandemic is likely to further increase the number of universities interested in having external certification or accreditation for their offers. It is possible that the type of offers or demands will have specific regional characteristics and this is something that I'm sure the EFMD will identify and respond to. Thus in future it may be the case that region-specific certification or accreditations will be of specific interest to schools who want to demonstrate the value of their offer in relation to their regional competitors. This offers new opportunities to use certification and accreditation in a way that is both local and global and adds specific value to institutions at different stages of their development.

The acceptance of greater online engagement and offers also now provides the opportunity for new partnerships, new types of student exchange and new ways for students to gain employability skills. The EFMD is already doing work to support and encourage creative engagement across the global business school network, and business schools are encouraged to participate in these discussions about the future models of learning and engagement.

The Future of Southampton Malaysia

The University of Southampton Malaysia was established as an international campus of the University of Southampton. In its early years it specialised in engineering programmes but the last few years have been focussed on the expansion of the university—both the construction of a new physical estate, and the expansion of the programme portfolio from four programmes to eighteen which now span all levels of learning—foundation programmes, undergraduate, postgraduate taught, postgraduate research and executive education. The new portfolio also includes new disciplines—business, economics, marketing, finance, actuarial science and computer science—and new models that allow students to study their full degree in Malaysia or to transfer and do part of their degree in Southampton UK.

Closer collaboration with the Ministry and the Malaysian Qualification Agency, and alignment of new programmes with the Critical Occupations List has supported the introduction of a portfolio of programmes that meets the needs of the country and the demand from prospective students. Most recently the University has established the University of Southampton Malaysia Business School which will engage with the global network of business schools through the EFMD to support the international experience of staff and students. The new estate provides all staff and students with state-of-the-art facilities to support their learning, including a Bloomberg suite and experimental labs. And the new University building is located in an established commercial centre which includes outstanding student accommodation, a multi-varsity sports centre and a wider range of food and beverage facilities.

The University is now introducing a new short course portfolio to further support student employability and to engage the wider network of commercial and government partners in a range of practice-based development opportunities. The new short course portfolio is categorised into different areas of development ranging from (i) soft skills to (ii) voluntary sector leadership to (iii) personal finance. Ultimately the goal is to position the University as a valuable contributor to the country and the region in which it functions, offering programmes that meet an identified need, undertaking research that contributes to core government priorities, providing students with a broad, international experience, in high-quality facilities that ensure a world-class learning experience.

The Role of Deans and Academic Managers

Experiences from the pandemic have shown that higher education leadership is multi-faceted. Deans and Academic Managers need to stay abreast of trends, market share, changes in employment needs and emerging student interests. Growing the student body enables universities to expand portfolios, introduce new innovations in teaching and provide a wider range of international learning experiences. This is a critical component in ensuring that offers remain relevant and attractive to future students.

The pandemic also demonstrated the need for universities to be more agile. Being able to respond to changing demand, provide greater flexibility, address changing employment needs, etc., will be critical to institutional sustainability in the years to come. The more agile an institution can be, the more they will be able to respond to the needs of their future students and to external shocks like the recent Covid pandemic.

Finally, the pandemic has shown the need for leaders to ensure that their universities are connected—internationally networked to provide students with increasing opportunities to understand global issues, and in partnerships that support student engagement and experience. These networks also help Deans to effectively manoeuvre external events that negatively impact on the immediate business of the university.

The pandemic has undoubtedly been a challenging time for all institutions and has created some very challenging times for students and staff alike, but it has also presented the higher education sector with an insight into how to work differently, how to be more agile, how to create stronger, more connected networks and how to internationalise across all aspects of teaching, learning, research and external engagement. The most important step now is for universities to reflect on their experience and consider how they can use some of the changes they have had to make through the pandemic, to create new more innovative models of learning and teaching for the future.

21

Transforming Organizations: Haier

Ruimin Zhang

Haier, one of the world's leading home appliance companies, has grown over the past two decades not only through organic development, but also through successful acquisitions based on an innovative implementation process that puts people front and center.

At the helm of this Chinese global home appliance giant is its CEO, Zhang Ruimin (1949, Laizhou, China), whose vision has transformed Haier into one of the most innovative corporations in its sector and on the international stage. CEO Zhang began his career working on the production line, and so understands the workforce's experience and concerns. Over time, he also completed an MBA. Here he discusses a career characterized by a passion for other cultures, as shown in the many examples he uses to illustrate his ideas.

CEO Zhang: We started the business in 1984, and we only made refrigerators at that time, but we gradually began producing other home appliances. Our objective at that time was clear: to establish an international home appliances brand along the lines of Matsushita, GEA and Sony. However, with the

---

Interview held on January 18, 2021. Edited by Santiago Iniguez.

R. Zhang (✉)
Haier Group, Qingdao, China

arrival of the internet, I adjusted these objectives, not with a desire to create a product brand, but to make an ecosystem-brand. In simple terms, products are now inexpensive, there are no consumer gaps, there are numerous players, and the same categories of products are all part of a discount price war. Therefore, I believe that certain products will be replaced by ecosystems. For example, you don't make a smart home based on just one product, or even from just one industry. So, if you don't make this product into an internet appliance and connect the two together, into a service for users, that is, a user-experience service, then this product will have no value. This is because everyone feels that the household internet is actually a personal internet, and that bringing people together creates a personal emotional experience and emotional needs.

Santiago Iñiguez: *One of the riskiest business growth strategies is mergers and acquisitions (M&As) especially among international corporations. They generally destroy value, as the objectives that justify them—exploiting synergies, scale or scope economies, entering new markets—are difficult to implement. In addition, the conflict between the two cultures of companies after an acquisition often hinders integration, along with other obstacles arising from the dynamic interaction between the various stakeholders. Were you aware of these risks, in addition to the potential negative reaction that procurement by companies in China can generate?*

CEO Zhang: When I merged with or acquired other companies, I was always looking at the experience of others, including those bought by Chinese or foreign outfits, and I noticed that many M&As had failed, which meant we had to act differently. This meant addressing the problems faced by companies which had failed. Where did their problems lie? Principally in the belief that the methods used to make their own companies successful could be replicated in the company they were merging with or had acquired. However, this is just one of the changes to the model. I believe that the most significant reason why these M&As were not successful was a failure to motivate the workforce.

I believe that within global companies, regardless of their nationality, everybody who works there all have one objective, which is to see their self-worth and self-respect reflected in that company. This was identified by the twentieth century psychoanalyst Carl Jung in his work on the collective unconscious,[1] that is, the realization our identity through belonging to a

---

[1] According to C.G. Jung, the human collective unconscious is populated by instincts as well as archetypes or universal symbols. "Collected Works" (H. Read, M. Fordham, G. Adler, W. McGuire eds.), vol. 9 (Princeton, NJ: Princeton University Press, 1957), p. I.

larger reality, even if we don't fully understand the process. So, we implemented our Rendanheyi model.[2] The basic meaning of Rendanheyi is that each employee should directly face users, create user value, and realize their own shared value by creating value for users. Employees are not subordinate to posts. Instead, they exist because of users. Without user value, there would be no employees.

Taking General Electric as an example, I knew that American society is highly individualistic, so I thought I could also ask them to take their original leadership services and change them into user services. When we bought GEA in 2016, the head of the company asked: "Now you have acquired us, how are you going to manage us?" To which I replied: "I have not come here to manage you, I am only your shareholder. We both have the same leader, and that is our users." This means that you only have to create value for your users, and this will reflect your own self-worth and self-respect. No matter for the individualism of the United States or collectivism in Japan, Rendanheyi model is worked for them, our subsidiaries in these two places have been enjoying double-digit growth during the current pandemic. Therefore, I feel that it is not just a case of buying a company, but that its subsequent development must be people-oriented, and therefore must reflect the maximization of an individual's personal self-worth.

Santiago Iñiguez: *Unlike other companies, where workers wait for their bosses to assign them tasks, Haier has adopted the Individual Goal Approach, whereby employees set their own objectives, work on how to innovate their products, interact with potential users, and their compensation is calculated based on the value they generate for customers. Haier has implemented this system in successive acquisitions, so that the workforce feels motivated and stays with the company, unlike happens with many other mergers.*

CEO Zhang: This is a problem being explored by companies everywhere. We previously collated various methods used by US corporations, that is, we carried out a personnel evaluation. We no longer do this, as we believe you cannot carry out a static evaluation; you cannot say that this person is doing well or not, because you do not know the potential that every individual has. But Haier is not a Western company where you can divide employees into different levels, and where you don't have KPI indicators, so what do you use?

---

[2] The literal interpretation of Rendanheyi is based on "Ren," which refers to the employee; "Dan" refers to the user value; and "Heyi" means combining the user value realization with created user value. A further explanation of RenDanHeY (Individual Goal Combination model) in: L. Zhou and R. Jing, "Management After Acquisition Inside Multinational Companies from Emerging Economies: The Haier Experience"; in S. Iñiguez de Onzoño and K. Ichijo (eds.), Business Despite Borders. Companies in The Age of Populist Anti-Globalization (London: Palgrave Macmillan, 2018), pp. 213–24.

If you have an opportunity to set up a business, you can create value yourself. So, Haier shed 12,000 middle managers, eliminated the middle management layer, and established 4000 micro-enterprises, each made up of approximately 10 people.

These micro-enterprises could create value in the market themselves, and they could collaborate and combine into a connected chain of groups, that is, an Ecosystem Micro-community (EMC), with between 10 and 20 micro-enterprises connected together. Ultimately, after implementing value-creation, they were able to go to market and become their own bosses. So, this method was a little like quantum mechanics. There is a very interesting phenomenon inside quantum management, known as Schrodinger's cat.[3] If you apply this within a company, it means, how do you know, if you have not given this person an opportunity, whether or not they are capable? So that means that we do not have the same evaluation system as the big companies in the rest of the world, who this person should be, who this person is, what kind of academic background or qualifications they have, and in actual fact, this is not how you create value, or reflect your own value.

Santiago Iñiguez: *One tends to think that the idea of hierarchy predominates in most Chinese corporations, and that distance to power should be one of the highest in comparative terms. However, in Haier, whose status is similar to that of a cooperative, you avoid talking about organizational levels, including the idea of managers as such.*

CEO Zhang: I would like to explain one particular point, which is that Haier doesn't currently have a senior layer. It does not have a senior management layer in the traditional sense, because according to Rendan-heyi, traditional management has subjective and objective management, with senior management levels being the main subjective body of management, and employees being the objective bodies of management. But in the age of the internet, since this uses a distributed system, and there is no subjective or objective, it should be egalitarian, because the information that every individual receives is the same.[4]

---

[3] The Schrödinger's is an experiment where a hypothetical cat is placed in a sealed box with a sealed vial of cyanide, above which is suspended a hammer attached to a Geiger counter aimed at a small lump of mildly radioactive uranium. The box is sealed, and the experiment is left to run for some set amount of time, perhaps an hour. In that hour, the uranium, whose particles obey the laws of quantum mechanics, has some chance of emitting radiation that will then be picked up by the Geiger counter, which will, in turn, release the hammer and smash the vial, killing the cat by cyanide poisoning. The idea is that until the box is opened and the cat's status is evaluated, it will remain in a superposition of both living and deceased. See D. Castelvecchi, "Reimagining of Schrödinger's cat breaks quantum mechanics -and stumps physicists", Nature 18 September 2018. https://www.nature.com/articles/d41586-018-06749-8.

[4] G. Hofstede, Capstone Encyclopaedia of Business (Hoboken, NJ: Wiley, 2003), p. 224.

Given that Haier is not a traditional large corporation with many management layers, everybody can focus on innovation and technology, and then these creators can connect together into one micro-enterprise, allowing the micro-enterprises to connect into one inter-connected group, which in turn can be trebled. Everybody is a creator, and this is the first foundation.

Santiago Iñiguez: *Haier's experience with Sanyo and GE shows that Rendanheyi can be applied to a variety of cultures as a way of identifying people's contribution to their businesses.*

CEO Zhang: We started using the Rendanheyi model in 2005, and since then a lot of people have visited Haier to learn about Rendanheyi first hand, which allows them to see it from different perspectives. Traditional management models see people as middlemen. In contrast, we believe that to be entrepreneurial, the workforce should be autonomous. This means that the enterprise does not manage people. This approach is beautifully argued in many of the maxims seventeenth century Spanish philosopher Baltasar Gracián's provides in *The Art of Worldly Wisdom*,[5] a classic book that became a best-seller again in the 1990s. For example, *The Art of Worldly Wisdom* mentioned: "More is needed nowadays to deal with a single person than was required with a whole people in former times." That means you shouldn't "deal with" a person, but to help a person to demonstrate his/her own wisdom.

In China, we also have a saying which translates as: "10,000 people seek autonomy." This means that even the most intelligent person in the world cannot deal with 100 people, and much less 10,000 people. Applying this to a company or an organization means that it is better to give the workforce a platform they themselves can develop. The solution is for everybody to be autonomous, this is the foundation. Our experience is that many people come to study Haier's Rendanheyi model but fail to grasp this concept because they are not willing to allow employees to become autonomous.

The second point is the organization. The Rendanheyi model has become a micro-enterprise, it has become an organization. Unlike traditional companies, it does everything itself. I went to Spain a few years ago, and was impressed by the Catalan architect Gaudí. He had a saying: "The straight line belongs to men, the curved one to God".[6] Companies are the same: traditional ones are linear, and we are creating one which is not. These companies are changing on a daily basis, and have full autonomy to be entrepreneurial.

---

[5] B. Gracian, The Art of Worldly Wisdom (New York, NY: Doubleday, 1992). Gracián notes: "There is more required nowadays to make a single wise man than formerly to make seven sages, and more is needed nowadays to deal with a single person than was required with a whole people in former times."
[6] This quote is attributed to Antoni Gaudí, the Spanish architect (1852–1926).

Finally, there's mindset. For many years, everyone thought that this model would fail. Everyone believed it was impossible, because the world doesn't work like that. However, we have insisted upon doing this until now, and we were compared to Don Quixote. I guess we have a little of the Don Quixote mindset, that is, to be single-minded in pursuing our objectives.[7] To date, the Rendanheyi model has proved a success, because the entire company has changed into an eco-system type organization, focused on the internet.

This is one of the outcomes of the organization during the process of its self-evolution. This outcome, you could say, presents both a scenario brand and an ecosystem-brand, and these are what the internet needs. However, what is the interlinking axis connecting these two things together? Value-added sharing. If you create value for the user, everyone is able to share that value. If you cannot create, then you need to disband. We do not have a human resources department, and we don't pay fixed salaries, so if I don't give you a fixed amount of money, then all I need is for you to create value for the user, and then, the higher the creativity, the more that you can share this. However, sharing and traditional organizations are not the same thing, it is not the sharing of any department, but the possibility of sharing this with the company's external collaborators. That is to say, traditional organizations might be a zero-sum game. This means that I don't care if others make money or not; as long as I earn money, that's all that matters. However, we create together and share together, creating value for the user together, and share this.

Santiago Iñiguez: *The rise of large Chinese corporations over the past three decades has generated interest in understanding the hallmarks of Chinese management. Analyzing Haier's evolution and listening to you suggests there is a synchronous ability to learn and adapt teachings from different cultures, as well as drawing on the ancient traditions of Chinese culture and thinkers such as Lao Tse or Confucius, what you call system theory versus the atom theory characteristic of the West.*

CEO Zhang: Yes, and this is an issue which we frequently research. First of all, I'd say that China did not have its own managerial system in the past. We have learned all of this totally from the West: China's companies in the 1980s were all studying Japanese total quality management theory. After that, and up until the 1990s, they were studying the US Six Sigma approach and salary and human resources systems, as well as KPIs, among others. Now, in the age of the internet, during the age of interconnectivity, we have discovered that these systems don't work, and can't be adapted to this new era. All

---

[7] M. Cervantes, Don Quixote (New York, NY: Penguin, 2003).

these systems are about zero defects in the production process, but that's a given, and now what the consumer wants is zero distance, which is to say that products should be wholly integrated with users, which has prompted us to seek out a new management model.

And we are basing this new model on aspects of China's traditional culture, which obviously isn't the same as Western traditional cultures. Western traditional culture means Newtonian mechanics and atomization, whereas China's ancient philosophy is based on system theory, as seen in the works of Yi Jing, Lao Tzu, and so on. So, system theory and atom theory are completely different. Atom Theory means taking something and dividing it up, the smaller the better, while system theory means seeing everything as a whole; so, we use this type of holistic thinking to engage in Rendanheyi. We no longer think about companies in terms of compartmentalized areas: research, production, sales and marketing, etc. Instead, we now allow all departments, for example, R&D, manufacturing, sales and marketing to encircle the product. Any one of them can decide to add entrepreneurial value for the user.

Let's say that the R&D personnel and creators are a single unit of say, 600 employees, and this cannot be divided up, because if you divide this up into teams of 20, they will not be able to research and develop refrigerators. For me, this is not the right way of looking at this situation. The reality is that if each individual from that group of 20 is connected to one or two external R&D institutes, then this is not a case of just 20 employees, but about actually being connected to 20 or 40 R&D institutes. So, this is the concept of the internet connecting everything together. You can integrate several resources, based on system theory, and each person's function has been brought into play.

I am happy to see that the West is now starting to turn toward atom management, which is a very dynamic form of management, and this is also system management and therefore, more or less the same as China's traditional culture. Looking at it from this perspective, China's traditional culture and Western atom management are taking different routes, but they will go hand in hand. Ultimately, I believe that global management should be integrated.

Santiago Iñiguez: *The pandemic seems to be marking the beginning of a new era of globalization. After the slowdown of the global economy, the new phase that opens may lead to a rethink of business models and how they generate value. The impact of technology is irreversible, and when international trade recovers, international corporations will have to act differently.*

CEO Zhang: I feel that the pandemic could be good for our Rendanheyi management model, which is gaining ever-greater global recognition: in March 2020, the *MIT Sloan Management Review* praised Haier for its organizational resilience. It (the review) has noticed how, over the course of the pandemic, many large corporations, including Google and Apple, have relatively rigid supply chains. Haier, on the contrary, is very flexible and can rapidly adapt to the changes of the era and has adapted to the difficulties presented by the pandemic. The reason for this is because, while adapting to Rendanheyi, many of these types of micro-interconnected groups have been able to create opportunities in the market. So, it's clear that the Rendanheyi model has provided greater confidence during the pandemic. Every employee is empowered to give full play to his or her capabilities, be deeply devoted to his or her work, and create value for users. In Haier's culture, the right to make decisions is delegated to the front line: everyone is his or her own CEO.

In my view, the main problem with globalization has been the way it is based on dividing things up; countries depend on raw materials, on processing, on consumerism. But I believe that globalization should actually be integrated with global consumer value. If, for example, you say that I have factories in several countries around the world, but these factories are not a manufacturing unit, that means that I understand local consumer needs. My consumer needs and those at local level are combined, meaning that I can create local user requirements or the requisite experience economy. In addition, in many other countries, if I have set up a factory, and this is in order to gain increased output, then this is completely different. In short, adapting the thinking of the nineteenth century British political economist David Ricardo regarding comparative advantage, the current internet era should evolve into a fully integrated global user experience.

Santiago Iñiguez: *Looking to the future, your mission is for Haier's workforce to keep thinking entrepreneurially, to maintain a start-up culture.*

CEO Zhang: This is an issue I have to consider every day. I hope that in 10 years' time Haier will still be a start-up company, which will mean breaking away from the curse identified by Alfred Chandler in his four-stage development of companies, the final of which is decline. However, I believe that this business model's biggest problem is during the stage of maturity, the third stage, when companies believe themselves to be mature, and can then go downhill.

But as Chandler pointed out, if the company's objective is scale and scope; if I am already the number one in my industry, this cannot continue to be the case. So, our companies, regardless of whether in business for several years, should all be like startups, that is, an entrepreneurial platform, with consistent creativity. What that means is that we now need to be able to split into parts, to make a smart organization, and to do great things as a smart organization, and then divide or split into two or more parts, and then make a second category, or split once again into a third part, thereby satisfying every type of requirement.

This is a little like the factual theory proposed by the mathematician Benoit Mandelbrot: an EMC (Ecosystem Micro-community) continuously breaks down into smaller parts, requiring we require consistent organization and division. I think that, regardless of however many years Haier has existed and will continue to exist, it should consistently continue to behave like a startup, and continue in its efforts, continue to innovate, continue to reinvent itself. We will be like a tropical rainforest, which will last forever.

Santiago Iñiguez: *Implementing this vision for the future will require visionary leadership, open to different cultures, lifelong learning. You were recently recognized by Thinkers50 as one of the most innovative business leaders of our time and have been rated by some analysts as the CEO of the twenty-first century.*

CEO Zhang: Like Schumpeter says, creative destruction creates its own problems. If the company CEO does a good job, then the company can develop well. However, if the CEO doesn't do a good job, or if he has any issues, then this company will have problems, and so, the company's fate is tied up in the CEO, and that's the wrong way to go about it.

In the future, the CEO will not exist just to embrace the organizational culture, and instead should enable each individual within the company to embrace the organizational culture. As Drucker has said, everyone should become their own CEO. So, if you do it in this way, the company is not controlled by one person, but everyone is entrepreneurial. Of course, from the beginning, the problems that can result from this is when these companies are being entrepreneurial, and whether it is all going in the same direction. The possibility is that it needs the CEO to come and take a look at this, which means, pointing out the direction that everyone needs to be working hard towards.

Take Haier as an example, what we are pointing out right now is that whatever you are doing, you need to surround a smart organization, or a smart society, you surround this, and it sounds like it is very different from the surface, but the direction is consistent, and this is what the CEO needs to do.

However, placing all the policies on the shoulders of the CEO puts the company in an extremely dangerous situation. So, my personal opinion is that the explanation for why the longevity of a company is being cut short is based on the fact that we are undergoing overly-rapid development. The CEO himself cannot keep up with this development, that is, if you do not allow every individual to become a CEO, isn't that correct? So, this is the reason why some companies do not succeed, and it is only the companies that keep up with the times that do so.

This means that for all companies, your so-called success is just keeping pace with the times, but it is not possible for you to just tread the pace of an era of success forever. However, if you become an entrepreneurial platform, there is always a part of the entire company which is a startup, and so, the company will most certainly be able to keep up. So, I feel that unless the position of the CEO changes, as it has to, companies will find it very difficult to keep up with these.

Part III

Innovation: Formats, Methods, Platforms

22

Using the Pandemic to Reset Executive Programs

Bala Chakravarthy

Executive programs are an important source of revenues for a business school (B-School). Even before the coronavirus (Covid-19) pandemic, competition in the executive education market was intense. It came not only from other B-Schools but also from new entrants like the massive open online courses (MOOCs), university affiliated corporations dedicated to executive education, and management consultants who had diversified into executive training. The pandemic has disrupted the programs of several of these providers, particularly the B-Schools. Participants can no longer travel freely to attend programs of their choice. The few programs that are still offered must meet the severe restrictions of social distancing and masking, making informal networking very difficult. This negates one of the biggest selling points of on-campus programs. Several executive programs have been cancelled and others moved online wholly or in part, as B-Schools struggle to salvage some of their lost revenues.

But the past few months have also delivered a pleasant surprise. Helped by the hard work of their IT support teams, B-Schools have been able to improve substantially the quality of their online programs. Participants are beaming in from different parts of the world and are actively participating in

---

B. Chakravarthy (✉)
International Institute for Management Development (IMD), Lausanne, Switzerland
e-mail: Bala.chakravarthy@imd.org

virtual classrooms and study rooms that closely replicate the facilities offered by a physical campus. Professors, after some initial reluctance, have jumped right in and have now mastered the new pedagogies. Online teaching has also given them some new tools. They have, for example, easy online access to participants' profiles, which helps them to orchestrate better class discussions. Muting a tedious and rambling student is also a lot easier and more polite online. While online instruction cannot fully mimic the drama and energy of a live classroom, it is here to stay post pandemic as a serious delivery option.

Corporate clients too have had their awakening. The pandemic has forced them to migrate from physical offices to virtual work. While this has limited the informal interactions and spontaneous brainstorming sessions at the proverbial "office watercooler," by some accounts overall office productivity has improved. Virtual working will form an important component of corporate work life post pandemic. This extends to executive development as well. Corporate HR departments appear more open to online options for executive education, especially if these are available at lower costs without seriously compromising quality.

Both the supply and demand sides of executive education have accepted online delivery as a viable option. Their support for it will only grow in the post pandemic world, as Zoom and other remote meeting technologies make rapid advances. But online delivery is both an opportunity and a threat to a B-School. While it extends the school's reach to new markets, it also legitimizes online competitors like LinkedIn Learning, Coursera, Udemy for business and Jolt. Unless a B-School can differentiate its executive programs, it will be dragged into an unwinnable price war with these competitors. They do not carry the overhead burdens of a physical campus and a full-time faculty, like it does.

The pandemic offers the perfect pause for a B-School to reflect on the changing dynamics of the executive education market, and to reset the way it designs and delivers executive programs. This paper discusses some of the opportunities that the school has for strengthening its functional, general management and custom programs.

Functional Programs: Migrate Online But Differentiate

Functional programs have been the bread and butter of many B-Schools. These programs provide executives an accelerated grounding in core functions like accounting, finance, operations, supply chain, marketing, and information technology. They teach the theories and frameworks used to manage these functions. The underlying knowledge is standard and well codified. It makes sense to deliver this knowledge online via self-learning modules.

The advantage of self-learning modules is that participants can master functional knowledge at their own pace and at a place and time of their choosing. They can test their learning by completing assignments online and getting real-time feedback via programmed algorithms. Advances in Artificial Intelligence (AI) will enhance the power of these algorithms over time. In contrast, conventional on-campus programs are lock step and do not accommodate the different learning styles of participants. The learning in class is often focused on the collective and not the individual. Given the advantages of self-learning modules, a B-School would do well to invest in them and migrate its functional programs online. But it should also differentiate its online programs to maintain a competitive advantage. There are three ways of doing this:

1. Offer the best portfolio of self-learning modules: The school can leverage the research power of its faculty to develop high quality self-learning modules that become market standards and a source of additional revenues for the school. When this is not possible, it should license modules from others. An advantage of online delivery is that it allows staffing from a virtual faculty pool that is richer than the school's own, including international gurus who can be brought in virtually via canned lectures. At a minimum, the school should offer participants in all its functional programs the best portfolio of self-learning modules, whether these are insourced or outsourced.
2. Provide custom electives: The school can complement online modules with online electives that customize the instruction to specific business contexts—firm size, industry, or geography. For example, there could be electives on how to apply the tools learned to problems of SMEs (small-and medium-sized enterprises), or the health care industry, or multinational companies (MNCs). The portfolio of electives offered will depend on the specialization of the school's faculty. It is a distinction that cannot be easily replicated by others and hence a source of competitive advantage for the school.
3. Deliver applied knowledge: The school can look at creative ways of blending the self-learning modules and customized electives with integrative exercises that help participants apply the knowledge gained to their work problems. Competing online providers have signed on practitioners to provide this applied knowledge; but their pedagogical skills cannot match the design and delivery skills of a trained B-School faculty. It is

important though for the faculty to stay connected with top practitioners in their fields and seek their help in designing the integrative exercises.

A school's brand name would be less important for functional programs in the post pandemic world. What would matter more is how its online programs are rated by participants. Price will continue to be an important factor in online delivery. B-Schools must trim their overhead costs, wherever possible, to stay competitive in functional programs.

General Management Programs: Focus on the Job of the General Manager

General managers are responsible for an organization's business, corporate, and enterprise strategies. Each of these strategies deals with distinct problems that are addressed by general managers at different levels in an organization. Business strategy is shaped and executed not within any function but by orchestrating multiple functions to play their part. Corporate strategy looks for synergies across the multiple businesses in a firm's portfolio. Enterprise strategy tries to align the firm's mission with the broader goals of society. Also, strategy formulation and implementation cannot be separated. Organizational and leadership issues must be addressed simultaneously when strategy decisions are debated. General managers add value through the trade-offs they make and the integration and alignment that they provide.

The skills needed by a general manager can only be honed through experience. But there are useful concepts and frameworks that a general management program (GM Program) can provide to help accumulate this experience. Participants learn by applying these ideas to a variety of strategy problems through case studies and computer simulations. This requires intense discussions and debates. What is learned is the process of problem solving; there are no right answers. It is difficult to transfer this inductive learning process online, though some are trying.

Working face-to-face in the contained space of a class or discussion room does concentrate the mind. Moreover, it exposes the body language and emotions of participants as they struggle with difficult trade-offs or tough ethical dilemmas in their deliberations. Also, the peer-to-peer learning that continues beyond the classroom over a meal or other informal interactions on campus are invaluable add-on experiences. These networks endure long after a program and provide a life-long source of support and counsel. For all these reasons GM Programs will return to the campus post pandemic, but B-Schools would have to make some important changes to strengthen them:

1. Provide a holistic design: Many of the GM Programs offered today do not really focus on the job of a general manager. What is typically offered is a loose collection of standalone topics, instead of a holistic view of the job. The focus should be on how to add value at the interface of functions, businesses, and stakeholders; and how to master the bureaucracy and politics of an organization to deliver this value. The emphasis should be on integration and alignment.
2. Teach in teams: Delivering a high-quality GM Program requires a faculty team that can integrate the disciplinary diversity that it brings. This is a far cry from what we have today. To deliver these integrated GM Programs, a B-School would have to bridge its departmental silos. Professors with different expertise must team up and improvise in class to create a seamless experience for the participants.
3. Bring in real-world experience: Also, the faculty teaching in GM Programs must have real-world experience to bring the holistic perspective that is needed. This can come through prior employment or consulting experience. Some schools host executives-in-residence. They are general managers who have either retired recently or on sabbatical between assignments. They can be invaluable in designing and delivering GM Programs.
4. Shorten the program: GM Programs are too long, some even stretching to ten weeks. The pandemic has built a strong sense of urgency. Executives cannot be spared for long absences from their jobs. B-Schools should offer their GM Programs in several short modules: online prework, a couple of short two-week sessions on campus, an individual project in between, followed by short periodic refreshers. This trimming should not be difficult since many of today's GM Programs devote a lot of time to the functional disciplines. For participants who need this knowledge, the school can direct them to its online functional programs.

This holistic perspective in design and delivery is the only hope for a B-School to retain its competitive advantage. If it continues to offer standalone topics delivered by its silo specialists (hoping that the participants will do the integration on their own), each of these topics and the GM Program itself will eventually migrate to online delivery. This will be bad both for the participant and the school.

Custom Programs: Cooperate to Address Difficult Dilemmas

Custom programs are an important revenue generator for B-Schools, often on par with the two open programs that were discussed earlier. These are designed to address the specific needs of an organization and delivered exclusively to its executives. Some client corporations have taken advantage of the growing competition in the executive education marketplace by putting their custom programs out for bids. Their purchasing department (and not their Executive Development department) takes the lead in negotiations with the B-School. This is the ultimate commoditization of custom programs. It has to be reversed.

Some of the custom programs are just functional programs tweaked to the needs of a client and perhaps open to price competition. However, a well-integrated general management program or a custom program that is designed and delivered to address an important strategic issue for the client are not commodities to be purchased. These programs must be co-created in close and extended partnership with the client company. The B-School's burden is to convince the client that it is the right partner.

The coronavirus pandemic has surfaced some tough dilemmas for corporate leaders. Should the focus be on workplace safety or continuity of business? Should the company aim for short-term gains or longer term performance? Should the focus in a multinational corporation (MNC) be on home country priorities or host country needs? These are dilemmas because these are not "or" problems but "and" problems; both goals are simultaneously important. Yet pursuing one of these goals will most probably compromise the other. Other crises will soon follow the pandemic: the climate crisis and the growing divide between the haves and have-nots in the world. Corporations must deal with the tough trade-offs between environmental, social, and financial performance. There are no good theories on how to manage these dilemmas. The balance struck will vary from company to company and even within a company vary over time.

A B-School can be an excellent partner for working on corporate dilemmas. Unlike management consultants it does not have a favourite solution to market or a large number of consultants to bill. Skilled faculty can work with the company's own experts in designing and delivering a step-wise process to understand the challenge, look at available theories, brainstorm on company specific solutions, experiment with these ideas, learn, and perfect what is executed.

The approach suggested is Participatory Action Research (PAR), a broad tradition of experimentation backed up by evidential reasoning, fact-finding, and learning. A B-School must have a core group of faculty skilled in the PAR methodology to successfully expand its custom program opportunity. Client companies will seek it not because it has the right answer (like what management consultants claim to offer), but because it brings different theoretical lenses to work on a client's dilemmas and has the action learning methodology needed to co-create acceptable solutions.

Conclusion

Even though this paper is about executive programs, the changes suggested here will spill over to a B-School's degree programs and to the school itself. Program delivery will have to be both online and on-campus, with the awareness that programs will inevitably drift online (with the attendant hit on profitability) unless the school can create stickiness to keep its programs on campus through differentiation. Creating this differentiation requires far greater inter departmental cooperation in research and teaching than we see in the faculty today.

23

Post-Pandemic Architecture and Education

Ignacio Dahl Rocha and Nicole Michel

We have the opportunity to take advantage of the technological advances that are revolutionizing our lives, to put them at the service of human beings and transform our cities and buildings.

We have all experienced how the pandemic has accelerated the changes brought about by technology. We also know that the crisis of the last year has highlighted the problems that plague our society, such as the environment or social inequalities, which characterize the cities that have emerged and expanded over the last century. This crisis offers an opportunity to reflect upon them and to find solutions. If instead, things simply return to the way they were before, we will have wasted a magnificent opportunity.

The dizzying pace of change calls for urgent action and forces us to anticipate the future. This already represents a huge challenge, given the difficulties of futurology and the risk of getting things wrong.

How are we to prepare ourselves for the transformation we so urgently need to undertake? And more specifically in relation to the subject in hand: what does educating for the future involve?

How do we prepare in order to address the changes brought about by science and technology, while at the same time preserving our deep-rooted

---

I. Dahl Rocha (✉) · N. Michel
RDR architectes, Lausanne, Switzerland
e-mail: i.dahlrocha@rdr.ch

humanist values? How will these changes condition the future of architecture and the city?

The ambitious nature of these questions forces us to exercise humility as we approach them from the point of view of our respective trades. Architecture offers the knowledge and skills required to meet this challenge, but its core lies beyond the limits of our discipline and instead requires feeding off culture in its broadest sense.

A new architecture can only emerge from an open dialogue with society, and in particular with educators and students, based on methods that ensure a creative, participatory and multidisciplinary process.

That said, we would like to share some thoughts and suggestions that have emerged over the last year. In the first place, we know that the pandemic, in addition to being the cause of innumerable traumas and opportunities, is also a symptom of a fundamental problem: the global ecological imbalance. Although this question goes beyond the purpose of these lines, we want to clarify that the greatest challenge facing architecture and urban planning lies, first and foremost, in a commitment to the environment.

The revolution of the virtual space.

In terms of the evolution of post-pandemic architecture, the transformations that will shape it will not necessarily be directly linked to health, but rather to the new ways of doing things that this crisis has brought about and that will persist in different ways. These new ways of doing things are modifying the essential material of our habitat: architectural space. Our daily lives have undergone drastic changes. Many of these are not new, but they have gathered an unexpected momentum. Most of us have reorganized our lives without leaving our homes. The boundaries between home and work have been blurred. We have worked online, shopped online, "visited" family and friends online, we have participated in or taught long-distance courses and seminars online, we have attended conferences and exhibitions online, we have even exercised or participated in religious services via our computers.

For many people, the last year has been a positive experience that has revealed opportunities for the future, even if the limits of the virtual world have been exposed in terms of replacing face-to-face activities. But other people have suffered as they contemplated these changes with resignation and helplessness, realizing how vulnerable they are.

Nevertheless, the fact is that we have become aware that the activities and social life that traditionally occurred in the home, public spaces or the office "can take place" in virtual spaces. Teleworking, online shopping and virtual classrooms are capable of replacing the traditional architectural spaces of the office, the shopping centre and the school.

This evolution in how we do things will necessarily be supported by an evolution in the concept of architectural space in which the boundaries between real and virtual space will gradually be blurred.

Information and communications technology are at the root of these transformations and will undoubtedly play an even greater role in the coming years, since in doing so, the virtual space increases its potential as a substitute for real space.

The concepts of real and virtual are in fact abstract notions and it is key not to see them as mutually exclusive options, but instead to understand the opportunities that lie in combining them.

The advantages of exploring this symbiosis between virtual and real space range from the quantitative, with the possibility of reducing current levels of construction (with the added benefit for the environment), to the wealth new ways of integrating both realms into new academic programs and methods.

Spaces such as auditoriums or classrooms may end up being replaced by dynamic, indeterminate and multipurpose spaces where the advances in communications technology as well as the development of new building materials will allow for a wide range of interactive pedagogical, social, recreational or sports activities beyond the limits imposed by the traditional compartmentalization of space.

Far from reducing the use of face-to-face, physical locations, we can imagine opportunities to enhance these spaces to favor formal and informal meetings, given the importance of in-person social relationships in the development of an educational community.

We also know that educational institutions are increasingly aware that the need to create lasting and wide-ranging communities is as important, or perhaps even more so, than the transfer of knowledge.

The academic community also possesses, thanks to the representative nature of architecture, an opportunity to communicate its identity and values to the world, and can do so by taking advantage of the potential to combine virtual and real spaces. In fact, virtual spaces have the potential to be used for architectural purposes, as they offer the possibility to house (or host) classrooms, meetings and interactive activities such as webinars, chats, blogs, on-demand recordings, book launches, among many others. Personal contact is irreplaceable, especially outside the classroom, and is, therefore, one of those aspects of our lives that hopefully will not change. Nevertheless, virtual spaces are here to stay, not as an alternative, but as a complement to their physical counterpart.

The importance of resilient architecture in managing uncertainty.

We should also explore the ability of architecture to adapt to the changes that occur with increasing frequency and are generating much uncertainty. The quality of accommodating change and learning from it is known as resilience and is a key notion in our thought process.

The term resilience in architecture is of relatively recent use and derives from the disciplines of human behavior. John Bowlby tackled emotional resilience and defined it as the ability of human beings to overcome periods of emotional pain and adverse situations, emerging from them with new strength. Similarly, while observing the natural world, C.S. Holling described resilience as a way of measuring the persistence of systems while absorbing change and disturbance: remaining in equilibrium in situations of instability.

Unlike sustainability, resilience looks not only at the end game but is also interested in what may happen along the way and how to take advantage of it, be it predictable or unpredictable. It takes into account long-term goals, but also deals with responding to the intermediate stages. It therefore progresses through immediate and sometimes-isolated actions, along with long-term coordinated efforts that look to build a lasting knowledgeable response.

A resilient architecture must reflect what we have learned over time. The mechanisms that allow it to evolve are based on continuous learning through feedback from past experiences that inform future decision-making. Its main characteristic is its flexibility.

In architecture, in the face of uncertainty, there is a need to generate flexible and adaptable spaces that can respond to variable conditions, changing needs, be they gradual or sudden, expected or unforeseen. This could potentially mean more "generic", less specific, more "adjustable" architectures.

We know that the most appropriate or specific design at any given moment is not always that which best resists the passage of time. Trying to forecast errors or unexpected changes could make it inappropriate or obsolete. Generic is the term used for an architecture that, because of its formal, spatial and technical characteristics, is adaptable and evolutionary. In general simple, clear and neutral forms prevail, often based on a modular composition. It is at odds with the notion of tailor made, which relates to very specific forms with links to a particular function, and that are therefore difficult to adjust to other uses or circumstances. Flexibility can be achieved through spatiality, which can be applied to constructions housing different configurations. It can also happen, in time, through the mutualization of a space used for different purposes at different times of the day or the week, or through the versatility of a space, that is, the fact that the same space is capable of accommodating different uses. The wide range of possibilities that the combination of these three notions opens up is further enriched by incorporating the concept of virtual space.

The flexibility of a building is also determined by its construction system, and the design of its elements should facilitate simple and quick internal reconfigurations. In addition, when construction elements are clearly articulated, the system allows for each piece to be renovated or replaced per its particular life cycle, while facilitating the permanent reconversion of the building, or in other words, its perpetuity.

Paradoxically, the need for resilient spaces could generate architectures that are less ephemeral and more robust in many aspects. The search for greater efficiency as a common, omnipresent criterion or as it relates to the objectives of sustainable development, minimizing the use of natural and energy resources, implies doing more with less. This constitutes a potential loss of redundancy, a key concept for resilience, since a redundant and robust system usually requires greater consumption of resources to allow the duplication of elements or systems and, therefore, is less efficient.

The most eloquent example of robustness is the extraordinary resilience that so many historic buildings have shown over the centuries compared to the ephemeral nature of most contemporary constructions. Regardless of their function, their formal and material robustness, as well as their aesthetic contribution to the urban environment, greatly valued in terms of patrimony, have guaranteed their permanence.

An example from our professional experience in school design illustrates the evolution of these central themes over time and the importance of resilience in a particular architectural project. At the beginning of this process, a major concern was that of investigating the ideal form of an auditorium, based on some well-known examples. A few years later, the very notion of an auditorium was questioned by many who preferred the flat-room typology, which led us to propose a flexible solution, conceiving the stands as part of the equipment. At the same time, the center of attention moved from the classrooms themselves to the common spaces, which provided areas for formal and informal exchanges based on the idea that "crucial things happen outside the classroom."

Today we now have virtual auditoriums, and the transformation of the architectural space sparked by advances in communications technology and paired with new educational methods and programs has resulted in a line of thought that questions the very notion of the classroom as a spatial and teaching unit. In fact, today's main teaching space could be perceived as a container that houses specific activities that could easily adapt, as we mentioned earlier, to a virtual environment. This innovation in teaching practices could result in a transformation of the typical learning space into a much more flexible one, where equipment, furniture, configuration, even walls and shape, could evolve in a number of ways to house diverse in-person and remote activities beyond traditional education. One could imagine it opening up by dissolving its enclosure to host myriad activities, potentially in the open air. The perceived simplicity of the container offers countless complex adaptable architectural responses to varying pedagogical needs.

An architecture at the service of society.

We mentioned earlier that a sustainable technology not just at the service of human beings, but all living beings and the planet, offers us a new opportunity to develop more harmonious forms of relating what is built in the natural environment, and transforming our buildings and our cities into true spaces of social integration.

The sharp decrease in mobility and its surprising and immediate positive effects on the environment, which occurred during this pandemic's first lockdown, illustrate what could potentially be achieved with a transport system based on renewable energies. We now have an opportunity to rethink cities that have been designed to meet the needs of cars.

How might such changes impact the future of the city? Cities could become much more technologically integrated, and at the same time more robust and adaptable; more diverse, less segregated cities that benefit from the potential synergies between different spatial uses; cities that are closely connected to, and supportive of, their occupants and their need of wellbeing and comfort. A balance between sustainability and resilience seems to arise as a possible way forward.

Technological advances led by an awareness of sustainable development and its associated socio-economic commitment provide us with an opportunity to recover the city for human beings. We hope that the new generations, in addition to saving our planet, will be able to create a habitat worthy of our ambitions as a society.

Architecture and urban planning take a generalist and synthetic view of problems that tend to be considered technical, yet are much broader and human in nature. The great challenge for these disciplines, both as cultural statements and given the complexity of these stakes, will be to shape an urban context that allows us to proudly declare that the city has always been the most polished expression of the human race.

24

How the Pandemic Has Demonstrated the Importance of System Leadership in Executive Education

Knut Haanaes and Katherine Brown

Introduction

Over the last 30 years, executive education has been in a long period of ongoing adaptation, mainly driven by established players in the realms of business and finance. That is now over. Executive education will change significantly going forward. We are today in what we can think of as a punctuated equilibrium, in large part because of the magnitude of Covid-19 which has driven an acceleration of changes that were already underway. We see executive education change because of new technology platforms, but also due to an increased awareness of the impacts of leadership decisions on people and planet. Many executive education providers still cater to the needs of the past, built on business models that are no longer viable. Many of these players will disappear if they are not redesigned to deliver the skills required for the changes ahead.

K. Haanaes (✉)
Lundin Sustainability Chair, International Institute for Management Development (IMD), Lausanne, Switzerland
e-mail: knut.haanaes@imd.org

K. Brown
International Institute for Management Development (IMD), Lausanne, Switzerland

Being competitive is still essential for a business to survive, but the means to remain relevant have shifted. In addition to the many skills of the past, we believe executive education will need to fully incorporate system leadership. In this chapter we will focus on how executive education institutions should move beyond focusing solely on competitive advantage and organizational leadership to also address wider ecosystem collaboration and system leadership. This comes in large part from the more proactive role of business in terms of sustainability and improving societal outcomes. Over the next decade competitiveness will also become more driven by collaboration, agility, and resilience. First, we will look at why these changes are taking place. Then, a short description of ecosystem collaboration and system leadership. We will then illustrate how this has played out during the pandemic before making some observations about the future of executive education.

Why Learn About System Leadership?

Our research shows how the business world is becoming more important in addressing global challenges. Business will play an essential part in helping solving climate change and social inequality—in fact, in addressing all the Sustainable Development Goals. In addition, the expectations from society are higher. Hence, companies need to recognize their increased responsibility towards an extended group of stakeholders. As such, executive education needs to shape leaders who can work effectively in multistakeholder systems, where corporate responsibility is a priority and will become actively tracked.

In his 2018 letter to shareholders, Larry Fink of the world's largest asset manager, BlackRock, wrote: "The public expectations of your company have never been greater. Society is demanding that companies, both public and private, serve a social purpose."[1] In our opinion executive education should no longer develop future leaders with a narrow view of capitalism. Just as excellent companies must combine the pursuit of purpose and profit, executive education players must demonstrate the ability to develop talented people who can navigate corporate responsibility, sustainability, and the new role of business in society. We believe that executive educational institutions should create societal impact by ensuring that leaders develop the mindsets and skills to be adept at combining profit and purpose.

Let's share some practical observations of what we are learning. Sceptics of the past would likely cast doubt on the ability of a company to remain

---

[1] https://www.blackrock.com/corporate/investor-relations/larry-fink-ceo-letter.

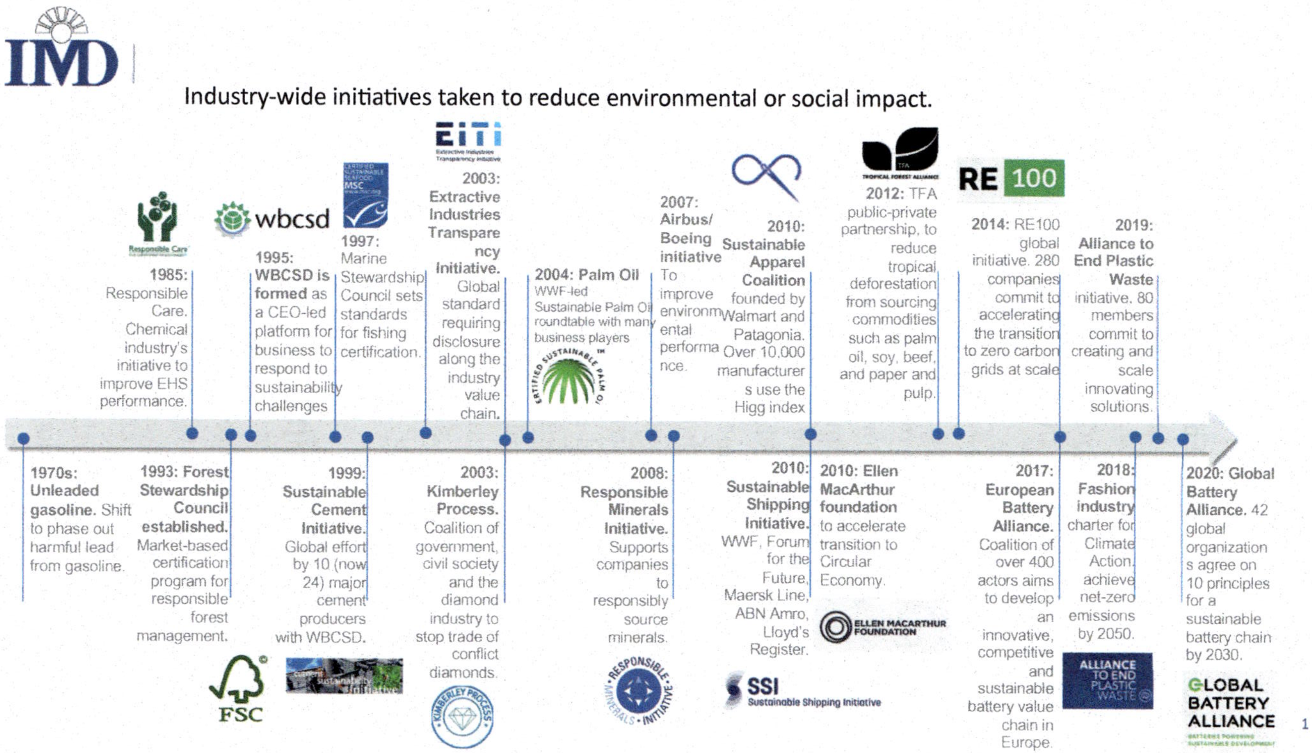

Fig. 24.1 A timeline of industry-wide initiatives (Elaborated by the Authors)

competitive in a collaborative landscape, where the focus of leadership goes beyond the sole concept of shareholder return. However, our research on the evolution of sustainability and ESG across industries indicates that big change increasingly happens through system collaboration, when an entire industry moves towards a certain set of social or environmental goals in step with public sector and civil society. This can best be described as a collective "raising of the bar" to a higher baseline to which industry players are held accountable.

The figure below shows the evolution of industry initiatives and collaboration. It shows an acceleration in engagement around sustainability issues across industries (Fig. 24.1).

In the last years we have also witnessed the emergence of significant cross-industry groups, designed under the playbook of systems leadership, that respond to the call for global transparency on ESG performance. One such group, the International Business Council of the World Economic Forum, released a proposal in 2020 that aimed to rally the existing landscape of standard setters behind a harmonized suite of measures that all companies and investors can use as a baseline for reporting their ESG performance. This milestone effectively saw business leaders at the highest levels using their collective voice to loudly call for a change in current reporting practice. Whilst the standard setting ecosystem had been working hard to meet the demands of better sustainability tracking for decades, it was examples of system leadership like this and related initiatives that dramatically accelerated the movement towards global standards.

We believe this is just the beginning, and that over the next decade we will see more and stronger collaboration to address big societal challenges, both within industries but also public–private collaborations as well as in operational ecosystems.

What Is System Leadership?

System leadership is necessary to develop strategies and inspire actions that solve big problems. It is about zooming out to understand the drivers of significant change at a more meta-level, the system level, realizing that most big problems can only be solved together since no individual party has sufficient resources or power to do so. Without understanding change, we cannot strategically attack societal issues like pandemics, climate change, circular economy, cybercrime, and corruption.

The academic area of system leadership initially came out of MIT, where Donatella Meadows, Jorgen Randers and colleagues built on the systems dynamics theory of Jay Forrester in their work on "limits to growth" in the early 1970s.[2] Later Peter Senge and colleagues described system leadership as the art of bringing together different parties (what they also called collective leadership) in creating societal solutions.[3] The World Economic Forum has over time been a strong shaper of and public advocate for system leadership, often in collaboration with thought leaders like Jane Nelson. Together with David Nabarro and Lisa Dreier, she provides a modern description of systems leadership as "a set of skills and capacities that any individual or organization can use to catalyse, enable, and support the process of systems-level change. It combines collaborative leadership, coalition-building, and systems insight to mobilize innovation and action across a large, de-centralized network."[4]

Despite serious attention—and promise—system leadership has so far gained limited application in business and in executive education. To a degree, this is due to the fact that we are still in the period of transition from older models of thinking, such as Milton Friedman's shareholder theory, that work against the grain of collective action for common good in the business context. As a result, examples of successful systems-level interventions, whilst increasingly visible, still get less attention than their classic forebears in practice.

Additionally, the influences and components that mark exemplary systems change are by definition amorphous in nature and hence difficult to teach in a classical sense. To this end, executive education can play a central role in delivering a more common understanding and practical application of systems change.

As a starting point, let's illustrate the key elements of system change:

(1) Change usually happens both deliberately and in a more emergent way; actually, systems are often surprisingly self-organized.
(2) System change is generally not linear, and outcomes are not predictable.
(3) Systems typically have positive and negative feedback loops. This does not mean that ambitions and plans are useless; they need to allow for adaptation and agility to meet the current context and updated projections of the future.

---

[2] Meadows, D. et al. (1972). "Limits to Growth, Potomac Associates," Universe Books.
[3] Senge, P. et al. (2015). "The Dawn of System Leadership," Stanford Social Innovation.
[4] Dreier, L. et al. (2019). "System leadership can change the world—But what exactly is it?" World Economic Forum.

(4) A multi-stakeholder view is required; we need to understand the key stakeholders, their interventions, and their interests. Different players with different interests create impact.
(5) Systems have leverage points, where a slight shift in one thing can produce significant changes in everything (the silver bullet, the miracle cure, the hero).
(6) Timing is essential; often, change happens because the "time has come."

We see system leadership and creating system change as a major opportunity for executive education providers.

How the Pandemic Has Demonstrated the Importance of System Leadership

Amidst the chaos of the Covid-19 crisis we have witnessed both a remarkable example of systems leadership in the rapid development of vaccines, as well as failures to exercise systems leadership in how policy decisions and vaccine distribution were handled at a global scale. As we evaluate both sides, we can start to see how our preparedness for collaboration in a crisis impacted the result.

On the positive side, the reflex to address widespread global health issues was already established via institutions that were built specifically for this purpose, such as the World Health Organization, Gavi (the Vaccine Alliance), The Coalition for Epidemic Preparedness Innovations (CEPI), and the Bill and Melinda Gates Foundation. Already operating at the system level, their ability to quickly mobilize their resources to create COVAX, the vaccine arm of the Access the Covid-19 Tools (ACT) accelerator, clearly laid out a process for the development and fair distribution of vaccines both quickly and universally. These actors were able to work alongside academia and government early on to both educate and advise on developments and actions as they unfolded in real time. Additionally, corporate actors raised their hands over the world to leverage their essential logistical capacity to aid in the delivery of critical supplies such as testing kits, masks, sanitizer, food, and ultimately vaccines. US companies such as Walmart and the pharmacy chain CVS, with significant physical footprints across the country, offered their parking lots for medical teams to efficiently set up testing and vaccination centres at short notice. This exemplified public–private collaboration at a time of highest urgency and set the world in motion for the ultimate example of systems leadership in action.

However, despite the strong start, traditional competitive instincts again began to emerge as vaccine rollout commenced following an extended period of social and economic hardship. Collaboration dissolved in many instances, and vaccine producers were forced to decide whether to honour orders from countries in need or stockpile for the use of their own nationals. Instead of the fair distribution envisaged by COVAX, many governments focused on their own economic interests by refusing to distribute considerable amounts of vaccine to even their closest neighbours. The European Union, itself an early example of ecosystem collaboration, failed to standardize the process of distribution of both testing kits and vaccines within its jurisdiction. This demonstrates that system leadership is in fact difficult even when it is the premise upon which an institution was created, as effective mobilization of the distributed actors—without ultimate authority—is paramount to success.

How to Learn About System Leadership?

We can best teach system leadership through application; we need to expose executives to action. Many executive education institutions are moving fast into action-based learning, especially technology-based start-ups. In terms of leadership development, this means moving from classroom to lab. Action-based learning focuses on solving real-life problems. Fundamentally, we need to think about learning more as an iterative process, not only on the "research-develop-teach" model. Action-based learning drives motivation by being relevant, by creating tangible solutions, and by showcasing impact. Importantly, this action-based approach must also clearly illustrate the average increase in positive outcomes and performance that are achieved through a systems-level approach versus one that is narrow and isolated.

Executive Education for the Future

To stay relevant, we believe that tomorrow's executive education institutions themselves will need to deploy systems-oriented and collaborative strategies. To lead by example, and to illustrate that competitiveness has its limits when the wellbeing of people and planet are at stake. The winners of the learning age will win together, not alone. We believe that this approach to system leadership can avoid the trap of addressing corporate responsibility in an intellectual vacuum. In the past graduates often left executive programmes feeling inspired, yet unequipped to truly affect change in the traditional business world for which they were now in charge. Many entered large corporate engines with visions of infusing collective purpose and impact into the business and course correcting the past yet became frustrated that their acquired tools and narratives failed to create the desired institutional change. We believe that the capacity of executive education institutions to gather their individual excellence in best-practice into a collective approach would greatly alter this outcome. That is a great opportunity for all executive education providers.

25

Executive Education Post-Pandemic: Some Reflections on the Role of Technology-Mediated Interactions Going Forward

Jean François Manzoni

Attempting to predict the future is a perilous exercise. In fact, it is probably a sure recipe to look like a fool more often than not. Nonetheless, you will find in this chapter IMD's perspective on the future role of technology-mediated interactions in executive education. Time will tell how far off the mark we are, but in the meantime these reflections will hopefully help stimulate your own.

First, let's agree on the scope of this reflection. Technology-mediated interactions refer to interactions between faculty and learners that occur "virtually" instead of occurring face-to-face. This technology-mediated interaction can be asynchronous (i.e., the learner can access pre-prepared material independently and on demand) or synchronous (meaning that a faculty member and typically other learners are also participating in the interaction).

Secondly, let me share a bit of information on IMD as it will help explain how we came to develop the perspective presented in this chapter. IMD is an independent academic institution (a not-for-profit, stand-alone business school), whose revenues depend almost entirely on program tuition fees, more than 80% of which involve non-degree activities and more than 90%

J. F. Manzoni (✉)
International Institute for Management Development (IMD), Lausanne, Switzerland
e-mail: jean-francois.manzoni@imd.org

of which required (overwhelmingly international) travel at the start of the Covid-crisis. In other words, in February 2020 we found ourselves with 90% of our revenues at severe risk.

Like most schools, we had started to integrate technology-mediated interactions in our activities. We had developed about fifteen asynchronous (on-demand) open programs, and we were selectively re-using some of these programs' material to support customized executive programs. We had also started to use synchronous modes (mainly webex and zoom) to conduct typically short interventions with executives we could not meet with face-to-face. We were convinced that technology-mediated interactions would continue to develop and we were very much intent on participating in this development, but we were also dealing with record volumes of activity in all of our programs, so it is fair to say that progressing on the technology-mediated front was not our number one priority.

This prioritization level increased very quickly in February 2020 when we realized that we would have to move our degree-program teaching "virtually", but also that our revenues risked falling *dramatically* if we did not *rapidly* (a) develop the ability to propose technology-mediated executive programs that (b) would be *sufficiently attractive* to convince executives and organizations to use these programs now, instead of postponing their program by who-knew-how-long.

IMD's culture is very collaborative and purpose-driven. Our faculty also understands the school's revenue generation model. As a result, IMD's fifty faculty members showed a very high degree of innovation and flexibility and invested substantial time and energy learning how to use technology-mediated interactions (TMIs) in a way that would live up to IMD's tag line of "real learning, real impact". The school was also willing and able to make substantial financial investments in hardware, software, and capability development. We decided to use this crisis as an opportunity to "progress as much over the next three months in our use of technology-mediated interactions (TMIs) as we would have normally done over the next three years".

I think it is fair to say that some of us were hoping—at least initially—that this move to technology-mediated interaction was temporary; as soon as executives would resume travelling, we could return to face-to-face interactions. Three convergent forces helped us to realize that this was not a short-term temporary phenomenon: First, we realized that the crisis would last longer than anticipated. TMIs would hence be with us for longer than anticipated. Two, we realized that executives and organizations would come to like the efficiency of TMIs and would hence *not* return 100% to face-to-face interactions and international travel. TMIs would remain beyond the acute part of the crisis. Third, and most important, we realized that *TMIs may in many ways be a superior approach to executive education than our traditional face-to-face interventions*. This realization came in two steps.

TMIs Enable a Greater Percentage of F2F Than We Thought

The first step was realizing that technology-mediated Interactions in fact allow us to do "more than we thought". If you had asked us pre-crisis what percentage of our impact we could have via TMIs, we probably would have said 50–60%. We would have explained that "face-to-face interactions are simply so much richer than TMIs and enable us to do a great many things that "you simply can't do online"."

We quickly realized that if we simply "lift and shift"—i.e., if we simply move on zoom what we do face-to-face, the result is indeed rather pedestrian. Much less interactive than face-to-face, much less energizing and frankly, more boring for both sides of the camera. The energy transfer does not operate as well on zoom as it does in an interactive, exciting face-to-face session.

But nobody sentenced us to "lift and shift"; we could also re-design each session to ensure that it would achieve its learning objectives with maximum effectiveness (i.e., achieving the objectives to a maximum extent) and efficiency (i.e., doing so with the minimum investment of learner time and energy). Through our initial attempts, we realized that sessions needed to be shorter than our traditional 3.5–4 hours face-to-face. We identified ways to introduce more interactivity in the sessions (more discussions between learners and between instructor and learners), and to make them more energizing and engaging by varying the pace and introducing more activities with a shorter cycle time.

We also realized that combining asynchronous and synchronous interactions could significantly contribute to enhancing effectiveness and efficiency.

- Asynchronous material is intrinsically efficient because it can be accessed anytime from anywhere by the learner. Also, its one-way communication component can be optimized in terms of compact and efficient delivery.
- Asynchronous modules designed intelligently and with modularity can also offer non-trivial *personalization* of the learning process. Personalization improves both the effectiveness and the efficiency of the learning process by enabling learners who get the material quickly to focus on more advanced

sections, while allowing those who need more time to process the basic material to do so calmly and fully.
- Last and obviously not least, moving a significant component of the "one way transmission of material" to asynchronous mode creates more time for interactive/discussion segments during the synchronous interactions, which has two advantages: First, it contributes to making these synchronous interactions more engaging. Secondly, more time for discussions and interactions increases the legitimacy of the synchronous module by leveraging more intensely the simultaneous participation of all the learners. Increasing the sessions' legitimacy translates into greater compliance and participation.

TMIs Enable Us to Do Things That We Simply Could Not Do as Well in F2F Programs

The second—and even more unexpected—stage of our journey involved the realization that not only can TMIs help us get closer to "100%" than we thought, TMIs also enable us to go beyond "100%". That is, an intelligent combination of synchronous and asynchronous interactions enables us to introduce features and benefits beyond what we can do Face-to-Face (F2F). Here are a few examples:

1. Synchronous technology-mediated programs enable us to bring into the program a much larger set of guest speakers. Where in a F2F world coming to Lausanne to give a one hour speech would have essentially consumed a full day of any European CEO, appearing in a liVe (with a capital V for "virtual") program now requires a much shorter commitment. This gives us extraordinary access to more guest speakers of greater prestige and quality.
2. Technology-mediated programs also make it much easier to integrate "discovery expeditions" into executive programs. In a F2F world, we had to choose *one* discovery expedition location and could only along bring a small number of executives. Getting to and from the location was also quite time consuming. In a technology-mediated world, we can benchmark an Asian company in the morning and a company in the Americas in the afternoon. We can also "bring along" a much larger group of individuals. By the way, these virtual visits are also less demanding logistically on the organizations welcoming us, which also increases our access.

3. F2F programs at IMD required individuals to travel to Lausanne (or Singapore). To increase the return on travel investment, we tended to run very intensive programs running over several consecutive days. On the positive side, we were able to have the executives' relatively undivided attention during these few days. On the negative side, the intense pace was more efficient for us from a capacity utilization point of view than it was effective for executives in terms of retention and internalization. They "drank from a firehose" for a few days and left the program very energized, but their retention level was probably lower than we care to admit.

   Removing the need to travel opens up the possibility of spreading the interventions over longer periods of time. Instead of doing a five-day program, we can and now do offer similar content over, say, two to five weeks. This spreading over longer periods of time requires a lower "absorption" pace, and offers more possibilities for revisiting key messages more than once and for repeated "mental retrieval" by learners. Given what we now know on the need for neurons to fire together in order to wire together and for repeated retrievals in order to solidify memory connections, we believe that (and are in the process of testing whether indeed) these "part time" interventions over longer periods of time will lead to greater retention and internalization.
4. Transforming intense, full-time programs conducted away from work into part-time interventions attended from work also enables us to design content and process in a way that better integrates it into executives' work life. For example, it is now easier for participants to invite some of their team members into parts of the program. It is also easier for us to integrate various kinds of application modules or projects into the journeys.

Our Vision for the Future, Including a Few Questions, Caveats and Concerns

We believe that international travel will start to resume by late Q3/start of Q4 2021. We believe that executives will start travelling again, which will lead to a resurrection of several F2F open programs and of the custom programs for which we were not able to convince the client to move to TMIs. We very much look forward to this return to a more normal life.

We are also *completely convinced* that the world will *not* revert 100% to pre-covid executive education practices. We are convinced that Technology-Mediated Interactions will become the norm and that in the future, (a) we will continue to have programs that are 100% technology-mediated and feature no F2F component, and (b) programs featuring a F2F component will *always also* include a blend of synchronous and asynchronous modules. In other words, we do *not* expect henceforth to offer *any* program that would be 100% face-to-face, something we were still doing in early 2020.

One reason will be that executives and organizations will demand blended designs from us. Another reason is that *we* will demand it from ourselves and from our clients. Please allow me a personal anecdote to illustrate this latter point:

> I was recently asked to meet with the CEO, CHRO and Head of Learning and Development of one of our partner companies. They were coming to discuss the design of the new intervention we will be conducting for them, and their expectations were very clear and explicit. This is a sophisticated client who's done many such programs over the years with many different partners, and they know what they want. Interestingly, what they wanted looked remarkably similar to a program we could have offered pre-Covid. In particular, it made very limited use of synchronous TMI and zero use of asynchronous modules. After discussing the situation with the IMD client team, I took the liberty of engaging our three guests on this point. Their visit went from ninety minutes to three and a half hours, and we now have a much stronger, richer, blended design. In this case, the impetus very much came from us telling the client: Of course we can do "face-to-face plus", but we can also do so much more today because of what we learned during this crisis.

These blended interventions (F2F, synchronous and asynchronous TMIs) delivered over longer periods of time will enable us, we believe, to offer more effectiveness (retention, internalization, and personalization) for a given (financial and non-financial) investment, or similar effectiveness at a lower investment.

You will of course have noticed my use of the expression "we believe", as opposed to "research/data shows". We do have some data to support these beliefs. In particular, we have relatively detailed measurement of learner perceptions at program end and four months later. Data collected from thousands of participants in open and custom programs suggest that well designed technology-mediated programs generate very similar positive feedback from executives to their face-to-face counterparts. The one dimension where we have not yet been able to reach the same levels is "benefits of networking"; F2F programs still get rated more positively on this front. This is not completely unexpected, but we still believe that we can introduce technologies that will increase value creation on this dimension as well.

But these data are suggestive at most. We need better impact assessment methodologies to be able to substantiate *conclusively* that one design is superior to another. In the meantime, we *do* know that *neurons that fire together wire together*. That's just a fact. It *is* also a fact that TMIs enable us to make neurons fire more often over longer periods of time. We believe this will prove to be a decisive asset.

A Quick Note on "Hybrid Programs"

Early in the crisis, the possibility of running hybrid programs (with some participants in class and others on screen) generated significant interest and hope. We experimented with it but quickly realized that it is a very challenging approach. First, the technical requirements are relatively high. For participants on screen to *really* see and hear *well* what's happening in class requires substantial financial investment to get sophisticated enough equipment. We initially invested into mid-range equipment and quickly got complaints from "virtual participants" objecting they didn't feel appropriately connected.

Beyond the technical challenge, hybrid classes present real pedagogical challenges. F2F participants have the instructor live in front of them and hence feel a greater energy transfer than the folks on screen. As a result, the instructor needs to pay particular attention to virtual participants. In fact, the instructor probably also needs to design the session based on the energy requirements of a virtual class, as opposed to a F2F one, which may not serve the F2F participants as well. Last but not least, instructors teaching two different groups simultaneously often struggle to share their attention optimally between the two groups. Too much attention to the F2F participants alienates the virtual ones, and too much attention to the virtual participants frustrates the physical ones.

We believe that hybrid technology will be useful in the future and have hence increased our investments to have a few rooms well suited for hybrid pedagogy. But we believe that the conditions under which hybrid will be optimal (as opposed to functional) are limited to cases where the *hybrid approach creates value for all participants*—that is, that both groups feel that there is solid benefit to having a hybrid class as opposed to two separate classes (one physical, one virtual). We think that this is more likely to happen in custom executive programs, where the client and/or the program requires the presence of individuals who cannot legitimately be expected to travel.[1]

Some Questions and Concerns

I have explained below what we think will happen in the next few years in executive education world with respect to technology-mediated interactions. We are very much preparing for this scenario. We also have a number of questions and concerns about this future. Sone of these concerns are more internal and pertain to the impact of the "TMI revolution" on business schools' faculty and staff. Others pertain to the "market side" of this equation.

More internal questions and concerns

1. As of now, technology-mediated sessions require much *more ex-ante pedagogical preparation* than face-to-face sessions. In a F2F setting, transition costs between lecture, discussion and buzz groups are very low; the instructor can shift gears and pedagogical mode almost instantaneously. Doing so during virtual sessions feels less seamless to us and we hence prepare more. Will our pedagogical fluidity increase as we become more experienced and new "technologies" develop? OR will TMI always remain less spontaneous and flexible than F2F?
2. On the positive side, part-time interventions attended from work enable us to offer more sessions over longer periods of time. On the negative front, these sessions create a real transition challenge for learners. Until, say, 14:00 their attention is fully focused on work matters, and suddenly they're supposed to shift gears and refocus on "us". Then, at 16:00 sharp their next meeting will start and if we didn't come to closure before 16:00, it is not entirely clear the learners will be able to get back to the material and reach this closure later. We must hence work hard at developing effective and efficient ways to support learners' intellectual and emotional transitions into and out of sessions. We must also ensure that we support them between sessions, especially when these sessions are spread thinly over long periods of time.[2]

---

[1] For more on this hybrid technology discussion, see my article commentary on "Hybrid Classes Transform Learning" by Ted Ladd and Johan Roos, *EFMD Global Focus* (Vol. 15, #1 [January 2021], pp. 38–39).

[2] This point actually raises an interesting research question related to the optimal intensity of sessions over time. What will be more effective between, say, 5 mornings in one week vs. 5 mornings spread over two weeks, vs. 10 sessions of 90 minutes spread one per day over two weeks or two per week over 5 weeks? Actually, this question is unlikely to have one simple universal answer independent of the organizational context and other aspects of the program design, including for example the

3. Another disadvantage of executive programs becoming drawn out over longer periods of time is the fragmentation that this spreading introduces into the lives of faculty and staff. Faculty and staff working at low intensity on more programs over longer periods of time create real challenges both in terms of efficiency (including on the scheduling front) and in terms of effectiveness (e.g., as it becomes a lot more difficult for instructors to remember what they said to whom when, and which point already came up with this group or that group). This lower intensity also raises challenges of emotional connection with the group(s) and could have a negative impact on faculty's ability to allocate focused time to research activities.
4. From a cost point of view, we find that technology-mediated programs actually generate *more costs* for us, rather than less. We save very minimal amounts on lunch and printing costs, but our costs significantly increase in terms of technology and participant support, both during sessions and between sessions.
5. As mentioned above, we at IMD have been very fortunate that our Faculty has agreed to invest significant time and energy transitioning to TMIs. Some of our faculty actually enjoy technology-mediated teaching—typically the more introverts among us. But the extroverts, or at least those who tend to genuinely *feel* almost physically the exchange of energy with their class participants, simply do not enjoy technology-mediated sessions as much. Beyond the enjoyment dimension, some of my colleagues also find these sessions more energy draining.
6. Some of my colleagues also start saying that they are *not learning as much* during technology-mediated discussions with executives as they used to in F2F discussions. Will the engagement and insightfulness levels of technology-mediated discussions improve as we all (faculty and participants) become more skilled at engaging in them?
7. An interesting tension is starting to emerge between faculty and non-faculty resources, as technology-mediated programs tend to involve a greater proportion of non-faculty resources than F2F programs. These non-faculty roles provide support, follow-up and/or coaching between but also sometimes during sessions. It is going to be interesting to observe how this shift may influence the relationships within and between these groups.

"Market-related" caveats and concerns

---

topics being covered, the kind of additional support provided between sessions or the level of peer accountability integrated in the program design.

8. Over the last twelve months, we have been more successful shifting custom programs to TMIs than we have been on the open program side. Corporate clients have tended to be quite receptive to the value of TMIs, while a greater proportion of open program participants has preferred to keep postponing programs in order to be able to attend them F2F. Is this an IMD-only trend, or will it be pervasive? What are the underlying causes of this phenomenon?
   - For example, we tend to think of our programs as being on a continuum between at one end the vitamin (good things happen when you take vitamins, but if you don't take your vitamins it's not a major problem) and at the other the aspirin (which you really *want* to take because it helps you solve a problem that is the equivalent of a headache or high fever). Are open programs more of a vitamin for executives and their organizations, while custom programs can be more of an aspirin for the corporation?
   - Or is the "networking" dimension such an important one for open program participants that they prefer to wait for the chance to do the program F2F?
   - And/or are open program participants attributing a high value to being away from office and home for a few days, in order to focus fully on their experience and/or simply because it's pleasant to be away from work for a few days?
   - How much of a factor is the pervasive "zoom fatigue" that we are currently observing across the world? Managers currently spending 8 to 10 hours a day on zoom may find it less appealing to *also* be doing an open executive education program via TMIs. How will the "zoom fatigue" evolve post crisis? Will executives be more or less likely to accept doing a TMI-based open program?

   How persistent in time is this open vs. custom program difference will depend on the persistence of its causes.
9. Last and potentially most problematic, will we be able to capture a high enough proportion of the value we are creating? Again, we at IMD believe that TMIs are creating comparable and in some cases even superior value for executives and corporations, typically at similar-to-higher-cost to us. Will we be able to demonstrate enough value creation to lead our clients to be willing to maintain or even increase prices? Or will they continue to associate "virtual" to "asynchronous online" programs, which tend to be priced at significantly lower levels?

During a recent virtual event gathering more than 300 executives, including a high proportion of learning and development managers, we asked them

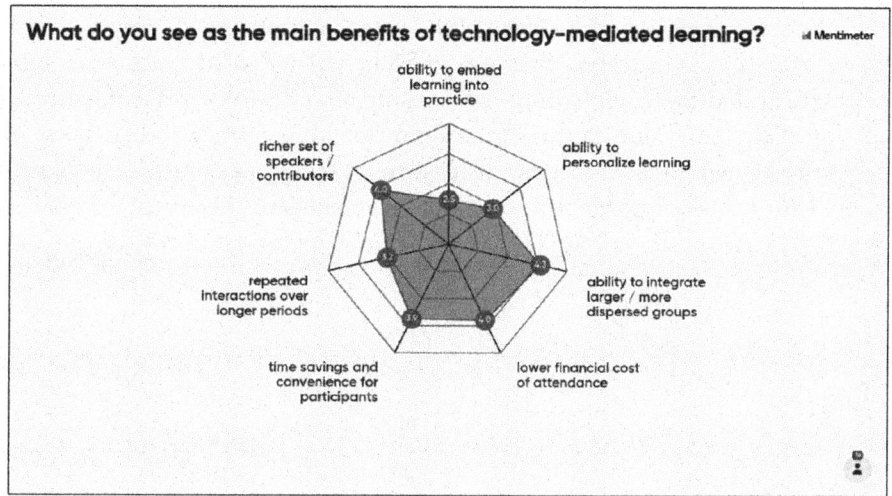

Fig. 25.1 *Summarized responses from 350 senior executives, collected online during IMD's Leading High Impact Learning Day, March 3, 2021 On a 1 (low) to 5 (high) scale* (*Source* Elaborated by the author)

to assess the absolute importance for them of seven benefits of technology-mediated learning. Based on the above, we expected—or maybe simply hoped—that they would attribute the same high value we do to the possibilities offered by TMIs in terms of ability to spread interactions over longer periods of time, to embed learning into practice and to personalize learning. Unfortunately, as indicated in the picture below, these three benefits do not yet register very much on our clients' radar screen. Clearly, a situation that we will have to correct if we hope for these TMIs to involve a sufficient amount of value capture for us (Fig. 25.1).

Wrap-Up

The caveats and concerns above are real and we at IMD will have to address them over the coming months and years. We believe we will have to address them because we believe that TMIs *will* become an increasing component of executive education in the months and years to come. New entrants *will* continue to propose very inexpensive (and sometimes free) asynchronous content, and learners and clients will expect from us the effectiveness and efficiency they believe they can receive from TMIs and blended programs. Professional service firms and ed tech companies are increasingly positioning themselves in this market as well.

For business schools who, like IMD, want to continue to play a leading role in executive education, the onus will be on us to increase our ability to design and deliver such interventions in an effective and efficient way enabling sufficient value capture to sustain our long-term viability. If we get it right, TMIs will be a fantastic new lever to enable us to continue to develop leaders who transform organizations and contribute to society.

26

Executive Education for Family Owned Portfolio Corporations: Needs and Challenges

Karin Mugnaini

Introduction

We must accept that executive education today can mean different things to different people. Companies as well are not spared from the diverse interpretation that these two words, "executive" and "education" yield. In this paper, I will address the term "executive education" as follows: Executive education is a tool for businesses to use to grow, nurture and inspire top leadership talent combining new knowledge and skills so their executives can gain fresh perspectives, cultivate accountability and ownership in order to achieve growth and continuity for the company.

In this short paper, the term executive education will not be used from the "user" or student perspective, which is often mixed with personal and professional development and thus not always identically shared by the employing organization. Instead, I will refer to executive education as something from the employer's perspective and in particular from the portfolio family firm's vision. Also, I will not refer to education as vocational, which is more prevalent in manufacturing or industry firms.

Finally, the word "executive" as I will use it in this piece, will refer to any company employee in a leadership and/or key management position.

K. Mugnaini (✉)
The Lorange Network, Zürich, Switzerland
e-mail: karin@lorangenetwork.com

For family owned portfolio organizations, this of course may imply a greater number of such employees as these types of firms typically employ family members as well as non-family executives who interface in some way or form with a number of businesses, investments or activities.

Additionally, before I begin, I would like to emphasize that although we are now living in what we are calling a "post-covid" or "post-pandemic" world, my strong feeling is that the way family businesses, and especially portfolio oriented family companies consider executive education should not be seen or blurred with a pre-, during- and post-pandemic lens. Rather, through our recent struggles and pandemic challenges, companies have witnessed an acceleration or intensification of issues that were always present. For example, questions involving how they can best play a part in the education, training and inspiration of key staff, whether family or non-family, as well as the sheer need to learn in order to achieve or progress. In other words, the issues are the same before and after the pandemic: a strong focus on the future, with an aim for continuous growth and wealth accumulation by properly preparing next generations for future highs and lows, unknown challenges, exciting opportunities. To summarize, I am taking the timing aspect out of my analysis of executive education. I shout out that all family owned portfolio companies must engage in the commitment for executive education for their employees. In fact, they should technically always have done so, but if they have not yet begun this journey, now is definitely the time to start! Learning is a necessity, pandemic or not. Learning is a "must-have," not a "nice-to-have"!

I will address the following questions: Why is executive education important?

Why is it specifically important for family owned portfolio companies? What are their needs? What are their challenges? I initially hesitated in switching the order to needs, challenges and importance, but changed my mind, believing that to begin with positivity—motivation and inspiration—as opposed to the problem, dilemma, pain or need identification—can further support my belief that executive education is foremost an investment with clear returns or upside, besides a necessity. I will conclude this piece with a list of suggestions for finding the appropriate program for the family owned portfolio business.

Why Is Executive Education Important to Corporations?

Investing in executive education means smarter, more alert employees, who make useful and broad, deep business contacts for the company, who are in closer touch with changing business environment, who have an ability to proactively shape and direct their business environment, and who can consequently help the firm to better guarantee business continuity. Executive education serves as an instrument for any kind of firm to future-proof, create greater value and build more wealth. "Growing executives translates into a growing organization" (Dishan Kamdar).

Why Is Executive Education Specifically Important for Family Owned Portfolio Companies?

Family owned portfolio companies, just as traditional, legacy or heritage family businesses, aim to create value, preserve wealth and grow. Yet portfolio oriented family firms typically operate in more eco-systems through often different areas of activities, either outside the main historical business sector or within. They are therefore even more challenged by complexity.

Executive education for family owned portfolio companies is thus an instrument they can use adeptly and efficiently to promote the optimization of opportunities that their portfolio offers, and discover or create new ones. The complexity and diversity of portfolio companies come from the fact that these entities are in touch with others outside the family firm's core business or center, often as well with multiple service providers such as consultants, lawyers, bankers, investors, etc., beyond the owners, management and staff of the companies in which they are investing. The sheer dimension of their activities makes it even more important for them to keep learning, sharpening skills and being closer to their markets. Simply put, the more one does, the more one has to learn.

What Are the Needs of the Family Owned Portfolio Business? What Are the Challenges?

Needs are multiple. Challenges are many. For many firms, needs may blur with challenges; it is not always so easy to separate a need from a challenge, and vice versa. When one is challenged by something or someone, to overcome that challenge produces needs. I will thus skim through the needs, which tend to be more organizational in nature, to concentrate more on the challenges, which may be driven more by external factors, are more opportunistic and thus highly relevant to portfolio businesses in order to live and thrive on creating and acting on opportunities.

Family firms who run diverse businesses or investments first need a solid strategy, a long-term one that can be adapted according to market impulses or changes. They need to build an organization or structure with and for trustworthy employees, partners and interfaces to run or manage the investments. They need to understand potentially multiple and often distinctly different businesses to efficiently select, run and manage the portfolio. They must continuously and simultaneously foster strong entrepreneurial and intrapreneurial spirit and skills. Finally, they need to make sure the family values are preserved and to guarantee positive family reputation and branding.

The challenges facing portfolio family firms obviously greatly depend on the core business, the type of companies in the family portfolio, the goals and the family itself. However, it is fair to say that generally speaking such firms face the following three main challenges: (1) to manage complexity (the portfolio) and thus to avoid distractions and stay focused; (2) to practice and promote project ownership, which can be facilitated through maximizing intergenerational relationships and the resources available in and around the family, motivating the next generations (nextgens) and employees, inspiring nextgens/employees to learn and engage; (3) to innovate continuously to assure business growth.

Point 2 above may be particularly delicate because it has to do with creating a cycle or a motor for progress and evolution. Practicing and promoting a type of circular ownership by the employee or nextgen whereby the ideas, investment or entrepreneurial projects and innovation is continuously feeding into new initiatives is key (Anil Sethi, Nicolas Berg). Creating this motor for continuous progress demands preparing, training and nurturing nextgens simultaneously with the other present generations. Also, in this circularity, all generations must build strong networks in the areas of present and future activity (i.e. for international partnerships, local market intimacies, franchises across multiple sectors, etc.) that help keep the business going and growing.

A final important point on the topic of challenges supporting Point 1 above, managing complexity, is that in order to manage that effectively, the family portfolio enterprise should track and analyze current, cutting-edge financial and systematic, active portfolio management knowledge, i.e. taxes, cash flow, mega trends, portfolio strategy optimization, risk management, portfolio evaluation (i.e. return multipliers, risks, timeline). Furthermore, the firm should understand investments and related topics such as founder team, product-market fit, IP, funding, sourcing, selecting, terms, supporting, scaling, monetizing, exiting, selling. This type of knowledge complements the creation of the circular ownership mentioned in Point 2. In other words, to keep the family "motor going" requires up-to-date information, data, knowledge and know-how.

In an interesting report by Kearney (Kearney Editors), the following specific issues are listed for Gulf Cooperation Council family businesses which I find useful in this discussion. Executive education has the potential to teach employees how to "fix" or improve these:

- True portfolio of individual assets and the portfolio as a whole
- Clear strategic direction and formalized risk appetite
- Anticipation of mid-term and long-term trends
- Capital with platform for competitive advantage
- Organizational complexity and potentially distracted management
- Asset value.

The authors claim that three pillars—performance transparency, investment strategy and active portfolio management—can build "sustainable, robust protected investment portfolios" (Kearney Editors). I believe a suitable executive education program should address and teach these topics.

The first or senior generation of a portfolio oriented family firm has however one main over-riding challenge, "the mother of all challenges," and that is the one that probably keeps the majority of owners awake at night: **how** to assure that things go on forever… that the money is there for generations to come.. that the family brand and reputation stays intact?

Some Suggestions for Finding the Right Executive Education Program

Hereby are some suggestions to consider when selecting a solution for executive education for your portfolio family firm. We have gleaned and presented many of these throughout our interactions with members and thought leaders at the Lorange Network.

- Look for a blended learning program that combines physical presence with online.
- Ascertain that the executive education offered is technology oriented; check that technology is well applied in the curriculum (i.e. internet, intranet, mobile technologies, Cloud computing, performance, communication, social media, data analytics, etc.).
- Find a program that integrates the relational, i.e. cultivation of student networking as these are relationships that will create future growth opportunities.
- Look for teaching/content staff who are more practitioner oriented than academic.
- Select a program with valid, relevant and renowned experts; aim high; quality counts!
- Make sure there is some flexibility in customizing the orientation to your company's focus areas and specific needs.
- Since this concerns a portfolio family business and a certain investment diversification is assumed, aim for a program whose instruction covers multiple sectors, markets and investment vehicles.
- Choose a program that fosters engagement and action!; your employee or nextgen needs to participate (learning by doing) and learning is multidirectional.
- Favor an executive education provider that builds accountability, responsibility and ownership into the curriculum. Learning has to create the drive or motor for management sustainability. Think of this as a circular process!
- Elect a provider that is truly international, and if not fully in English then at least mostly.
- Take a solution that is fully linked to industry; connectedness and real-world wins over research or observation. This has to be here and now!
- Don't be obsessed with size; even small programs are good, and at times even better!
- Dare to work with relatively new providers. Education is ever evolving and there are innovative and exciting developments being born constantly.

The pandemic has not only boosted education as a past-time but it has also jolted the more traditional providers to be seriously self-critical and fine-tune offerings to suit a more difficult world. Additionally, some newcomers in education are coming from completely unexpected places such as networks, corporations, foundations, so look for sources broadly.

- Check the financial stability behind the education provider. A new-on-the-market program is fine but make sure that it is financially healthy.
- Look into the business mentality behind the program; is the proprietor open-minded? Is he/she well-reputed? A doer not a talker? Someone who recognizes the value of breaking down silos? And is this mentality or personality reflected in the program offered?
- Visit the physical location and sample an online session; nothing beats having a trial experience.
- Make sure your employee or nextgen wants to do this and is committed! He/she must buy into this; it cannot be forced.
- Assure that he/she can do it; are expectations met? Can he/she continue doing the regular work assignments whilst partaking in the program? Is there an easy and simple way to facilitate the completion of a program?
- Be fair and anticipatory, making sure this works for both of you. Think of it as a partnership or a team, maybe family adventure and investment!

Conclusion

To no surprise, I am a staunch supporter of executive education, no matter what! Who does not benefit from learning? Education is an ongoing process. "Education isn't something you can finish" (Isaac Asminov). "We now accept the fact that learning is a lifelong process of keeping abreast of change. And the most pressing task is to teach people how to learn" (Peter Drucker). "Wisdom is not a product of schooling but of the lifelong attempt to acquire it" (Albert Einstein).

The authors of the book in which this piece appears, Dr. Peter Lorange and Santiago Iñiguez de Onzoño, have committed years to doing just that. They believe continuous learning should be "real-world"—practical, combinable with an employee or family member's regular work, and blended (creatively combining asynchronous and synchronous learning).

So in summary, I encourage family owned portfolio companies to jump into the thrilling, beneficial wheel of executive education, a wheel that keeps the car going no matter the road.

And remember the wise words of the Chinese Confucian philosopher for your future generations, "Tell me and I forget, teach me and I may remember, involve me and I learn" (Xun Kuang). Continuity and inclusivity in executive education is paramount.

27

Learning Analytics: A Science in Rapid Expansion That Is Shaping the Future of Education

Martin Rodriguez Jugo

For many people, data science, learning analytics or artificial intelligence (AI) models applied to education, are still a thing of the future. But in my opinion learning analytics is a science that whilst new, is already being used in different ways in the education sector. In this chapter, I will analyze this fascinating area, its potential, its future and how the Covid-19 pandemic has affected the use of related tools in order to enhance the learning process, support faculty, raise student/participant engagement and increase satisfaction in higher education and executive education programs.

The use of learning analytics and AI models in education has grown significantly in 2020. Some university presidents, provosts and deans are assigning teams to work in this field in order to develop a new generation of courses supported by different forms of analytics, data science and even AI in its different formats, such as machine learning and natural language processing. Universities having a Data Chief Officer (CDO) is something that is becoming common, and from my perspective, it's very needed.

This wave of innovation, which has been accelerated by the transition to online class delivery due to the Covid-19 pandemic has not only been about technology, it has also enhanced course design as well as course delivery. The

---

M. Rodriguez Jugo (✉)
IE University, Madrid, Spain
e-mail: Martin.Rodriguez@ie.edu

© The Author(s), under exclusive license to Springer Nature Switzerland AG 2022
S. Iñiguez and P. Lorange (eds.), *Executive Education after the Pandemic*, https://doi.org/10.1007/978-3-030-82343-6_27

right strategy for its deployment must include a diverse team with members from teaching and learning design, as well as a team with a data science and visualization background. In other words, this is not just investing in technology, it is also about building capabilities and arousing the curiosity of those working within program management, as well as the faculty itself. This will lead to situations where teams have to ask a lot of questions, document the results, define the models during the process, iterate them, analyze what to do with the output and set up action plans. More data does not mean better decisions, but instead, more information will help us achieve a better analysis if we ask the right questions and maintain a growth mindset. Moreover, it is essential to involve all the key stakeholders in the process, since learning analytics will benefit them all in the final analysis.

How the Covid-19 Pandemic Has Accelerated the Implementation of Learning Analytics

An Acceleration of the Digitalization of Education: More Relevant Data to Process

As mentioned, there is no doubt that the Covid-19 pandemic has accelerated the digitalization of education at all levels, as well as the shift to online or hybrid education. During the crisis, academic institutions had to begin live streaming their sessions almost overnight as they were forced to deliver their classes through remote teaching models. After a period of remote teaching approaches and "Zooming", some institutions transitioned to more sophisticated teaching models which included other approaches such as hybrid classrooms, where part of the student body could be online and other parts in the classroom. There was also a move to asynchronous components like videos, interactive activities, simulations, multimedia cases, peer-interaction: altogether a much richer array of teaching methods that are evolving day by day and are under continuous enhancement.

It is expected that after the pandemic, universities, business schools and executive education units will return to face-to-face teaching. However, we expect that it will be a renovated learning approach which will be enriched with elements of the digitalization previously adopted and that it will include much more interaction between students and learning platforms/edtech solutions, as well as engagement apps. All these new digital elements and interactions within and outside the typical classroom represent a great opportunity to continue the implementation and deployment of learning analytics models as more data is generated, collected and processed.

This leads us to see there has been an important challenge related to learning analytics in recent years. As data has now become much more available, this issue has been partially solved. We must consider that to be able to apply learning analytics models, we need a large quantity of data from learners. In the past, we relied on fully face-to-face teaching environments. This data was not collected as it was much more difficult to do so via automated processes. As learning models evolve with the addition of new digital elements and interactions along the learning journey (both inside and out of the classroom), new opportunities arise to collect and process this data. Culture and mindsets change as well, meaning that faculty and program management are now more open to experiment and apply learning analytics models whilst at the same time, new questions and needs arise.

This digitalization and the efforts that institutions are making with respect to the application of data science to education is allowing higher levels of efficiency whilst at the same time enabling us to reach larger audiences. Learning analytics can also support the experimentation of more scalable teaching methodologies for specific courses or for specific areas across different levels of education.

Amplifying Learning Environments: The Value of Mixing Synchronous and Asynchronous Models. More Flexibility

We have to be aware that an important part of the learning process occurs outside the formal classroom. Learning also occurs in different environments, doing exercises before, during and after the class, along with group and team discussions. Learning also takes place when working with peers on assignments, doing different activities and even within informal conversations with faculty, classmates and colleagues. In executive education, discussions and debates are an extremely important part of the learning model.

Depending on the class level and learner profiles, universities are including self-paced and/or asynchronous online components for students to come better prepared before each class. This is an effort to maximize the impact of class time, so that more time can be spent on activities that are more practical and analytical by nature (and which reach the higher levels of Bloom's taxonomy). Institutions can rely on a number of options which include their own developments, incorporating learning resources from external collections, or even Massive Open Online Courses (MOOCs). Students and course participants find real value in how content is curated and presented by their teachers. They also find value in the mix of learning resources which are being used as part of the learning experience. That said, creating a minimum knowledge threshold benefits class time and creates optimal experiences.

A common practice in MBAs, executive MBAs and ExecEd AMPs is the use of pre-programs on specific topics such as accounting, finance, data analytics, marketing, economics and even people skills in which participants with low/mid-level knowledge in these specific areas reach a minimum level and get ready for the core courses of these programs. These pre-programs can be used as refreshers for those who have studied these topics in the past, but need to review the content again or update their knowledge. Taking advantage of analytics during the process of taking these pre-programs can be very useful for faculty in order to adapt the course in the first sessions with debates, exercises and explanations. It can also help identify areas of interest, or areas that need special support from an academic perspective. This practice of including pre-programs can be implemented on elective courses or complex subjects as well. At this point, the reader may be thinking that we're entering a world of more adaptive and personalized forms of learning.

As said, flexibility and my freedom of choice is more appreciated than ever. Executive education and management education are not escaping from this trend either. More digital learning formats, with interactive learning resources, hybrid classroom experiences and a mix of synchronous and interactive asynchronous models are here to stay in the coming years. The challenge we have is to find the right balance among them in order to amplify the effect of the learning journey without losing touch with faculty and students.

Different Uses of Learning Analytics

Enhancing the Learning Process and Student Success

Enhancing the learning process and student success is the crux of the matter. Management education and executive education need to adapt their teaching models so that students can reach higher levels of concept mastery, application of tools or frameworks and develop decision-making skills in shorter periods of time and with the use of much less effort. This scenario calls for a symbiosis between learning science and data science; in other words, we need to be more efficient by enhancing the learning process.

This new scenario is a great opportunity to test new approaches and pedagogies across the entire learning journey. There are many possibilities in this area, and the discussion could cover a whole book and a number of discussions. Below is a brief analysis:

1. **Relevant course management function**: By applying analytics, this could help us increase person-to-person interaction, as well as other types, with learners. This includes engaging with platforms, systems used for course delivery, engagement, edtech apps, simulations, discussion forums, and many others. Other factors could also be taken into account such as personal circumstances, personality, culture, professional background and other socio-demographic elements.

    Gathering, tracking and processing all this information allows course management to provide better service during the course and anticipate learner needs by applying AI models.

2. **Applying predictive models to detect the learner's academic needs**: Analyzing participant and student behavior as well as their interactions across the learning journey is important. If this analysis is done ethically, with structure and rigor, new possibilities are created. Predictive algorithms created with the application of AI supervised models to begin with, and then with the application of AI models at a later stage that include unsupervised techniques can have a great impact on the learning experience. These algorithms can be designed to anticipate the academic needs and interests of the learner, and can also help identify learners who are at risk of underperforming at a later stage during the course. In addition, it can also help identify triggers which could cause problems later in the class.

    These predictive algorithms will support faculty and course management in many ways, one of them is being able to personalize and adapt the class to the audience they have in front of them.

3. **Better, more personalized experiences and feedback**: Personalization and more tailored learning experiences are key and can be included in different ways, given that each new course, with new students is different from the previous one. Some possibilities are described as follows:

    - One of the possibilities is supporting faculty in the preparation of synchronous sessions. Professors can take advantage of learning analytics dashboards in order to tailor their live classes to specific areas of interests and needs with respect to their students. Professors can also use the dashboards to identify the areas where their audience may need some reinforcement and additional explanations.

- Regarding feedback, we should think big. One example is natural language processing (NLP), which is a reality today and is under constant improvement. Professors will be able to train AI models to grade essays and assessments, providing personalized feedback by using the rubrics developed previously by faculty. There are many advantages of these new possibilities, namely, reaching higher levels of personalization and immediacy for receiving feedback. Learning analytics and AI models can help detect plagiarism and cheating and it also helps make sure students behave ethically.
- In some institutions synchronous sessions are recorded and they are available for students to watch at a later time. This practice can be seen as a great opportunity to collect data, for instance, to analyze which sections of the synchronous session are viewed repeatedly. With that information, faculty can ask themselves if these areas are related to the concepts that students find most difficult to understand.

4. **The possibilities of adaptive learning**: Many of us have been thinking about this type of personalized learning where hundreds of different paths are developed for learners. Today, some solutions are available on the market, mostly focused on K-12 and undergrads, but this is still costly to build and implement in the right way. It requires collaborative efforts from data science, AI modeling, learning science and content development working together for specific academic areas.

We have to be aware that all these possibilities and many more need work in order to collect data at different parts of the learning experience, and from different sources like those already mentioned (click interactions, NLP, participation, discussion forums, likes/dislikes related to specific content, connection time and pace, among others). Other sources can also be considered like facial recognition, eye gaze tracking, student response to specific stimuli and other kinds of sensors.

Our experience at IE University shows that efforts related to enhancing the learning process and student success are key. One of the pilots that we have launched is the application within executive education online programs. We have designed a model that tracks and measures two macro level variables: the mastery of concepts (knowledge and competencies acquired) and the engagement of participants. During the course, both of these macro level variables are tracked every day and this information is used by both professors and program management (see Fig. 27.1).

There are many conclusions that can be drawn from the practice of tracking engagement. In this case this macro level variable is calculated by

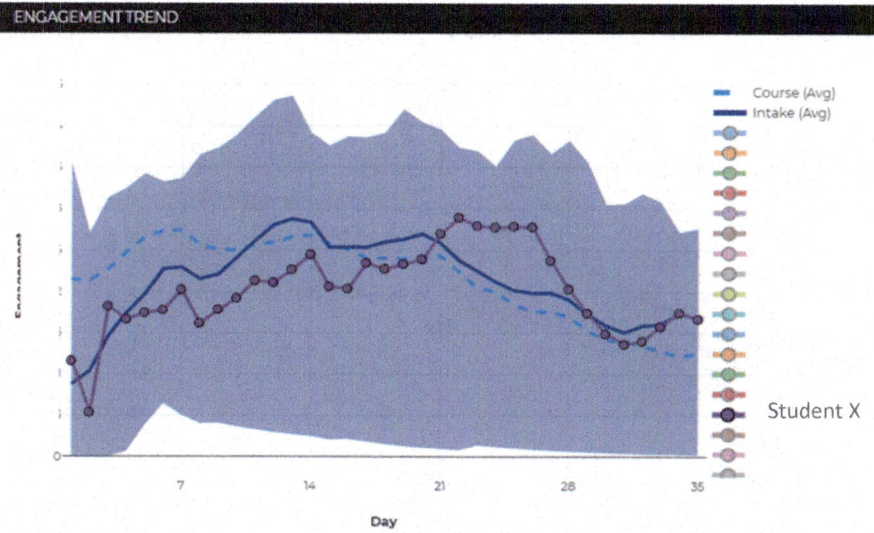

Fig. 27.1 Engagement evolution tracked in a five week-long executive education online program[1]

individuals for the entire intake/cohort and then compared to the average of previous intakes. This approach helps us provide a more personalized service in an almost just-in-time response. If you analyze the tendencies, you can see that engagement increases at the beginning of the course, is stable for several weeks and then it decreases toward the end. This behavior is typical and can be explained due to the fact that at the beginning of the course, activities start slowly during the first two days, until it reaches an optimum plateau. Toward the end, class engagement tends to decrease because participants may finish three or four days before the course formally ends, as these courses have important components of self-paced methodologies.

Something similar is done for the knowledge and competency mastery macro level variable. In the image below this graph is presented for another class. In this case, again the increase of knowledge can be assessed by individuals, intake and the class average by measuring the impact of the course on each student and class as a whole (Fig. 27.2).

This information about knowledge and engagement is used separately as well as collectively in order to maximize the learning experience. Other tools are measured in these courses from IE University including predictive algorithms. We use this data, these models and dashboards as an advanced

---

[1] Image taken from internal dashboards developed by IE University.

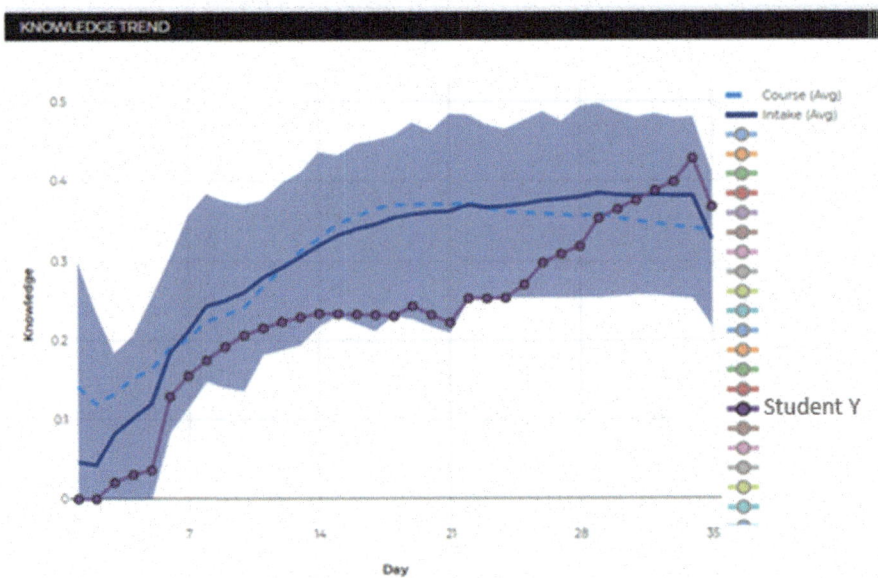

Fig. 27.2 Mastery of concepts and competency evolution tracked in a five-week long executive education online program[2]

tool to monitor participants, tailor communication strategies and assess the effectiveness of each course.

Improving and Updating Courses

Apart from enhancing the learning process and student success, learning analytics have huge potential in the areas of improving and updating courses. This means that during and after course delivery, academic teams integrated by faculty, tutors, program management, learning designers and analytics specialists can all analyze the course performance and present improvements for future presentations or intakes.

There are several ways in which a course can be analyzed, for instance, it can be analyzed by measuring the learning efficiency as well as at what level the learning outcomes were reached. However, there are other ways that can also be considered such as the following: interest raised in the audience, learner engagement, completion rates and whether participants would recommend the course to similar audiences.

---

[2] Image taken from internal dashboards developed by IE University.

Some analysis based on analytics that can help the academic team improve their courses for future students is as follows:

1. **By analyzing the results of machine graded assignments and quizzes.** What happens if an important segment of the student body makes the same mistakes in these assignments; in other words, some specific questions have a high rate of wrong answers. This situation should ring bells for those professors involved. They then need to carry out a proper analysis in order to answer these questions: are the instructions clear for students? Is the question well stated and easy to understand? In the case of a quiz: Is each option presented as a clear solution?—The previous questions are focused on how the assignment or quiz is presented, but it is even more important to question how the content is presented within the actual course and how the theory in question is explained during the course. In other words, now the course itself is under analysis in order to see whether the content is explained well, in a clear manner, is easy to follow and to understand and that it also fits with the audience knowledge level and area of expertise.
2. **How students and participants interact with the content and the platform for asynchronous activities:**
    a. If they followed the paths suggested and if not, how they navigated the different content and activities.
    b. Find any patterns of repetition with relation to content views, examine how the content was consumed, particularly with the videos.
    c. What time and days are students more likely to take the asynchronous components of the course.
    d. Find areas of interest and assess every piece of content through likes and dislikes.
    e. Which areas were skipped.
3. As mentioned previously, if we apply sophisticated facial recognition techniques (ensuring that they work with diverse audiences) to live sessions, they can provide much insight. Professors can analyze to find moments where students were interested in the discussion, engaged or even surprised. Moreover, they can use this to find when students were distracted, not interested, bored and very importantly when they did not follow or understand the class content.

With all this information and with other questions that the academic team may have, professors, instructional designers and program managers can enhance the course. It is key to carry out the analysis objectively and with the goal of improving future classes. It is key to bear in mind that this is not to punish any participant or student when taking the course, but instead to provide enhanced learning experiences in the future. If every faculty member or facilitator reviewed their courses after being taught, they would be able to enhance the learning process and student success rate as well, now consciously making an effort to find areas of improvement for the next iterations of the course. This will take the course to the next level.

Learning Analytics: The Future and Some Challenges

It is always difficult to predict the future, and this is not my intention. However, in this final section I would like to share some trends that we are seeing.

The first trend is that learning analytics will be linked to more long-term approaches for each person. This means that instead of just focusing on a specific subject, course or program, analysis will be carried out over longer periods of time and by adding other personal and life-long data.

In 2020, the EDUCAUSE Horizon Report™ Teaching and Learning Edition reported an example of an academic institution applying "ML algorithms to predict a student's grade performance – even before courses begin." The institution in question is Penn State University, which is using data collected from more than 10 years from admissions, applications and other transcript data. This is an interesting way to support their admission process. If we consider this as a possibility that could be extended to other institutions, we would soon arrive at a situation where admission processes could count on more tools in order to make decisions and they could base their decisions on qualitative data (interviews), quantitative data (the results of admissions tests) and Machine Learning (ML) algorithms. If we go a step further, we may reach situations where not only academic performance can be predicted, but also career paths and even professional success, simply by adding more data prior to and during the program itself. In other words, fostering a lifelong relationship that will include additional input, even once the program has ended. This is highly relevant to the application in corporate learning environments and also for lifelong learning approaches. In these contexts, recommendations, in terms of courses and trainings which could be taken in our institutions and in others will be given in order to support their growth.

Another important thing to mention is the discussion around the following three topics:

- **Ethics and Integrity**: Making sure that the data is used for having a positive impact on the people and society, but also on each individual. All these efforts should comply with regulations associated in terms of use and cybersecurity.
- **A "one size fits all" approach doesn't always work**: An important challenge when building these models is treating each person as an individual. Learning is a complex process, and exceptions should be understood as well as identified by the models because each person is different, with different circumstances, backgrounds, cultures, etc. Due to this, it is very important to have humans monitoring the models applied. The people behind these initiatives must be able to understand the way the model works, how it evolves, how the output is given and how conclusions are drawn. The output has to make sense to these people and they must question their models periodically in order to make sure that they are evolving in the right way and under their control. At IE University, diversity is one of our values, thus we have taken this as a serious matter when applying learning analytics approaches.
- **Learning analytics to support the faculty and the learning process**: As I have outlined, learning analytics models should be applied so as to create a better learning experience. More and more parts of the learning journey will be automated, but the function of teachers and faculty shouldn't be replaced. The main objective is for better and more productive courses and programs.

Online learning, technology-based learning, learning analytics and AI models are here to stay and will increase in the future. Current systems and edtech solutions will incorporate more and more tools to support universities, business schools, executive education and corporate learning. It will be important to put into practice an approach of asking questions, improving and learning, but don't forget that technology and these models are the means rather than the end. The objective is to support our students and participants so that they can learn more efficiently and easily through a more engaging process. In terms of data science and analytics, this requires a mentality that shifts from data capture and processing to thinking, asking questions and doing proper analysis with the data collected in order to obtain beneficial outputs.

References

Inside HigherEd

https://www.insidehighered.com/news/2020/11/10/authors-discuss-new-book-big-data-campus.

https://www.insidehighered.com/blogs/university-venus/why-higher-ed-needs-data-ethics.

https://www.insidehighered.com/views/2020/08/06/due-covid-demand-analytics-has-risen-significantly-information-doesnt-mean-action.

Educause

https://library.educause.edu/-/media/files/library/2020/3/2020_horizon_report_pdf.pdf?la=en&hash=08A92C17998E8113BCB15DCA7BA1F467F303BA80.

https://library.educause.edu/topics/information-systems-and-services/analytics.

https://library.educause.edu/topics/emerging-technologies/artificial-intelligence-ai.

https://library.educause.edu/topics/information-technology-management-and-leadership/higher-education-transformation.

https://er.educause.edu/podcasts/educause-exchange/the-ethical-issues-around-learning-analytics.

28

Learning Platforms: edX

Anant Agarwal

The early last decade ago saw the appearance of the main MOOC (massive online open courses) platforms. Those that have prospered have scaled up their operations considerably, during the pandemic, while diversifying their educational services, mostly through partnerships and agreements with universities around the world. One of the leaders in this sector is edX, founded by MIT and Harvard University, which operates its opensource learning platform worldwide. Its CEO and founder is Anant Agarwal, a professor of electrical engineering and computer science at MIT, an empathetic, approachable and deeply cross-cultural academic entrepreneur. Born in Mangalore, India, he obtained his Ph.D. in electrical engineering and IIT Madras, and was, until joining edX, the director of MIT's Computer Science and Artificial Intelligence Laboratory. His experience, strategic vision and current position makes him one of the best qualified people to formulate an accurate vision of the future of higher education.

On June 29, 2021 it was announced that "2U will acquire substantially all of edX's assets for $800M in cash. Together, 2U and edX will reach over 50 million learners globally, serve more than 230 partners, and offer over 3,500 digital

A. Agarwal (✉)
edX, Weston, MA, USA
e-mail: agarwal@edx.org

programs on the world's most comprehensive free-to-degree online education marketplace."

"As edX looks to its next phase of growth and impact, joining forces with 2U marks a major milestone in our evolution",[1] *said Anant Agarwal on occasion of the announcement of the deal.*

The following chapter is extracted from an interview held on January 26, 2021.

The Vision for edX

When we look back a few decades, adult education was the preserve of the universities, which enjoyed a virtual monopoly, similar to large companies like AT&T in the early 80s, which controlled every aspect of telephony: from the phone itself, the line, service and international calls. But if you look at communication systems today, there are any number of players: Apple and Samsung lead the handset market, while long-distance calls are provided by Sprint and AT&T and others, and of course can be made via internet. Information and applications are provided by Google and other entities.

In other words, we've seen an unbundling of services. And unbundling is the key word. Unbundling has created rapid advancement in technology, rapid benefits for all stakeholders, particularly the user. Today, I can make international calls virtually for free; only three decades ago, when I was a student, I was paying four dollars a minute to call India. So, these companies have created huge value for their shareholders.

What I would like to see is unbundling within the education industry. Generally, each university, whether it's IE or MIT, does everything: admissions, education, degree granting, career counseling, technology, content creation, everything is done by the university.

This is where edX comes in. Our vision of the future is one where education is unbundled, where we try to create worldwide networks of suppliers and collaborators. An example: edX brings digital technology and outreach and networks to the university. The way we work is to augment the university. We are a platform company. We partner with the many institutions in the world where their content is available on edX as a platform.

We see ourselves at edX as forming a part of an unbundled university educational ecosystem where we partner with universities to provide a set of

---

[1] https://press.edx.org/2u-inc.-and-edx-to-join-together-in-industry-redefining-combination.

services that augments the key value and core competencies at universities, which are professors, education, academics, degree granting and we bring in the other components. That's how we see a future where education and learning all over the world becomes unbundled and we become a partner of universities and colleges providing these services to the world.

From MOOCs to Educational Platforms

When we founded edX, some of my colleagues at other MOOC platforms talked about how within 10 years there would only be five universities left in the world. Those were alarmist statements, because we have evolved as complementary to universities. Content, teaching, research, all of this is happening at the great universities around the world. What we do is compliment them and provide certain services that universities are not developing.

Over the past 10 years, the main contribution of MOOC providers has been to provide access to education to learners all over the world. Think of this as the twenty-first century supply chain of education, which is global and networked.

The second big innovation has been in credentialing. Before, students would have to study for two years or four years to get a degree. In response, we launched a number of very innovative micro credentials like MicroMasters® programs and MicroBachelors® programs. A MicroMasters program credential is about 25% of the cost of a master's program, which can be completed in four to six months. 91% of students who have earned the MicroMasters program credential tell us they had a career advancement within about three months, a pay raise, a promotion or a new job. They take micro credentials as a new way of learning, to learn new skills in a short amount of time without having to spend years in a degree program. These new complementary models of education fill the gap in the middle, offering micro credentials that can be earned in about six months.

Micro Credentials and Stackable Courses Complement Traditional Degrees

These new credentials will not completely replace traditional degrees. They offer more choices, as in other businesses. Today we have a lot more options as consumers of communications technology and smartphones. We see a world which is modular and stackable, like building with Lego. You take small

Lego blocks; you combine them to create bigger units and then you combine the units to create bigger blocks. Modular credentials are the Lego blocks of education.

A learner can come in and they can earn a MicroMasters program credential or a MicroBachelors program credential and many of them stop there and put that on their resume and get the job. But many other people will decide to take another, and another qualification. They can get additional MicroBachelors program credentials or additional MicroMasters program credentials and stack them up and learn new skills until one day they realize they have enough of these stackable credentials, enough credit, for a full MBA or a full masters or a full degree.

Our approach is to build bigger units from smaller chunks. Many people can't afford a full MBA or they don't have the time, so they opt for the MicroMasters program. I believe that the two are complementary. One is not going to replace the other.

Engagement of Participants in MicroMasters

The traditional approach to education is outdated. For example, we believe that if someone doesn't get the whole degree, they ought to drop out. When I was growing up if I went to college for two years and then went back home, I would be considered a dropout and sent back. But the beauty of modular education is that it offers as much learning as the client wants. If somebody takes two MicroMasters programs and stops, what's wrong with that? That's all they want. In the past, they had to spend two years to get a full degree and so many people never even started because it was too daunting.

Now, many more people are starting to look at some sort of education, education has become a funnel where previously it was a cylinder. Previously, everybody started and almost everybody finished as if through a cylinder. What we're doing is converting a cylinder into a cone. A lot of people come in at the bottom of the cone, and they just do one MicroBachelors program and one MicroMasters program, and that's enough for them. Some people might do two or three and then some might go on to do the full degree, going all the way through the cone.

An example: we have a MicroMasters program in Supply Chain Management from MIT. Thousands of students are completing this program. A small number of students will apply to MIT because the MIT campus can only admit about 60 or 70 students per year, but thousands of students are completing the MicroMasters program and getting value along the way, stopping when it suits them.

This creates an opportunity that elite universities cannot cover, since they require people to come to campus. But now, they can educate hundreds of thousands, or even millions of students. And of course, digital technology is the key enabler.

The Post-Pandemic World of Education

The pandemic has seen an exponential increase in edX enrollments. In fact, in April 2020, the number of learners was 10 times higher than in February. In fact, in April of 2020 we registered five million new students, which equaled the number of new students that came to edX in all of 2019.

The pandemic has created a huge upsurge in people looking for online education. Firstly, because people have more time on their hands, but secondly, many people are looking for a new job. They have been laid off and they want to emerge stronger after the pandemic. They're looking for short programs. They don't have much time and they don't have a lot of money. So, they're looking for short programs that are skills-focused.

The pandemic has impacted learners and universities and created a new culture of lifelong learning. A lot of people have now tried online learning and will continue this culture. For universities, I think online will become a part of the culture going ahead, and the pandemic will make blended learning the new normal. Before the pandemic, online learning around the world was close to zero. But after the pandemic hit in March 2020, everybody went to online learning; every university switched to 100% online learning. Now, as the vaccines are rolled out, my guess is that over the next few years, the new normal will be 50/50 online and residential teaching. In short, the future of learning is blended.

How Technology Will Next Impact on Education

Let's compare the past and the future. So far, online platforms have adopted the findings from learning research. As early as 1972, the Craik and Lockhart's Level of Processing Model (2) showed that active learning has much better outcomes, whereby people are given a small amount of information and the application of that information is checked. So, edX has active learning pedagogy built into the platform, whereby people learn a small amount and interleaved with that process are interactive questions. The students discuss, learn and interact, all in a seamless, interleaved manner, that is active learning.

Learning platforms have substantially improved learning outcomes by introducing cutting-edge research and learning. In the future, I see some amazing gains coming from three key technologies: one is AI (artificial intelligence); the second is cognitive science; the third is AR-VR (augmented reality-virtual reality).

At edX, we've collaborated with some universities such as Berkeley who have done research to show that using AI techniques they can predict when a learner is going to drop out. This means they can intervene and provide encouragement. Cognitive science has shown that retrieval learning or spaced learning is a good thing, whereby knowledge checks are provided at increasing intervals of time. You tell somebody something, then ask them a question about it a week later and then another a month later. This technique is called spaced repetition, and has been shown to improve learning outcomes. MIT has built some early prototypes of their research in this field into the edX platform. Finally, we will use AR-VR techniques to replicate labs and provide rich and engaging experiences to learners.

The Role of the Professor in the New Learning Process

As a professor at MIT, I believe that the role of the instructor and the professor is very important. I don't think AI and machine learning will be taking over these roles any time soon. I think AI and machine learning have a long way to go before they can replace humans.

We use analytics a lot at edX. I'll give you an example. One lecturer was looking at the data and he found that at minute seventeen in one of his videos, people lost interest in it. The analytics showed what happened. But the predictive part, the prescriptive part was up to the professor, who was then able to address the problem by improving the video content.

I think we've reached a point where AI and machine learning can tell us when there is a problem. But in terms of the solution, there are things that the human, the faculty member has to do. We will create content, but AI and machine learning will create personalized pathways. I believe personalized learning is the next big thing in education where the content will be created by the professors, but the personalized learning, the pathways, what should I teach the student next, that could be done by adaptive mechanisms. And we have prototypes running on edX today that are experimenting with these techniques.

Lifelong Learning

When the pandemic hit, executive or professional education at universities went from residential to completely online or non-existent. I've talked to many deans of professional and executive education at universities, and they are suffering. At the same time, there is still considerable interest in online executive or professional education, which is why we are launching a professional education course online from Wharton on connected strategy. This means somebody sitting in Madrid can be taking a course from an expert in strategy, from wherever I choose and at whatever time I choose. It is completely flexible. In the past, this would involve travel and spending a week away, it was very expensive and very difficult. That said, I believe that in-person executive education still has a place. I don't think it will go away, but I think it will be augmented by online learning. I think a lot more executive education will happen completely online because it's so much more flexible, it is so much easier and it's so much more accessible, and of course technology makes this interaction much, much better.

The difference nowadays is that I can learn from many different sources. Today, I could be learning from a professor at IE. Tomorrow, I could learn from a professor at Wharton, the day after tomorrow, I could be learning from a world expert in Bangalore. I think people will be looking for the best in class for executive and professional education and go to that place to get it.

So, I really do believe that lifelong learning, which is a continuation of education and professional education and executive education, is going to be very, very important for lifelong learning. And I think the pandemic has shown us that it can be done very effectively online as well.

Obstacles to Reforms

In the past, if you asked academics about reforming the learning process, they generally pointed to university leadership or government accreditation agencies for not doing so. However, by and large, in my experience talking to university and government leaders around the world, I have found that university and government leaders want to implement changes and are ready to do it.

The challenge is that faculty and students have proved resistant to change. Let me illustrate this with my own story. I suggested to a fellow professor that we teach a course fully online. They weren't very comfortable with the idea, because they were worried about what they were going to be doing if they weren't giving lectures. Their discomfort diminished when I explained that instead of giving lectures in class, the professor's role changes to creating new content and working with students who might be having trouble with the material. Professors can create new exercises and examples and constantly update their courses.

Professors can serve as a guide and a role model and lead discussions. Online teaching will free them up to spend more time leading discussions and answering questions one on one. There is some resistance, and I think it takes time for students and teachers to understand the potential. Students felt that unless they came to class and learned directly from the professor, what they learned had no value, but the pandemic has shown us that professors can teach online, students can learn online. In other words, the biggest challenge was not administrators, not institutions, but the lack of familiarity with online learning of professors and students.

But now that both professors and students have tried it during COVID, and, by and large, even though most people may not like 100% of it 100% of the time, but many like at least 70% of what they're seeing, they like the flexibility, and students like the fact that they can now watch videos at midnight as opposed to going to a class at nine o'clock in the morning. They can pause and rewind. So, I think what you're seeing is that more and more people, faculty and students, are now willing to give blended learning a try, now that they have become more familiar with it. And there's a lot of room for improvement as we incorporate the best of blended and online learning more thoughtfully the next time around when there is not such an immediate rush to go online.

Teleworking

COVID has changed the future of work, and the subsequent shift to remote work will not just change corporations. It will change the world. Let me explain. Before the pandemic, people went to work, virtually 100% of the world's population that was working, who had a job, went to a workplace, and then the pandemic hit. Then, everybody who could, started working remotely. We have 250 people at edX, and from working in the office we pivoted overnight, and all of us started working remotely. It's been over one year now. We've been working remotely and we've found that it's been more flexible. Productivity is much higher. For me, I don't have to spend two hours every day sitting in Boston's nightmare traffic jams. As a result, I'm much more flexible in terms of my work. I'm more productive and I'm happier. My experience suggests that most companies will move to a blended model combining both in-person and remote work. But I think the balance could be much more online than in person. For most jobs, particularly in technology, there will be much more remote work than in person.

This will change the world in so many ways. Obviously, there will be less traffic and perhaps governments won't need to spend so much money on transportation. I also think we will see productivity increase. I think we will see companies being able to hire from anywhere, whereas previously, a company could only hire people in the area where their physical office was located, people who could physically come to work on the campus. Now, companies can hire people from anywhere.

Our European team is in Barcelona. Before, I used to come to Madrid and Barcelona very often as we were growing the team. And now I have a dream that if we can work remotely, maybe we should hire a lot more people who can work from home, and who can be based anywhere in the world!

As a result, I believe we will see increased social mobility. You will no longer have to be in Silicon Valley or Madrid or Boston to find a good job. I can go and live anywhere in the world. This has to have a positive impact on many nations or areas. It will change the real estate market.

I'll give you an example in the Boston area: if you look at house prices in Cape Cod, which is on the beach, and New Hampshire at the Lake Sunapee area, which is in the mountains, the price of homes in these areas, which are a one and a half hour commute from Boston, have risen 50% during COVID. Why? Because people are deciding to live where they really want to, rather than where they have to.

In short, remote work and remote learning will completely change the world. And as soon as politicians and companies and others see that, we'll experience a tidal wave of change. The question we have to ask ourselves now is what will the world look like as a result of remote work? It will completely change the world: politics, dynamics, economics, real estate, communications, housing, transportation, everything.

Who Will Be the Next Disruptor in Technology-Based Education?

No company or business model is unbeatable: edX is a disrupter, so people often ask us, who will disrupt your company? I think any company or any institution that is not moving quickly will be disrupted. I think, in general, institutions, whether edX or universities or companies, if they don't move quickly in these times of digital transformation, will be disrupted, which means that just like everybody else, we have to keep moving quickly.

In terms of where the next disruption might come from, for edX, it could come from anywhere. We are seeing that many Indian companies are raising hundreds of millions of dollars from venture capital firms and creating massive, massive online education programs. And India has a tendency to leapfrog. For example, the mobile phone in India leapfrogged the landline generation and similarly online education might leapfrog campus education, because very few students have access to a quality campus. And so online learning may take off in India. So, I think that disruption can come from anywhere. I think India has a huge opportunity.

Part of how edX addresses this market for global disruption, is that we have created an open-source platform called Open edX and there are 3000 sites around the world using open edX.

In fact, France Université Numerique, the French national platform, is on Open edX. Israel's national platform is open edX. Russia, China, Hong Kong, Japan, Korea, Jordan: all of these national platforms use open edX.

The Future of edX

If there's one thing I'm good at, it's dreaming. When we started edX almost 10 years ago, my dream was to educate one billion people around the world. And today, if you count the number of students learning on open edX and on edX itself, we've grown to more than 100 million, with over 37 million learning on edX and the remainder on Open edX platforms, but we still have a long way to go. I want us to find a way to get to a billion using Open edX and edX over the next 10 years.

I would like to see the edX platform become a leader in applying AI technology, cognitive science technology and AR-VR technology and creating cutting-edge experiences in the open edX platform. We are partnered with over 165 institutions, but there are more than 40,000 universities around the world. I would love to see a day when we could help thousands, tens of thousands of universities all over the world take their programs online and create this new future of blended learning.

29

Enhancing Social Reach: OpenClassrooms

Pierre Dubuc

One of the most successful online course platforms in Europe over the last decade has been OpenClassrooms, created in 2013 by Pierre Dubuc and Mathieu Nebra in France. Initially conceived as a platform to provide universal access to quality education, mainly vocational and applied, the company has been diversifying from a B2B segment increasingly to institutions, social organizations and companies, keeping a social mission. Dubuc is also the CEO of the company, a young entrepreneur who felt the need to improve education, taking advantage of the contribution provided by technologies, while studying telecommunications engineering in Lyon, France. Since then, despite the prevailing regulatory barriers in Europe, the company has grown significantly, increasing the number of online programs during the pandemic.

Interview held between Pierre Dubuc and Santiago Iniguez on February 17, 2021.

P. Dubuc (✉)
OpenClassrooms, Paris, France
e-mail: pierre.dubuc@openclassrooms.com

The Impact of the Pandemic on Online Learning

The pandemic has been a great opportunity for online education business. We've experienced significant growth, both because of the B2B segment, which has really taken off, and also because of our social programs. As a result, it's clear that there is huge demand for reskilling jobseekers and trying to diminish the consequences of the social and economic crisis.

The environment is very exciting. Now it's very important to help those people in need to get new skills and new jobs: it's a special priority for us. It's also exhausting. Our team has been working non-stop remotely for almost a year. We have more than doubled the size of the team and half of them have never been in the office yet. They've been working for us remotely, which has been a very different experience for us.

Our mission at OpenClassrooms is to make education accessible. Our vision, which is a short-term statement, is to make professional education available for as many people as possible, meaning education that leads to jobs, to an improvement in people's employability. In essence, our areas are competencies and jobs. We can call that education too: employment programs are gallery-oriented programs. We're at the crossroads of higher education and vocational training. The outcome for the student should be related to an improvement in their employability or just simply getting a job or switching careers; or even creating your own job or having internal mobility if you're already working.

We started as a B2C company and then created the B2B segment, which has become the main source of our revenue. This is logical, because obviously, if you want to increase the employability of your students, then you need strong connections and relationships with employers and companies, hence the B2B segment. So, we've been growing and we now have more than five hundred B2B clients.

This B2B segment has more than doubled during the pandemic. In total, we have three market segments. The main one is employers, which means companies. We've got the B2C, we call that students. It's directly getting in touch with students and they pay for themselves.

We also have what we call social programs, which are more related to public policies and programs funded by foundations, nonprofits or governments for five target populations, which are job seekers, refugees, people with disabilities, school dropouts and people living in underprivileged areas. This segment has been growing significantly during the pandemic because of the social crisis. In response, the French government doubled its public policies investments on job seekers and young people.

The Value Added of OpenClassrooms

As said, our core focus is on B2B, the employers, the professional world, but we also partner with higher education institutions, universities, schools and other training centers: we design programs together and some of them are our clients. We also help them to digitize their offer. One contribution is, again, career orientation to enhance the students' employability. We help them not just to digitize their curriculum but also to bring more competency-based mindsets into their teaching.

The group of academic partners is growing because our blended learning programs fit well with brick and mortar colleges and universities, where they operate the full program, teaching in presence, the marketing and the management of the programs, among other things. And we operate behind the scenes, we run the online components, which makes a lot of sense. I believe that these types of partnership will continue growing in the future.

Demand for Online Programs After the Pandemic

It's hard to predict how demand will evolve in the coming years, because there isn't much visibility in the market right now. We are convinced that it will remain high for this year, 2021. That's pretty much a given, and we think it is going to continue in 2022. But after that, there may be a decline at some point when things return to normal, although I'm not sure what normal means and when this return will actually happen, there might be a slight decline, and then demand will continue to grow again. I think the drop in demand might last six months, a year. But generally, I don't think we'll return to where we were a year ago, notably because we're very exposed in the B2B segment. Furthermore, I don't think that executives at companies will resume business trip at anything like the previous level of say, five years ago, or that they will send people all over the world for vocational training.

At the same time, I think there is another effect beyond not being able to attend class in person because of lockdown, which means you have to study online. This effect is more structural and relates to the fact that the sectors of those companies impacted by COVID have been forced to accelerate their transition to online business. Consequently, if you were in retail, then you are now doing more e-commerce.

The example can be extended to other industries. It means that the transformation of those businesses has experienced a significant acceleration.

Behind this transformation, the issue of skills and jobs rises as an important one. Upskilling and reskilling programs, because they become more and more strategic and more and more large scale, have to be deployed very quickly. This is structural and it's here to stay, and in fact will only grow and grow. In response, HR departments and CEOs realize that to do so, to deploy upskilling and reskilling programs for 10,000 employees in three or six months, you need to be online, because quite simply, it is not possible any other way. And this is here to stay.

The Freemium Model

Freemium is a program targeted at our B2C customers. Most of our courses are MOOCs, with free access online. You can access more than 500 online courses on an international platform for free, including watching videos, reading text content, taking the exercises and related activities. Then on top of this, obviously, if you want to be involved in a degree program with certification and diploma, mentorship, career coaching, then you start paying fees.

We have two million students in total taking free courses every month. Some of them will upgrade into the paid tiers and get access to a mentor and receive a qualification. But the way we look at it is that we're going to train students and lifelong learners. It doesn't really matter who pays for the tuition fees. It could be the students themselves. It could be their companies, or it could be some funding body like the government and the public employment agency or foundation, some sort of scholarship.

At the end of the day, we will train a student. In other words, it's the same program, no matter the segment and the markets we address, and for us as a mission-driven company, because we want to make education more accessible, we understand that this is also about making it financially accessible. Right now, more than two-thirds of our students don't pay, meaning they have access to our educational programs, but somebody else pays for them, and mostly this will be funding bodies and employers. This is core to our strategy. We want to make sure that we've got financial aid and we've got many ways for students to access their education.

Evolution of Online and Degree Programs

Technically, we have the status of a school in France, and we offer our own professional diplomas, not academic degrees. Academic degrees can only be granted by public universities in France, as in most other countries, and this area is regulated by the government. We do offer just a few academic degree programs in partnership with universities already accredited. Basically, we operate most activities, but under license.

I think down the road we can expect regulatory challenges. It's not that we cannot deliver degree programs, because we already do. But to us, the outcome, the end goal, is not the degree, it's the job and employability. We think that degrees are first, a proxy for quality, I mean, for the students or employers, it's a proxy that says, okay, this person has the skills I need, the right level of qualification, the right level of education, etc. So, this proxy aspect is important, but it's also a gateway to financial aid in many countries. In many countries, you have access to some sort of scholarship or student loan or some funding options, because this is an accredited degree. And if it's not, you don't have access to that financing. So we return to our mission of making education accessible, which also means making education financially accessible.

We want to offer more financial options to improve access to our programs. This is not so much about entering the degree segment, but more as a way to expand the options for all students to access education-to-employment programs. I don't think that we will compete against brick and mortar colleges, for example, because we don't really address the same segments.

Badges, Certificates and Degrees

There's a big difference between the size of two markets: degree programs on the one hand and non-degree with certificates on the other. The degree market is huge, and depending on the countries, it can slow down or be stable or grow slightly, depending on each market. Today in the United States there are fewer college students than before. So, you could say the market is stable or even falling. In emerging markets, due mainly to demographics, it's exploding.

On the other hand, the market for certificates and stackable credentials and related offerings is growing, but it's still very small compared to the degree market. I think the main question is around accreditation and recognition of those credentials. Right now, accreditation bodies, generally speaking, only focus on degrees and not so much on certificates and badges. As a result, badges and certificates are still not widely recognized. This means that new providers might create their own, but it's hard to compare quality based on one badge, one certificate. And if you take just data science, let's say, you can find online 50–100 programs.

As a student, a consumer, it's really hard to compare, because some of them last 20 hours, some of them 200 hours, some of them 500 hours. And the quality of the curriculum varies. What's more, you're obviously not going to cover as much ground in 20 hours as in 500 hours. I mean, this is obvious, but still the name at the end is still a certificate. So, it's really hard to gauge the difference for the end user. Whereas, when you talk about a bachelor's degree, a master's degree, no matter which university or which college you're talking about, there may be variances on the quality, but the time frame is always similar.

I think the big challenge will happen when accreditation bodies start to look at those credentials and start to build accreditation processes to standardize and make them comparable. And I think they will. It will also take time, but it's also when public policies will funnel financial aid toward those credentials. Obviously, both will go hand-in-hand because when the US federal government decides to redirect Title IV funding and Pell grants [1] toward bootcamp companies along the lines of stackable credentials, and that's going to start, they're going to pump a lot of money into it. So, accreditation bodies will be forced to give accreditation to those newly identified programs and then a new standard will be set.

I think this is when we'll see a tipping point. But degree programs won't disappear, to be replaced by certifications or badges. I don't think that's true. I think degrees ideally will be built as blocks and one block could be tied to a certification as a stackable credential. So, you could do a sub-part of a degree. And we can link, in a smart way, degrees to certification.

That's kind of what we're trying to be at OpenClassrooms. But obviously it depends on the accreditation bodies. At the end of the day, if they don't allow it, then it's going to be hard. But I think they will. And they are increasingly moving in that direction. For example, in France, the national accreditation body for degree programs, is now forcing colleges to describe their degree programs as blocks of competencies, and they're forcing them to give certificates to students if they validated only one block.

How Demand for Education Will Evolve After the Pandemic

If you look at traditional college students in markets like the United States or in Europe, the demand is likely to be stable or, depending on the demography, to slightly improve or slightly increase. But, generally speaking, it is going to be stable. However, there'll be a huge new market, which is the reskilling markets for working adults. In the US market now there are more working adults in colleges than students between 18 and 24.

So now, the universities and colleges, community colleges in the United States, train more working adults in their 30s, in their 40s, along with high school dropouts or people who want to accelerate or switch careers. This market is growing significantly and will continue to grow in the coming years.

So, if universities focus only on the 18–24 year-old segment, their activities may remain stable or maybe even decrease. And it's going to be hard. But if they expand into the lifelong learning segments, even with degree programs, helping people with reskilling, they will need to adapt and be more flexible so as to accommodate their schedules and that kind of stuff. But we're not just talking about vocational training, we're also talking about longer programs, and I think there is a huge opportunity for universities and colleges to expand there.

After the pandemic, executive education will continue growing but will remain online to a large extent. People are now used to be working online, studying online, being educated online. So, that a given. I'm a more concerned with traditional higher education, because I think what most students experienced at a typical university was definitely not what online education should be like. Replicating the traditional lecture through Zoom meetings from nine in the morning to six in the afternoon is a horrible experience for anybody. Obviously, students are not really happy. Teachers are not happy. Everybody is exhausted.

There might be a tendency to say online education doesn't work and that we need to get back to in-person education completely. It's clear most online education was not designed or structured properly, and was really done in a hurry. It was not done properly. That said, some universities and colleges are leading the way and they have platforms and content and instructional designers and they really offer a better experience.

I think it will be clear in the next couple of years which institutions created a good experience. And those who didn't will go back to in-person education. This is actually a big threat, I think, to traditional colleges. They didn't really invest because I think they will revert to what they did before, in person, and not be fully technology-enhanced, not blended. And the rest will have just accelerated that transformation and will continue on that transformation and will be more flexible. It's going to be hard for traditional universities in two years' time to say: "oh, no, you cannot study online, you cannot follow your course online. You know, it's only in-person." This would eliminate the flexibility that has been achieved over the pandemic. Students will be similar, but we will then be in 2024, and students may want some of their courses online, maybe not all of them, but at least with the flexibility to do so.

And I think they will go to institutions where this is possible. In traditional higher education, I don't think institutions, generally speaking, invested enough in building good online quality education for lifelong learning, vocational and executive education. It's gone. And it won't come back.

New Developments in Technology-Enhanced Education

In the coming years we will see many new methods and formats. Programs may include more asynchronous pieces, I think this teaching approach also brings more flexibility to the model because as a student, you can do it at your own pace. You can do it again and again if you want to. For the institution, it's also a way to scale, because when it's asynchronous, usually you scale it once and for all and then you maintain it. But then it doesn't really matter if there are a hundred or one million students behind your unsynchronized module.

It's a challenge to traditional mindsets because it requires a team to build this material and then to update it, instead of teachers instructing live. And it means that one single teacher cannot do it by themselves. They need a full team of specialists. They need video stuff. Then you need studios, you need instructional designers, you need certification experts, you need faculty and teachers, obviously. But you also need people with public speaking skills. You need so many different jobs and skill sets that one single person can't really do it at scale. So, it's really an organizational challenge, a controlled challenge for a university, because it means it's not just the teachers doing their own thing from A to Z. It's more of a collaboration with a team.

In short, it's a big challenge. And from an institutional standpoint, there's the question of the investment needed to build or buy a platform. You need to build or buy content. You need to maintain this content and you need to have a certain volume to make it sustainable. If it's only for 10 people, then it doesn't really make sense, if it's for 10,000, then it probably does make sense.

This is a move that should be led by the top management, the president, the deans, and then to drive this controlled challenge within faculty. So, it's not easy.

Training Senior Management Using Hybrid Formats

For top management in the future, executive education will probably offer blended approaches, and we will see a cultural shift over one generation. If I'm being blunt, top management is usually older. And then over time, when you start having the younger generations coming and moving up the ladder and they will have worked remotely for years, they will have been trained remotely, maybe they even got a degree online in their previous academic experiences. it will be kind of a given for them to continue their training online, so I think it will take a bit, a few years, a bit of time to get there. I think social networking will be needed with blended approaches to make sure that institutions connect with people and have real human-to-human interactions. That can also be done online, I think. But it will remain an in-person experience.

I don't think in five years' time you'll have a lot of only in-person classes for senior managers. I don't think it's very realistic, to be honest, because people won't have the time. Companies won't allow employees to travel abroad for training. Already it seems strange that over the course of 18 months somebody fly to the United States to take three classes and then fly back. Nowadays, because of the pandemic, the cost, and also for environmental reasons. Companies need to reduce their carbon footprint. And this is a pretty good way to do it.

The Future of OpenClassrooms

Our goal is to provide employability to our customers, and the way we track our success in that endeavor is by measuring the number of students we place in the workforce, meaning getting the first job, then a new job, a salary increase, a promotion or some sort of positive professional mobility. We set ourselves a target for 2025 to place one million people a year in the workforce: young people applying for their first job; job seekers switching careers; working adults getting upscaled or rescaled in their own organization. It means the focus is on employability and career development, as well as on volume, because the mission is making education accessible to as wide a public as possible.

We started in Asia last year. And interestingly, the way we started is with senior management and executive education fully online. We began training senior managers in companies like Dentsu, in digital transformation, leadership, change management in English and online. At some point, we will have to translate or train them as well, because the language barrier is very high.

We see big developments. We don't have short-term plans in China right now, because this is a really specific market. But it's clear that the education market in China, in India, is growing at an incredible rate. It's a market by itself. And it's growing much faster than anywhere else in the world.

For the moment, India, China, the United States, and the rest of the world are all separate markets. There are some bridges, but to be honest, not many. I do think in maybe three or five years you will see more and more institutions able to go from one market to the other and be big in another market as well. The problem is the different regulatory environments and the need for licenses and accreditation in each region.

Reference

1. Title IV is Federal Student Financial Aid. These programs may be 'free' money or grants such as a Federal Pell Grant or Federal SEOG (supplemental education opportunity grant) or borrowed money such as the Student Federal Direct Loan or Parent PLUS loan. https://studentaid.gov/data-center/student/title-iv.

30

Chinese Executive Education in Perspective: CKGSB's Innovations in Business Education

Bing Xiang

Today, we find ourselves in an era of major transformations—including technological, economic, social, political and geopolitical disruptions—coupled with dysfunctional global governance, rising protectionism, nationalism and populism, as well as reconfiguring global investment and trading systems. Humanity has been confronted with serious challenges, such as income and wealth inequality, diminishing social mobility and climate change, which are difficult to address partly due to collective myopia. Meanwhile, the COVID-19 pandemic has only made these challenges more pertinent and urgent. In this era of tectonic changes, business schools have an unshakable responsibility in helping individuals and institutions (companies and NGOs) to better navigate through these turbulent times, and to make the world a better place both economically and socially.

Since our inception on November 21, 2002, Cheung Kong Graduate School of Business (CKGSB) has been innovating beyond the traditional boundaries of business education in order to play a catalyst role in addressing some of these societal and environmental challenges. Our mission is to cultivate transformative business leaders with a global vision, sense of social responsibility, innovative mindset and ability to lead with empathy and

---

B. Xiang (✉)
Cheung Kong Graduate School of Business, Beijing, China
e-mail: bxiang@ckgsb.edu.cn

compassion. In this connection, CKGSB has been and will continue to expand the traditional focal points of business schools, to help generate economic prosperity and social advancement. This chapter highlights some of our innovations in the past, areas for growth, along with planned initiatives for the coming decade.

"Top-of-the-Pyramid" Approach

A major innovation at CKGSB is our unique "top-of-the-pyramid" approach, which we have been spearheading since our school's establishment, that addresses the learning needs of decision-makers (such as chairpersons and CEOs) of prominent companies and successful entrepreneurs. This new segment extends beyond the professional managers that most MBA and EMBA programs traditionally target. We believe that top business leaders need to be committed to lifelong learning to meet the challenges posed by today's technological, economic, social, political and geopolitical changes. Our success in serving this group rests primarily with the new insights, skills and perspectives that we offer to help them stay ahead of the curve and better navigate through the world's transformative changes. For this elite group of business leaders and entrepreneurs, their choice of program is fundamentally insights-driven, and much less shaped by rankings or accreditations.

CKGSB has succeeded in developing such insights on China business for several reasons. First, many of our professors tenured at the globally leading business schools, prior to joining CKGSB; and, thus, they offer cutting-edge management theories and practices from around the world and provide a global perspective in understanding China's business and economics landscape. After joining CKGSB, they have continued producing original research, particularly on China issues—which is made possible thanks to the generous support we have received from the Li Ka Shing Foundation. Moreover, most of our faculty members are ethnically Chinese and, therefore, have an advantage in understanding the Chinese language and culture. At the same time, they have their fingers on the pulse of China's economy and business environment. For example, three of them have taken up Chief Strategy Officer positions at Alibaba Group, Ant Financial and JD.com. This, combined with CKGSB's students and alumni network that represents a Who's Who of China business, gives our professors access to the leaders of China's top private and state-owned enterprises, as well as multinational companies in China, allowing them to co-develop business knowledge.

To meet the learning needs of senior executives in China, CKGSB has developed structured, proprietary and fresh insights on China business and economics. Our unique insights and approach have enabled CKGSB to attract the decision-makers of China's most respected and innovative companies like Alibaba, ByteDance, CITIC, Fosun, Huawei, Midea, Sinopec and TCL. More than half of CKGSB's 16,000 alumni are at the CEO or Chairman level, and they collectively lead one-fifth of China's most valuable brands. The prominence of CKGSB's alumni network in business may be unparalleled in China.

To serve global business leaders, CKGSB offers practical knowledge on issues such as how to do business in and with China, and how to compete and collaborate in China, one of the world's most dynamic markets. In light of China's growing importance in the global economy, we provide an in-depth and up-to-date look into the potential global implications of China's transformation, as well as innovations stemming from Chinese companies like DJI and ByteDance (TikTok) with potential global applicability and impact. To date, CKGSB has trained more than 3,000 senior global executives and successfully delivered custom-designed programs to the senior management teams of multinational companies like Agilent Technologies, Clifford Chance, Cummins and Lego Education.

A Global Ecosystem Fueling Economic Disruptions

CKGSB's experiments in fostering a new generation of economic disruptions represent another innovative focus. The idea of economic disruption is central to economic development and social harmony, as it is indispensable in generating upward social mobility among young people. China is noted for its substantive and continued economic disruptions as evidenced by newly emerged large-scale companies and newly minted billionaires in the past two decades. For example, mainland China today has 117 companies on the Fortune 500 list (in 2020), while in 2000 it only had nine. Moreover, when you look at the company level or at the wealthiest individuals in China, there are always newcomers, and the lists of the wealthiest individuals and largest corporations in China are always changing. According to the 2020 Hurun China Rich List, China added 257 new billionaires (in USD), as of August 2020, despite the pandemic, achieving an over 300% increase in the total number of billionaires (in USD) in a span of ten years. Meanwhile, the number of Fortune 500 companies in Mainland China and Hong

Kong also increased from 12 in 2001 to 124 in 2020. While China may not have been as strong in innovation as the United States, it may have been the best in generating economic disruptions in the past 20 years. Japan is noted for its excellence in innovation, yet it has not performed well in generating economic disruptions. Five out of the 641 unicorn companies globally are from Japan (as of April 2021).

To foster these types of disruptions in China, since 2015, CKGSB has been working with key players such as Tencent, Baidu, JD.com, Microsoft, Softbank, Bytedance, Alibaba and others, to set up an ecosystem in China that focuses on developing unicorn and soon-to-be-unicorn companies. With an emphasis on social innovation, we hope to develop a new generation of business leaders who are not only successful, but also socially-minded, long-term oriented and who have a global perspective.

Building on our success in China, we have extended this initiative to European and ASEAN markets (in partnership with Churchill College, Cambridge University), and are in the process of expanding it to other markets like Japan, Korea, and countries in Latin America and Africa. China's experience in generating economic disruptions and our school's experiments in this regard may be of global relevance. In light of the current COVID-19 outbreak, our initiative to build a global ecosystem, which cultivates economic prosperity while emphasizing social innovation and responsibility, may be more pertinent and urgent than ever before.

The Humanities in Business Education

CKGSB also systematically incorporated the humanities—such as history, religion and philosophy—into our business curricula starting from 2005. Our introduction of the humanities has been motivated by the following considerations. Firstly, on the individual level, we hope to inspire business leaders to aspire to not just a "rich" life, but also an "enriched" and even "enlightened" life. Secondly, we believe that the humanities—particularly courses engaging global history, religion and different philosophical traditions—are essential for the business leaders of today and tomorrow to manage global and diverse teams. Lastly, the humanities can help mitigate humanity's collective myopia, and foster a long-term vision and a broader view of business for the greater and global good.

Social Responsibility and Social Innovation

CKGSB's experiments in social responsibility focus on the whole wealth cycle—not only on how we do business, but also why we do business, and how we apply the wealth generated.

Since 2010, CKGSB has been requiring its EMBA students to complete 48 hours of community and philanthropy work (equivalent to 6 days of course work), in order to graduate. This initial experiment with our EMBA students was later extended to other degree programs at CKGSB in 2012.

In 2017, we started offering a compulsory social innovation module. Key issues humanity faces today—such as income and wealth inequality, diminishing social mobility and sustainability—cannot be solely addressed by the business, government or non-profit sector alone, but rather require collaboration among all parties to effectively address them. This is the reason we promote collaboration across government, businesses, NGOs, civil society and international organizations by experimenting with social innovation.

CKGSB's Challenges and Areas for Growth

With efforts of nearly two decades, CKGSB has become the preferred choice among business leaders of prominent companies and a new generation of economic disruptors in China, as well as among world-class scholars returning to China. CKGSB's brand has also been well recognized in ASEAN countries, Japan and Korea. However, our brand awareness is limited in other regions and markets, as we are a relatively young school and only started to expand into overseas markets in 2011 by establishing representative offices in New York and London. We also recognize the need to diversify our faculty to become more global, since most of our professors are Chinese by heritage. The ongoing decoupling between China and the United States is another challenge we face in our globalization efforts.

CKGSB does not enjoy the scale and size of endowments like some of the world's top schools. Moreover, given that the Chinese government has in recent years increased its financial support for state-controlled business schools and is expected to continue doing so in the future, the competitiveness of private business schools, like CKGSB, within China will be impacted. In addition, CKGSB also faces increasing challenges from new players, like Hundun and Dark Horse University, in the Chinese ecosystem of management education. In light of these, CKGSB has been relentlessly innovating, which is essential for us to thrive in China's fast changing business environment.

Going forward, we seek to work with schools, businesses, governments, civil society and multilateral institutions worldwide to continue pushing the boundaries of business education and play a constructive role in addressing some of the most pressing challenges facing the global community. Particularly in light of the COVID-19 pandemic and its ramifications, it has become more urgent and imperative for business schools to play a catalyst role in advancing cooperation among the different stakeholders. More than ever, we need globally minded and socially responsible business leaders, who can compete with compassion and empathy. We, at CKGSB, will continue to stay positive, future-oriented and innovative in driving that agenda forward.

Printed by Printforce, United Kingdom